PUBLIC RELATIONS

THE BASICS

Public Relations: The Basics is a highly readable introduction to one of the most exciting and fast-paced media industries. Both the practice and profession of public relations are explored and the focus is on those issues which will be most relevant to those new to the field:

- The four key phases of public relations campaigns: research, strategy, tactics and evaluation.
- History and evolution of public relations.
- Basic concepts of the profession: ethics, professionalism and theoretical underpinnings.

Contemporary international case studies are woven throughout the text ensuring that the book is relevant to a global audience. It also features a glossary and an appendix on first steps towards a career in public relations making this book the ideal starting point for anyone new to the study of public relations.

Ron Smith is professor of public communication at Buffalo State (SUNY), where he has served as department chair and associate dean for the School of Arts and Humanities. A public relations practitioner accredited by the Public Relations Society of America, he is the author of *Strategic Planning for Public Relations*, *Becoming a Public Relations Writer* and (as co-author) *Media Writing*.

The Basics

PUBLIC RELATIONS

THE BASICS

Ron Smith

Routledge
Taylor & Francis Group

LONDON AND NEW YORK

First published 2014
by Routledge
2 Park Square, Milton Park, Abingdon, Oxon OX14 4RN

Simultaneously published in the USA and Canada
by Routledge
711 Third Avenue, New York, NY 10017

Routledge is an imprint of the Taylor & Francis Group, an informa business

British Library Cataloguing in Publication Data
A catalogue record for this book is available from the British Library

Library of Congress Cataloging in Publication Data
Smith, Ronald D., 1948-
Public relations : the basics / Ron Smith.
pages cm. – (The basics)
1. Public relations. I. Title.
HM1221.S769 2013
659.2–dc23

2013005178

ISBN: 978-0-415-67584-0 (hbk)
ISBN: 978-0-415-67583-3 (pbk)
ISBN: 978-0-203-79890-4 (ebk)

Typeset in Bembo and Scala Sans
by Taylor and Francis Books

CONTENTS

Part I

Understanding Public Relations

A FIRST LOOK AT PUBLIC RELATIONS

This chapter introduces you to the profession of public relations: What it is. What it isn't. It outlines the practical benefits that public relations offers organizations and society at large It also introduces the ethical base of the art and science of public relations.

Understanding public relations is something like the story from ancient India about the blind men and the elephant. The parable tells of six blind men, each feeling a different part of an elephant. One touched the side and thought it was a wall. Another touched the tusk and thought it was a spear. The man touching the trunk thought he had a snake. And so on: The knee a tree trunk, the tail a rope, the ear a fan.

The story points out the pitfall of looking only at parts and not perceiving the whole. Public relations is like that. Public relations is publicity and research, special events and speeches. It is strategy and evaluation, community partnering and fundraising. But none of these, individually, reveals the totality of what public relations is about.

Some people see corporations hiding safety information from workers or covering up inept decisions by managers. They see politicians deceptively attacking opponents with money from unnamed backers. By focusing only on such negatives, the critics fail to see the benefits that public relations provides to society.

So what is public relations about? That's the focus of this book.

Public relations is one of the **humanities**. It is an aspect of culture with ethical norms and a social perspective as an element capable of uplifting society and making sense of human experience. As such, it is associated with language and philosophy.

Public relations also is associated with the **arts**, particularly through the important role that design and visual communication plays in the discipline.

Finally, public relations is a **science**, specifically an applied social science with theoretical models based in research, driven by data, and focused on solving a practical problem.

Together, these concepts of public relations set the stage for looking at a discipline that helps us understand society and human behavior.

WHAT PUBLIC RELATIONS IS NOT

Many misunderstandings surround public relations. Some are understandable, the result of confusion or outdated information, or perhaps only partial information (the elephant analogy). Other misunderstandings seem more deliberate, the result of willfully looking only at the dark side and believing that the worst example is the norm.

Delusions and misconceptions? Or untruths and lies? We'll use a term with more neutral nuance and call these erroneous statements **fallacies**. These simply are false, no blame implied. It may seem unusual to begin a book with a list of criticisms, but by airing these fallacies we can actually glimpse a bit of the positive side of public relations.

Fallacy: PR equates to lying, hype and exaggeration.

Reality: Truth is a foundation of public relations. "That's just PR" overlooks the standard of verifiable performance and sees only the illusion of smoke and mirrors. If public relations was so negative, it couldn't last. After all, you can put perfume on a skunk, but it's still a skunk. Public relations is about accuracy, honesty and information in context.

Fallacy: PR is just a form of propaganda.

Reality: Propaganda lives in a world of half-truths, innuendo, misrepresentation and hidden bias. Public relations focuses on the polar opposites. Once the two terms ("propaganda" and "public relations") were used interchangeably, so it's not hard to understand that some people have not updated themselves on the nuances of the terms or the fact that no reputable public relations professional engages in anything like propaganda.

Fallacy: PR is secretive and insidious.

Reality: Stonewalling means trying to hide information or delay its release. Public relations seeks to work with journalists and others to tell an accurate and timely story about their organizations. But much of the work of public relations is behind the scenes: researching, advising, counseling, strategizing, planning. So it is generally off the radar for most journalists and other observers. However, secretive means uncommunicative, and public relations is anything but. Open, honest and timely communication is at the heart of public relations.

Fallacy: PR tries to keep the public ignorant about what's really happening.

Reality: Public relations flourishes only in a democracy, wherein many voices participate in debate on public issues. It enables people or organizations with different viewpoints to advocate and argue toward consensus—or, if that isn't forthcoming, at least toward a fair policy in which the majority accommodates the concerns of the minority.

Fallacy: PR tries to control unsuspecting people.

Reality: Public relations definitely does not try to control anyone. It couldn't even if it tried, because mind control doesn't work, at least not in the public arena. Public relations does, however, seek to influence. It does this by building relationships to add value to organizations by increasing willingness of publics to support rather than oppose those organizations. And that's more than a semantic difference between control and influence.

Fallacy: PR is only about spin, making bad guys look good.

Reality: The term "spin" is wrong on so many levels. It suggests a hired gun who tries to make bad things look good, or at least less bad. Rather, public relations allows organizations, advocates and individuals to openly share information, criticize policies, suggest alternatives, and otherwise engage in dialogue. Public relations serves the public interest by providing a voice for all in the court of public opinion. It advances society just as does its legal parallel, in which even people charged with a crime and presumed by some observers to be guilty deserve a vigorous defense by ethical attorneys. The court of public opinion isn't always fair. Both sides may not have equal representation, and there's no wise judge, no impartial jury to deliberate. Still, public relations gives every party an opportunity to present its case to perhaps the only jury that really matters—the public.

Fallacy: PR works only for powerful groups with deep pockets: corporations, government, lobbyists and others who work against the best interests of average people.

Reality: Public relations enhances democratic values by providing for multiple voices in the marketplace of ideas. For every cereal manufacturer advertising sugary food to kids, dozens of nonprofit groups use public relations to educate parents on childhood nutrition, to expose the false claims of the marketers, and sometimes to advocate for effective public oversight on marketing practices. The same can be said about issues from nuclear energy to workplace safety, from animal rights to climate change.

Fallacy: PR is only publicity, and nobody reads newspapers anymore.

Reality: Remember the elephant parable from the beginning of this chapter. Publicity accounts for only a small slice of the public relations pie. Public relations is so much more. With the fragmentation of the mass media and the mushrooming of new and interactive media, organizations now can go directly to their publics without needing the assistance of journalists. "Mere PR" dismisses the profession as being inconsequential and unnecessary, neither of which is true. It also misses the point that—in addition to being skilled writers, editors, graphic designers and so on—public relations practitioners also are experts in strategy, management and other problem-solving aspects of organizational life.

Fallacy: Anybody can do PR.

Reality: It's true that public relations doesn't require a license as does dentistry, law and funeral service. So anybody can call himself or herself a PR person, and who's to disagree? But public relations is a profession rooted in research, ethics, strategic planning and evaluation, as well as effective written, spoken and visual communication. It is based on a course of study. So it's more appropriate to say that anybody who has acquired the skills and adopted the ethical standards can do the work of public relations.

Fallacy: PR is the guy with the shovel following the elephants in a circus parade.

Reality: Sometimes public relations is asked to clean up the mess caused by others, usually managers who made bad decisions with even worse consequences, often because they failed to consider public relations perspectives before they acted. But rather than being the band aid (to switch metaphors), public relations has become the wellness program and preventative medicine that helps avoids the problem in the first place.

Fallacy: PR has a dark history, such as campaigns to get women to smoke and books that guided the Nazi propaganda machine.

Reality: In the past, research sometimes looked at how the uneducated masses could be influenced and manipulated. That's where research was in the early 20th century. But theory and research also have developed, as has the rest of society. It's true that an early public relations campaign aimed for social acceptance of women smokers. That was when society discriminated overtly against women and when even doctors and nurses smoked, before we learned of the associated dangers. So it's more accurate to point out that public relations, from its early foundations as a profession, has been used in many ways to uplift society and help people who have been oppressed and marginalized—and yes, to sell cigarettes and all the other consumer products that corporations provide.

(In case you haven't observed a pattern yet, professionals do not generally use the abbreviation PR. The shorthand is associated with all the misperceptions about public relations. So in this book, we consistently use the full term.)

It's easy to criticize any organization if you focus only on the excesses, exaggerations and aberrations rather than the best practices, high standards and good work. Schools? Look at all the dropouts, cost inefficiencies, bullying and poorly educated graduates. Military? Consider the rogue killers, suicide and rape. Churches, scouting programs and college athletics? All that sex abuse and underage drinking. Hospitals? Accidental patient deaths and nurses' strikes. Manufacturing companies? Plenty of pollution and inferior products. And so it goes.

Focusing only on such negatives is an exercise in paranoia. It may be fun for folks who enjoy reading about conspiracy theories, but it's not useful for understanding real-world relationships. On the other hand, it's never helpful to deny the negatives, because we learn from them. Especially, we can learn how to overcome them, relegating bad practices to the dustbin of history.

WHAT PUBLIC RELATIONS IS

If there's confusion about public relations, it may be because the term is used in so many different ways, many of them just plain wrong. A company advertises for a PR representative, only to have the job turn out to be a sales rep or a telemarketing caller. A restaurant has a job in PR, but only for young women with great bodies willing to wear sexy outfits. A politician wants a PR person to do opposition research to distort another candidate's record. That's definitely not public relations.

To get a real look at anything, it's always a good idea to go straight to the source. Here's what public relations people say about their profession.

Three-quarters of a century ago, Harwood Childs (Princeton University professor and founder of *Public Relations Quarterly*) wrote in his book *An Introduction to Public Opinion* this classic and still insightful definition:

> Public relations as such is not the presentation of a point of view, not the art of tempering mental attitudes, nor the development of cordial and profitable relations ... . The basic problem of public relations, as I see it, is to reconcile or adjust in the public interest those aspects of our personal and corporate behavior which have a social significance.

Here are eight contemporary definitions by leading public relations organizations:

> Public relations is a strategic communication process that builds mutually beneficial relationships between organizations and their publics.
> Public Relations Society of America

> Public relations is defined as the planned and sustained effort to establish and maintain goodwill and mutual understanding between an organisation and its public, such development being for the benefit of the practice of public relations in commerce, industry, central and local government, nationalised undertakings, professional, trade and voluntary organisations and all practitioners and others concerned in or with public relations.
> International Public Relations Association

> Public relations is the art and social science of analyzing trends, predicting their consequences, counseling organizations' leaders, and implementing planning programmes of action which will serve both the organization and the public interest.
> World Assembly of Public Relations Associations

> Public relations is the deliberate, planned and sustained effort to establish and maintain mutual understanding between an organisation (or individual) and its (or their) publics. It's the key to effective

communication in all sectors of business, government, academic and not-for-profit.

                                    Public Relations Institute of Australia

Public relations is the management, through communication, of perceptions and strategic relationships between an organization and its internal and external stakeholders.

                              Public Relations Institute of South Africa

Public relations is the discipline that looks after reputation, with the aim of earning understanding and support and influencing opinion and behaviour. It is the planned and sustained effort to establish and maintain goodwill and understanding between an organization and its publics.

                    Chartered Institute of Public Relations, United Kingdom

Public relations is the strategic management of relationships between an organization and its diverse publics, through the use of communication, to achieve mutual understanding, realize organizational goals and serve the public interest.

                                      Canadian Public Relations Society

Public relations is the discipline that looks after reputation with the aim of earning understanding and support, and influencing opinion and behavior.

                                 Middle East Public Relations Association

There isn't a single definition because the profession is still evolving. But nowhere in these definitions do you find room for untruth or propaganda, exaggerations or stonewalling, publicity stunts or media gimmicks. Rather, the definitions of public relations, as they are articulated by the leading professional organizations in the field, all focus on strategic management, organizational goals, mutual understanding, goodwill and public interest.

Rather than giving readers of this book another definition, here is a narrative about the attributes of contemporary public relations. These qualities apply equally to corporations and nonprofit organizations and social causes, and to endeavors both large and small.

Public relations operates on a principle of *mutual benefits*; that is, it seeks not only to assist the sponsoring organization but also to advantage its publics. It is committed to the *public interest* and the betterment of society.

All communication associated with public relations adheres to high *ethical standards* of honesty, accuracy, decency and truth. Growing numbers of organizations have clear credos or *codes of ethics* outlining such commitments.

Public relations operates with *transparency* in an open environment, aligning itself with *democratic ideals* of the right of people to know the source of messages and to accept or reject those messages. It appreciates *diversity* and the cultural distinction of its publics, and particularly respects the rights and dignity of minorities within its publics.

Spurred both by regulation and customer demand, organizations must be *accountable* to their publics. Most publics are increasing their expectations for *quality performance* and *open communication*. Organizations are successful only to the extent that they perform at a high level, delivering quality products and services. All organizations operate in a *competitive environment*. Publics besought by rivals will remain loyal only to those organizations that earn their loyalty consistently and continuously.

As part of the *management function* within an organization, public relations counsels organizational leaders. It brings to the decision-making table *theories* born of ongoing *research* and both original and existing *data* to drive decisions through *strategic planning*. It seeks to develop systematic and sustained programs to address issues in common with its various publics.

Much of the theoretical base is drawn from *social psychology*. Theories useful to public relations include *cognitive dissonance* and related *consistency theories* (how people deal with information contrary to existing information, attitudes and biases), *diffusion of innovations* (how information is transmitted from groups to individuals), *selectivity* (what people pay attention to and remember), as well as many theories associated with persuasion and conflict resolution.

Public relations maintains an *ongoing dialogue* with the organization's various publics. Such dialogue seeks to represent one to the other and to nurture an environment in which each can influence the other. This involves *listening*, not only hearing but also understanding another perspective. In this *boundary-spanning capacity*, public relations can assist the organization in *adapting* its products, services and ideas toward the interests of its publics.

Within an organization, effective communication involves *cooperation* between public relations and other organizational functions such as marketing, legal, human resources, quality control and fundraising. Just as each knight was an equal participant at the round table in King Arthur's court, so too should each discipline have an effective and equal voice around the boardroom table.

The consumer philosophy has taken hold of all aspects of society, and organizations must answer with a *customer-driven response*, focusing on *benefits* for their publics. People support organizations that serve their interests and needs.

Mergers, downsizing and restructuring have led both businesses and nonprofits to seek ways to operate with *lean resources*, and the duplication that exists when marketing is isolated from public relations is too great a price for organizations to pay.

Strategic communication is part of an organization's *management role* and *decision-making process*. It is rooted in the organization's mission as lived out through its *bottom line*. This bottom line goes beyond money earned or raised; it focuses on the organization's fundamental purpose or mission. Strategists plot courses, set objectives and measure results.

Many *media changes* are affecting the way organizations communicate. The "mass media" have fragmented to the point that none rules supreme anymore. Lines have blurred between news, opinion and entertainment, further confusing audiences. Meanwhile, increasing advertising costs and tighter promotional budgets have led organizations to look at the more cost-effective communication and promotional tools from the public relations side of the house.

Strategic communication uses *multiple tools*, drawing from all communication-related disciplines to talk with various groups of people. *Established media* such as newspapers and television remain useful. *Emerging technologies*—particularly those involving digital, interactive and portable media—make it easier to supplement general media with more personal and targeted communication vehicles.

The strategy of choice in a competitive environment is *proactive, two-way communication*, in which organizations plan for, and initiate, relationships with the people important to their success. This approach emphasizes *dialogue* over monologue.

Organizations are successful to the extent that they enjoy a strong *reputation*, which results from neither accident nor luck. Strategic planning can identify and evaluate an organization's visibility and reputation. No organization can afford to be a "best-kept secret" among a relatively small number of supporters.

All kinds of organizations are realizing more keenly the need for long-term, mutually beneficial *relationships* between the organization and its various publics and market segments. Public relations practitioners long have recognized this, and marketing more recently has been discussing the need for *relationship marketing*, which really is a form of public relations.

With this growing awareness comes the fact that public relations is one of the fastest-growing professions and one of the most competitive. Universities find that the number of students wishing to study public relations often exceeds their ability to hire enough faculty to keep pace with the enrollment trend. Employers report receiving hundreds of viable applications for a single job opening.

All of this signals a healthy future for public relations, and for people who are willing to develop their skills in communication and problem-solving making themselves competitive in the profession that knows few boundaries.

THE BENEFITS OF PUBLIC RELATIONS

If a political candidate with limitless funding from unidentified supporters blasts opponents without regard for truth, that's a problem for democracy. When a corporation hides mismanagement of financial, quality and safety issues, that's a problem for society. The fault lies not in public relations but rather in the corruption of public relations strategies and techniques by powers more interested in expediency than in ethical service to society.

Just as corporations and politicians can misuse public relations tools, these same tools are used for good by social reformers and advocates for the environment, social justice, minority rights, education and so many other issues of importance to non-profit organizations, small businesses, local government and other groups.

Here are some of the ways that public relations helps society at large, as well as the organizations and people within society.

- *Financial Well Being.* Companies and nonprofit organizations can save money with programs that retain customers, increase productivity and influence legislation. They can make money by generating new customers and by attracting interest in new products and services, as well as by enhancing the support of stockholders and donors.
- *Safety.* Public relations can save lives through programs advocating behaviors related to seatbelt use, bicycle helmets, organ donation, child abduction and many other causes.
- *Health.* Public relations can lead to healthy lifestyles with advocacy and education programs such as those that encourage people to control obesity, eat more nutritious meals, exercise regularly and check for early signs of disease.
- *Recreation.* Public relations within the sports and entertainment worlds can help people enjoy their leisure time. Sports teams, entertainers, recreational facilities and travel destinations use public relations to publicize events, promote offerings and engage fans. Every leisure activity from bird watching to football, gaming to painting engages in public relations.
- *Civic Awareness.* Military units use public relations to recruit, foster public support and report their progress to members, families and legislators. Government agencies and lawmakers promote programs and services to their constituents.
- *Community Service.* Nonprofit organizations such as schools, churches and charities promote their services and share their expertise. Hospitals and medical organizations promote health literacy and thus help people make healthy choices.
- *Reputation.* Public relations helps organizations to gain support and minimize opposition by generating favorable publicity, encouraging alliances and coalitions with other groups, and testing plans against the interests of the organization's publics.
- *Survival.* Public relations helps organizations weather crises, survive lawsuits and reverse negative opinions.

THE PUBLICS OF PUBLIC RELATIONS

When public relations people talk about the organizations and the people they engage, they sometimes use the language of systems theory, which provides a framework. **Systems theory** provides a framework for understanding how organizations interact, both internally and externally.

The concept of open or closed systems indicates the extent to which an organization interacts with its environment. **Open systems** interact frequently and easily; **closed systems**, not so much. Public relations generally operates best with open systems; that is, with organizations that are ready, willing and able to engage their many publics.

Systems theory offers the idea of **linkages**, patterns in which an organization interacts with its various publics. Every public can fit into one of four linkage patterns: customers who use the product or service, producers who make it, enablers who create supportive conditions and limiters who create negative conditions.

So who are these publics of public relations? Let's take a university as an example.

Among the **customer publics**, students and potential students are obviously important as **primary customers**. But we don't stop there. A grouping of **secondary customers** includes the graduate schools that eventually will receive applications from graduates of our university and businesses that eventually will hire the graduates.

Among **producer publics**, the university's employees are obvious matches. But these can be subdivided: faculty and staff, veteran and novice employees, tenured and non-tenured faculty, full-time and adjunct instructors, volunteer members of university boards and councils, and so on. Take it a step further and include book suppliers. Then add an important component of people and groups that help the university produce its "product" (i.e., education): alumni, donors, foundations, state and federal grants, perhaps state legislators in the case of public universities, and others who provide the financial base.

Enabler publics offer wide possibilities for potential interaction, because they provide support and foster a positive environment. For the university this category includes parents and career counselors who help students make academic choices. It includes regulators such as state education departments, educational oversight agencies and accrediting organizations—groups that can create a positive academic environment.

Community colleges that serve as feeder programs for transfer students and other universities that function as colleagues are also enabler publics. This category includes elements of the surrounding community: neighbors, local government, police agencies. Also counted among enablers are quality-of-life venues such as restaurants, bookstores and entertainment sites, and landlords providing off-campus housing.

Two other groups can serve as enablers when the relationship is positive with the university: the media that can extend the university's message to other publics, and unions that can influence employees.

Limiter publics, on the other hand, are groups that may negatively impact the university. Media and unions potentially fit into this category if the university cannot nurture them as enablers. Other limiters could be activists who are potentially critical of the university's role in issues such as environment, animal testing, minority rights and dozens of other topics that confront modern higher education. Limiters also include competitor educational institutions seeking to attract the same students. Limiters also can be threatening environmental factors, such as high interest rates on student loans or demographic factors such as fewer people of high school and college age, as population trends sometimes reveal.

Each of these groups is in a relationship not only with the university but also with each other and with additional groups unrelated to the university. Thus each is a player on the public relations stage.

HOW ORGANIZATIONS USE PUBLIC RELATIONS

What type of organizations use public relations? All kinds. Every kind. It's hard to think of any organization that doesn't engage in public relations in some way. Some practitioners work for departments within corporations or nonprofit organizations. Others work for public relations agencies that are hired by corporations or nonprofits to handle particular public relations needs.

In either setting—in-house or agency—the work generally falls into one of several categories. Here's a look at some of these, along with related case studies.

Corporate public relations provides the vehicle for businesses to publicize products, gain customers, motivate productivity and workplace safety, and maintain a communication link with investors, regulators and industry colleagues.

Public relations is an everyday aspect of business in most corporations—the automobile, pharmaceutical and fashion industries; small businesses such as garden centers and corner cafes; service providers from hospitals to hair salons; and leisure entities such as sports teams, resorts and travel agencies. Even newspapers and television stations, as well as public relations agencies, have their own public relations people to engage their customers, attract new business, and promote their role within the community.

Most corporate public relations people today are engaged in a new trend within their profession toward **integrated strategic communication**. This is an evolution that blends public relations with marketing. It allows companies to coordinate their promotional activities and use every tool possible to engage and communicate with their customers and other significant publics.

Practitioners who work in corporate public relations are committed to helping their businesses or client companies. They also are committed to the ethical ideals of the public relations profession, and pragmatic enough to understand that the ethical practice of public relations is, in the long run, also in the best interests of their company. They have observed that corporations that hide behind pseudo public relations to deceive customers, or mask corporate wrong doing, inevitably find themselves in the public spotlight.

Consider some well-publicized instances of corporate misconduct: Halliburton overcharging government contracts, Compass Group bribing UN officials, Enron hiding debts, Tyco evading taxes, Olympus hiding financial losses, NewsCorp hacking phone records, and dozens of other scandals involving corruption, bribery, tax evasion, illegal political contributions, sex scandals and environmental offenses. Usually, the stonewalling and attempted (and always unsuccessful) cover-up is the greater crime, at least in the court of public opinion.

Thus for both ethical and pragmatic reasons, public relations practitioners often find themselves as the corporate conscience and voice of reason, urging companies to operate with transparency, integrity and accountability.

EARTH MONTH

With about 4 million customers each day in 16,000 locations around the world, Starbucks easily can be called an industry leader. Thus when it recognized its own vulnerability and turned its attention to an environment problem, the potential impact was huge.

Starbucks research showed that the environment is the top social concern to its customers internationally and that customers in general are more supportive of companies that practice good environmental policies. It also recognized an opportunity, because Starbucks itself was damaging the environment by using millions of disposable drinking cups every day.

Recognizing a silver living by correcting its own problem, Starbucks turned to its public relations people. They created "Earth Month," a diversified campaign among employees and customers to encourage the use of reusable mugs. They obtained the endorsement of celebrities and environmental organizations, and engaged reporters and bloggers.

The public relations strategy began with in-store promotion with free coffee for customers with reusable mugs was launched in the US and Canada, Europe, Latin America and Asia-Pacific venues. The company produced a global responsibility report highlighting Starbucks' commitment to environmental issues. Starbucks also convened meetings of suppliers, manufacturers, academics, even competitors to work toward common acceptance of reusable cups.

The program was successful, with 1.2 million customers participating in the opening promotion and 50,000 pledging to always use reusable mugs.

The public relations plan generated much favorable publicity for both Starbucks and the recycling cause—more than 265 local broadcast stories and 20 national reports, with 12 national print stories in the US alone. The program also increased positive consumer attitudes from 57 percent to 80 percent for Starbucks' environment responsibility.

In retrospect, Starbucks said it should have used social media more, something it added to its ongoing promotion of reusable cups.

GOVERNMENT PUBLIC RELATIONS

Government public relations covers a wide range of areas, including agencies and military. From the White House to Whitehall, every government agency throughout the world has to communicate with constituents.

Government public relations involves lobbying of governmental agencies by corporations and nonprofit organizations seeking to impact public policy decisions. Unions, corporations, churches, small businesses, professional organizations and cultural groups—all sometimes mount public relations campaigns for or against various issues. The issues come in many flavors: health care, smoking, business regulation, product safety, scientific research and so on.

PANDA EXPRESS

When it was time for US zoos to return two giant pandas to an animal preserve in China, they turned to FedEx to deliver the "packages." This was a logical choice. It built on an earlier FedEx delivery of penguins temporarily relocated after Hurricane Katrina. When the birds were returned to the New Orleans zoo, the fanfare included a parade led, appropriately enough, by an emperor penguin.

The panda program had all the opportunities associated with two nations cooperating in a conservation program to save the endangered species. It also had the obstacle of groups opposed to the "repatriation" of the pandas for economic and pseudo-patriotic reasons.

FedEx wanted the panda return to be celebratory. It focused on news media, US and Chinese government officials, community leaders in Atlanta and Washington DC where the zoos were located, and FedEx employees and customers around the world. It held news conferences and farewell zoo events in Atlanta and Washington, with police escorts to an airport departure celebration. It also organized welcome-home ceremonies in China.

FedEx produced a behind-the-scenes video of the "Panda Express," as the record-setting cargo flight was named. It also promoted the event on its website, blog, online newsroom, Twitter feeds and employee intranet. When the successful return was completed,

FedEx counted nearly 1,500 placements in 175 international media reaching more than 1 billion people.

FedEx has had subsequent "Panda Express" flights to deliver other pandas from China to France, Scotland and Memphis, Tenn.

PUBLIC DIPLOMACY

Public diplomacy is related to government public relations. Formal state-to-state diplomacy usually is conducted in secret. Public diplomacy is the overlap area in which governments use the power and influence of the media to impact public opinion in another country or perhaps within a nongovernmental organization, corporation, political faction or nonprofit organization.

An example of this is Israel's campaign to position itself as a gay-friendly country in the midst of intolerant regimes. The plan isn't likely to change neighboring nations, most of which outlaw homosexuality or deny even that any gay people live within their boundaries. But the pro-tolerance stance can strengthen support for Israel by many citizens—gay and straight—in democracies such as the US, Canada, Australia and European countries.

There have been many times when, during a civil war or internal uprisings in various countries, an outside government would float ideas and allow leaks to encourage the strife-torn country to accept internal reform, make peace with warring factions, or otherwise resolve the conflict. At times, the public diplomacy has been directed toward a third country with influence over the leaders of the conflicted nation, encouraging them to make the necessary concessions or allow the needed reforms.

The tools of such resolution include traditional publicity vehicles, social media, opinion leaders, and public appeals to religious and cultural leaders.

FREE SILVA

In 2008, Silva Harotonian was arrested in Iran for plotting a "soft revolution."

An Iranian-American of Armenian ancestry, Silva worked for the International Research and Exchanges Board, a nonprofit organization providing education and training for grassroots social workers. Her work focused on public health professionals working with mother-and-child projects.

Seven months after her arrest, Silva was convicted of attempting to overthrow the government of Iran. She was sentenced to three years in prison. Within a week of sentencing, her employer hired Edelman public relations firm to help secure her release.

Edelman prepared an international public-awareness campaign that required a delicate balance. Outside influence would be needed, but Iran would take a hard line if too much pressure became evident. Understanding Iran's suspicion toward Americans in particular, the plan sought to engage people who might influence Iran's president and top religious leader. It tried to maintain a respectful tone toward Iran as it reached out to human rights organizations and to Armenians in the US and Europe. Ironically for a public relations agency, much of Edelman's strategy involved behind-the-scenes private activity.

The campaign developed an advocacy website to leverage international support, provided interviews with Silva's family, targeted international media, and arranged for the French and Armenian governments to appeal for Silva's release. After 11 months of detention, Silva was released from prison. A condition of her release was elimination of the advocacy website, so successful had it been.

POLITICAL PUBLIC RELATIONS

Political public relations is an area that focuses on the process of getting elected and staying in office. Practiced by ethical professionals, political public relations can positively impact public opinion and generate support for candidates and issues. Though the environment may be highly partisan and the players often confrontational, nevertheless, there is an important role for civic-minded experts with skills in polling, issue analysis, strategic planning and writing.

The day-to-day work of political public relations involves research into a candidate's image and constituents' take on public policy issues. It deals with publicity for candidates and their positions.

Two broad areas of tactics are common in political public relations: special events such as press-the-flesh gatherings and public debates, and media relations with an increasing emphasis on social media.

Political campaigns around the globe give witness to the fact that bloggers are becoming as important as mainstream journalists. Fundraising and political advertising also play a huge role in this subspecialty.

Unfortunately, political public relations also is the setting for many of the most egregious excesses and irregularities associated with public relations. In too many situations, political public relations involves negative strategy (name calling, dirty tricks, attack ads, vilification of opponents, misrepresentation and outright lying). It is public relations stripped of its ethical base, commitment to honest communication, and any vision of mutual benefits and social responsibility.

WRITE-IN CAMPAIGN

It's almost impossible to buck the system when it comes to party endorsement in US politics. But a strong public relations plan fed an upset when Lisa Murkowski became the first write-in candidate in 56 years to win a senate seat.

Murkowski, a Republican, had been a US senator from Alaska. She was beaten in a primary, largely because of opposition from the Tea Party faction of her party. But when polling showed that she had strong voter support, she launched a write-in campaign. The task had all of the expected goals related to funding, visibility and appeals to voter interests, plus one additional factor. Write-ins required proper spelling of the candidate's name, and Murkowski isn't your typical Brown, Smith or Jones. So the campaign distributed 50,000 bracelets with the Murkowski's name.

Other than that, the public relations plan relied heavily on Facebook and Twitter, which was especially effective in countering Tea Party opposition messages. It also featured the standard fare for political public relations: news releases, speeches, TV and newspaper interviews and news reports, meetings with editorial boards of newspapers, issue papers, televised debates, e-mails and phone calls to voters, websites with frequent updates and redesigns to attract repeat visitors, and downloadable videos.

The result was that she received 10,000 votes more than her nearest rival, the party-endorsed Republican.

NONPROFIT PUBLIC RELATIONS

Nonprofit public relations involves a wide variety of organizations: services such as education; health care; cultural and religious groups; human service agencies and charitable organizations; membership organizations such as unions and professional groups. The nonprofit sphere also involves travel and tourism, entertainment, and some aspects of sports and recreation.

A key element of nonprofit public relations is that journalists in both established media and emerging social media are more likely to be supportive. Consider these likely endeavors by nonprofit organizations:

- Introduction of a fundraising campaign for a new hospital wing to extend cancer treatment.
- Announcement of a grant based on promising research into a childhood disease.
- Appointment of a new religious leader for a denomination with many members in the community.
- Final preparation in staging a benefit performance by the local symphony or a touring musical artist.
- Creation of a foundation for inner-city children by a sports celebrity who just signed a multi-million-dollar contract.

Reporters don't cover these news stories with the same skepticism and watchdog mentality with which they approach corporations and politicians. That is one reason that many practitioners prefer nonprofit public relations, particularly because they can deal every day with causes that serve the public good and contribute to a better society.

Nonprofit organizations have learned the same lesson as corporations: Taking a public stand on a social or public policy issue can both gain and lose support. About 2 percent of Californians are Mormons. After the church spent $30 million (more than 70 percent of the total raised) to oppose gay marriage there, the church's own public opinion polls showed a decrease in acceptance for the religion. Several Mormons publically announced their resignation from the church. In response, the Mormon Church undertook a reputed $40 million multimedia campaign drawing on their own polling and using print and broadcast ads, a new website, and TV spokespersons dispatch to help rebuild its image.

Sometimes the rivalry is internal. For decades, the Catholic Church advocated for universal health care in the US. But during the political debate the bishops' conference opposed the Obama proposal, which was supported by the Catholic Health Association representing 13 percent of all hospitals in the country. In the pews, Catholic sentiment for and against the health-care reform plan was little different than among other sectors in the population.

GUIDE DOGS

The British nonprofit organization Guide Dogs for the Blind needed a low-cost, high-impact plan to create pre-event publicity for a major fundraising event with wealthy donors.

Research identified dog-loving celebrities who could be invited to act as ambassadors for the event, which aimed to attract donors to an exhibition and launch party. Twenty-one personalities volunteered their time, including actors Felicity Kendal and Britt Eckland, government officials David Blunkett (himself blind) and Baron John Prescott, and sports celebrities Gary Lineker, Sir Ian Botham and Roy Keane.

They participated in photo shoots by Adrian Houston, with the celebrities posing with their own dogs. This became the basis for the fundraising photo exhibition at a London art gallery, where the photos were to be auctioned online for the Guide Dogs charity. The donations would go toward the organization's goal of providing training and placement for more than 800 guide dogs.

The celebrities also gave media interviews, participated in talk shows, lent their names to columns in print and digital media, and attended the launch event.

The strategy was to create an event with celebrity involvement to attract media interest and donor appeal. The result was nationwide media coverage, with pieces in 16 publications and full-page articles in three papers.

The budget for the entire project was £7,000 ($11,000, €9,000).

The goal was to attract 50 donors, but more than 300 wealthy contributors and celebrities attended the launch event.

PUBLIC RELATIONS FOR SOCIAL REFORM

Public relations for social reform has an ancient—and many would say, glorious—history.

This sometimes overlaps with nonprofit public relations and nongovernmental organizations, though it differs in that it generally is movement-based rather than linked to a specific organization. For example, Amnesty International focuses on international social reform on behalf of prisoners of conscience and political prisoners. In that sense, working with AI is an example of NGO public relations.

Yet the movement for fair treatment of political prisoners is broader than that one organization. It involves many educational institutions, religious groups, legal organizations and human rights entities all working toward a similar end, but without the coordination of a single organization.

One of the most significant social reform movements involved the abolition of slavery or the slave trade in many countries—England, France, Australia, the US and many European colonies and possessions. Public relations played a big part in the abolition cause with publicity, speeches, books and pamphlets, lobbying, advertising, and eventually newspapers, radio and television.

So successful were anti-slavery campaigns over the past two centuries that institutional slavery is now banned throughout the world. Yet there remain dark shadows: human trafficking, child slavery and the sex trade. Public relations practitioners use not only traditional tactics but also the emerging social media on behalf of their cause to eradicate the remnants of such captivity and abuse.

Other reform movements similarly have benefitted from public relations support: suffrage campaigns for the right of women to vote, safety standards for food, animal rights, educational reform, gun control and reduction of gun violence, humane treatment of the mentally ill, elimination of child labor, prisoner's rights, pro-peace/anti-war campaigns, and elimination or regulation of prostitution, smoking, drugs and alcohol.

Today the public relations fight continues with activism dealing with environmental protection, religious freedom, gay rights, education of girls and other aspects of the women's movement, rights of aboriginal/native peoples, abolition of the death penalty, pornography, gambling, pro-life/pro-choice and so on.

HUMAN TRAFFICKING

An estimated 17,000 people are brought to the US each year against their will—kidnapped, tricked or coerced, beaten or blackmailed into prostitution and other slave-like working conditions.

The US Health and Human Services Agency created a program, "Restore and Rescue," to identify victims of human trafficking and help them return to a better life. The campaign eventually gained the participation of more than 40 national partner agencies.

Extensive research by Ketchum public relations agency indicated that addressing a campaign directly to victims wouldn't work, because they have little or no access to the outside world.

Instead, the strategic planning team focused on opinion leaders: social workers, law enforcement personnel, religious personnel, emergency-room medical staff, labor groups, women's organizations and similar groups. Working with more than 300 intermediary local organizations, the project urged people to "look beneath the surface" to identify victims of trafficking among people they encounter.

Tactically, the campaign created an information website, launched a 24/7 multi-language hotline, and distributed 625,000 pieces of print informational materials.

In evaluating the success of the program, Ketchum noted three objectives for the project, which began in 2005 with 10 major cities and rolled out to 24 cities over the next few years.

The first goal of the campaign was to increase the number of trafficking victims identified. In the first year of the hotline, more than 5,000 valid calls were received, and 1,000 victims were identified and referred for assistance by social workers.

The plan also aimed at bringing media attention to the problem. During the introductory year, more than 70 million media impressions were counted in national outlets and in local media venues in 10 inaugural cities targeted by the campaign.

Finally, the campaign sought to raise awareness among opinion leaders and intermediaries who could help identify trafficking victims. Restore and Rescue generated nearly 60,000 visitors to the trafficking website.

PUBLIC RELATIONS, PERFORMANCE
AND ADAPTATION

"Words are merely words and they can be purely cosmetic if they aren't backed by convictions, actions and policies." That's what Harold Burson, co-founder of the global public relations agency of Burson-Marsteller, told students at Utica College of Syracuse University.

Public relations practitioners no longer ask how to say something effectively or even what to say. Instead they focus on what to do. Act appropriately and strategically, and the words will follow.

A contemporary understanding of public relations involves the notion of helping organizations adjust to the social environment. This builds on the advice of one of the founding fathers of the public relations profession, Edward Bernays, who advised that the "engineering of consent" rests on information, persuasion and adjustment by the organization to its publics.

Some organizations see the difference between performance and pronouncements, between word and deed.

Narcotics Anonymous, for example, says "our public relations policy is based on attraction rather than promotion." That's a good formula even if you are not an addict in recovery, because it reflects the humility and transparency that underlies any good public relations program. Trustees of the organization note that "most addicts will only hear of us through media reports and announcements, through professional referral, or through direction given by members of the community-at-large—or they won't hear of us at all." For that reason, says Narcotics Anonymous, cooperative relationships within the community are necessary to the organization's ability to help people in need.

Some groups go out of their way to engage critics. Ford Motors has been applauded by the Sierra Club for developing a hybrid SUV, but the same environmental group also denounced Ford for having the most gas-guzzling cars in the industry. Yet Ford meets regularly with the Sierra Club, noting that such interaction gives it signals of what consumers want and expect. Even if they can't agree on everything, both sides see the engagement as a positive.

BETTER BANANAS

The Rainforest Alliance has criticized poor farming practices as a major source of pollution and deforestation in Central and South America. Chiquita Brand International is one of the accused companies. Instead of countering the criticism, Chiquita cooperated with the alliance to promote the Sustainable Agriculture Network, a coalition of environmental groups in eight banana-growing countries.

The company imposes strict environmental standards on its contract farmers. In return, SAN provides a certification protocol for farmers to earn the Better Banana seal. The program is open to any exporting company.

This cooperative venture has not been without criticism. In general, businesses sometimes feel that they may be exposed to criticism by stockholders and competitors, and nonprofit groups may worry about being co-opted by big corporations. With the SAN-Chiquita venture, critics called it "greenwashing," merely pretending to respond to environment issues without making substantive changes. The company and the network counter that these are steps toward solving the bigger environmental issues.

The program also initially alienated trade unions. But when SAN became aware of this, it reached out to them and involved the unions in setting and applying the environmental standards.

Meanwhile, the Rainforest Alliance said it is receiving requests from other companies to begin discussions on cooperating on environmental concerns.

ENVIRONMENTAL DEFENSE

Working with wayward corporations is a new strategy for the Environmental Defense Fund. The president of the environmental advocacy group explained: "Our informal motto used to be 'Sue the bastards.' Now our official tagline is, 'Finding the ways that work'."

FedEx boasts that it delivers packages anywhere in the world, though it has been criticized for fuel inefficiency and contributing to air pollution. In a collaborative effort, FedEx worked with EDF and Eaton Motors to develop a fleet of delivery trucks that were more environmentally friendly, including hybrid diesel-electric delivery trucks. The goal was to have the entire 30,000-truck FedEx fleet using the hybrids or all-electric models, but it later found more cost-effective ways to improve the efficiency of its entire fleet by 20 percent.

FedEx, EDF and Eaton shared an award for environmental partnering from Harvard University.

PUBLIC RELATIONS, IMAGE AND REPUTATION

A squirrel is a rat with good public relations. This statement light-heartedly links public relations with reputation. What people know and think of something—whether that something is an organization, a person or a rodent—is important with regards to how they treat it. Reputation spells the difference between like and dislike, support and opposition, feeding the cute critter or setting a trap for it.

But the squirrel-rat allusion misses much of what reputation is about. While part of reputation is based on image, a bigger part is based on action. Reputation is rooted in how a person or organization (or rodent) acts. Regardless of the cuteness quotient that Disney gives squirrels, any farmer or gardener knows that destructive behavior means that the furry beast is no friend.

From a public relations perspective, reputation is the result of what you do, what you say, and what others say about you. One reason for the continuing growth of public relations is that organizations are paying more attention to this, realizing that what people say affects the bottom line.

Reputation is probably the single most-important asset an organization has. Reputation is the single basis for the financial dominance of Coca-Cola, the world's most valuable brand worth $60 billion (£38 billion, €48 billion). After all, it's only soft drink and, arguably, not much better than (or even different from) other brands. Yet Coke's reputation and branding make it the No. 1 soft drink around the world.

Warren Buffet, one of the world's most successful business investors of the 20th century, famously told employees of the scandal-riddled Salomon Brothers investment bank: "If you lose money for the firm by bad decisions, I will be very understanding. If you lose a shred of reputation for the firm, I will be ruthless."

As many people learned from their mother, reputation is built up with consistent action over time, but it can be lost with a single bad decision. Ask Penn State about its decisions not to report or investigate charges of child abuse. Attempting to avoid bad publicity, the university jeopardized its 157-year heritage, destroyed its place in the football record books, and risked its future as an athletics program, while earning an immediate $60 million (£38 million, €48 million) football fine and the likelihood of perhaps $500 million (£315 million, €399 million) in legal costs and fines.

Here is some current thinking on these and related concepts. (Fair disclosure: Theorists and practitioners in public relations are not at all of a single mind about these terms. You may find them used differently or even interchangeably. But try these on, and see how they work for you.)

Reputation is the general, overall and long-term impression of an organization on a specific public. It, thus, is the prevailing impression of an organization and the social evaluation that people make of it. Reputation is rooted in what people know, or think they know, about an organization and what attitudes they hold based on that information.

Reputation management is the process of seeking to influence the way publics view and understand the organization. Reputation management begins with tracking and identifying what others say and feel about an organization. It focuses on building and maintaining a desired reputation with key publics. In critical times, reputation management can be part of crisis communication, with the organization attempting to recover from a negative environment.

Image (aka **perception**) is a more general and short-term evaluation of an organization's messages. It is drawn from the way an organization projects itself toward its various publics. Image is what people think about the organization based on both word and deed; that is, on the verbal, visual and behavioral messages, both planned and unplanned, that come from an organization and leave an impression. Not all publics receive the same messages or process them the same way, so image can be inconsistent and can vary from one public to another or from one time to another.

Some confusion exists about the relationship between reputation and image. Reputation is interactive and closely associated with public relations, image is linked more with advertising and the production/presentation of branding messages.

Rosanna Fiske pointed this out in AdWeek in 2011, writing in her role as chair of PRSA: "Public relations is not about image; it's about reputation, trust and credibility. Advertising ... is about image—the visual, the look, the controlled viewpoint." Both are important, she wrote, adding: "Reputation is hard-earned and long-standing. It comes from years, not moments, of doing and saying the right thing."

Positioning or **branding** is a process of managing how an organization wants to be seen and known by its publics. A concept drawn from marketing, positioning specifically deals with establishing and maintaining a distinctive place for an organization vis-à-vis its competitors. It is the organization's competitive posture.

Organizational **identity** is the way an organization consciously projects itself visually as an expression of its personality. An **identity system** involves tools such as the organization's name and logo, brochures, news releases, interviews, advertisements, letterhead, posters, manuals, signage, publication layout and design, correspondence, websites, social media sites, videos, voice mail and telephone answering, uniform use of color, and other means of communication.

NOTHING BUT NETS

The leading pest-control company, Orkin, has positioned itself as a protector of public health with an array of marketing and educational materials to help homeowners protect themselves against mosquitos and other pests, along with the diseases they carry.

As part of a reputation-enhancement campaign with its employees and customers, Orkin signed on as a sponsor with the United Nations Foundation's "Nothing But Nets" program. NBN raises funds to purchase and distribute mosquito netting in Africa, where malaria is a leading killer of children. The disease can be controlled simply by using bed nets when children are sleeping.

The plan was inspired by Sports Illustrated columnist Rick Reilly, who in turn was motivated by a BBC television documentary. Since the program began in 2006, it has raised $35 million (£22 million, €25.5 million) and provided more than 4 million nets in 20 countries in sub-Saharan Africa. Since 2008, 11 nations on the continent have seen malaria deaths cut in half.

Nothing But Nets has enlisted dozens of sponsors, including NBA Cares, the charity of the basketball league. MLS Works, the community outreach program of Major League Soccer, also signed on, as did *Sports Illustrated* magazine. Because of its natural connection with mosquitos and other pests, the NBN program seemed to be a natural fit for Orkin, which has 400 outlets in the US and international franchises in Africa, Canada, Europe, Central America, Asia, the Middle East and the Caribbean.

Internal company research indicated that three-quarters of Orkin customers are sports fans, another plus for the campaign that itself has a strong sports theme. Being based in Atlanta, Orkin enlisted the participation of the local NBA team, the Atlanta Hawks.

Internally, Orkin called its plan "Fight the Bite." The campaign focused largely on Orkin employees, using print and social media to equip its employees to serve as "viral communicators" about the benefits of mosquito netting. It also reached customers through a media relations component. The campaign also had a community relations element, with a World Malaria Day event in New York City, Sports Zoolebrity Day at the Atlanta zoo, and arena night with the Hawks and with the Atlanta Dream of the WNBA.

Orkin also developed "Bug Battle," a free iPhone game to spread awareness about malaria.

The company vowed to donate one mosquito net each time a customer purchased its pest-control service. It asked its employees and customers to donate to the cause, with each $10 paying for the purchase and distribution of a bed net. Each year, Bite the Bug has increased its goal, from $100,000 when it was started to $225,000 three years later—and each year it surpassed its goal. In four years, Orkin's program contributed $1 million (£630,000, €797,000) to Nothing But Nets.

ETHICS AND PROFESSIONALISM

With the power to influence comes the responsibility to act responsibly. One of the hallmarks of public relations is a strong ethical base and a commitment to contribute to the public good while also serving the interests of the boss or client. Indeed, ethics is the distinguishing characteristic between a real public relations practitioner and someone with communication or persuasive skills merely pretending to do public relations work.

The professional organizations in many countries of the world are strong upholders of ethical practice. Living as we do in a borderless world, the practice of public relations spans the globe, extending ethical norms that developed in North America, Western Europe and Australia into new areas, such as the former Soviet Bloc republics and emerging democracies in Africa and the Middle East.

Because of their size and influence, the professional organizations in the US, Canada and UK are among the most influential across the globe. The code of professional standards of the Public Relations Society of America, for example, is similar to the code of conduct of the Chartered Institute of Public Relations in the UK and the code of ethics of the Canadian Public Relations Society.

Additionally, professional standards are established by several wider organizations. The International Public Relations Association's code of conduct serves as a model of ethics standards worldwide. Other groups are regionally focused, such as the European Public Relations Confederation, the Middle Eastern Public Relations Association, and the African Public Relations Association.

Use a search engine to find the websites of professional groups associated with IPRA. Altogether, nearly 100 national organizations exist to promote the work of ethical and effective public relations. Here's a partial list of some countries with professional public relations organizations:

- In Europe: France, the UK, Germany, Greece, Iceland, Ireland, Latvia, Italy, Switzerland, Norway, Poland, Slovenia, Spain and Ukraine.
- In the Middle East: Azerbaijan, Turkey, Syria and Israel.
- In Asia: Bangladesh, China, India, Indonesia, Japan, Malaysia, Philippines and South Korea.
- In the Americas: Brazil, Cuba, Venezuela, Canada and the US.
- In Africa: Egypt, Sudan, Nigeria and South Africa.
- In Australia and Oceania: Australia and New Zealand.

A question sometimes comes up: Why isn't there some kind of **licensing** to make sure that people who call themselves public relations practitioners actually know what they are doing and are committed to working ethically? After all, it requires a license to do acupuncture and physical therapy, to practice law or medicine, to be a teacher or pharmacist, and to operate a funeral home or work as a landscape architect or a realtor. Some of the licenses come from governments, others from professional groups. Most have educational requirements and testing.

All of these professions in some way impact the people whom they serve, making licensing a reasonable rule. After all, just because your neighbor thinks she'd be a good dental surgeon doesn't mean she should be allowed to open a dental clinic in her garage.

But public relations is different. As the case has been built earlier in this chapter, public relations serves the public good. But it's also part of the wider issue of human rights. The United Nations and most countries have provisions for freedom of expression, open communication, free and generally unrestricted speech and freedom of opinion. Allowing governments to limit these to people in a certain profession generally has been considered an unwarranted intrusion into individual liberties.

But the profession has devised a middle ground between no limits and government approval for doing public relations. It's called **accreditation**. This involves the profession setting and maintaining its own standards, rather than having them imposed from outside.

In some countries, the professional organization has created a program of study, testing, sponsorship and/or portfolio review. Practitioners voluntarily submit themselves for the accrediting process in return for the right to be acknowledged as an accredited practitioner of public relations. The APR designation serves as a mark of distinction given to public relations practitioners by public relations practitioners, attesting to the demonstrated expertise and commitment to the profession and its ethical standards.

In the US, the Universal Accreditation Board includes PRSA, several regional public relations groups, and discipline-specific groups such as the Religion Communicators Council, the National School Public Relations Association and the Agricultural Relations Council.

Public relations associations in Canada, Australia and the Philippines have their own accreditation process. Efforts are underway in India to introduce an accreditation component to the public relations profession there. In the UK, CIPR issues several certificates and diplomas in specialized areas such as crisis communication, public affairs and internal communication.

Additionally, professional groups in many countries—Ireland, the UK, Australia, the US—have a voluntary process to accredit or approve universities to teach public relations.

PUBLIC RELATIONS IN SOCIETY

This chapter provides an overview of the history and evolution of public relations. Rooted as it is in all social interaction throughout history, public relations has come into its own as a legitimate profession contributing to the betterment of society.

Public relations is as ancient as clay tablets in Mesopotamia and as contemporary as the next generation of digital tablets. It is as traditional as a political speech in the public square and as cutting edge as an international social media campaign for human rights.

HISTORICAL ANTECEDENTS OF PUBLIC RELATIONS

In tracing the development of public relations, we look back not out of nostalgia or for the sake of trivial knowledge, but rather to support the premise of this chapter: *Public relations is a natural, essential and recurring element of human social interaction.*

Public relations is part of what makes us human. As such, it is one of the oldest and most foundational aspects of society. In fact, it's difficult to imagine a society in which effective communication and information, advocacy and positive relationships are not among the most basic components of everyday life.

Edward Bernays, one of the founding fathers of contemporary public relations, observed that "The three main elements of public relations are practically as old as society: informing people, persuading people, or integrating people with people." Thus an understanding of the evolution of public relations give us glimpses into what the professional has become in today's world.

It's not accurate to say that this look back through the centuries reveals people who were consciously practicing public relations as we understand it today. But it does show that the various elements of public relations have been present in society since the earliest of times. [In this chapter, these elements are printed in italics, so you can better observe some aspects of public relations throughout the ages.]

Be forewarned. This look back also reveals that common practice has not always been consistent with ethics. Some past practices employed elements of dubious moral principles.

Traces of some of these remain today, generally disavowed by public relations practitioners but nevertheless part of the underbelly of persuasive communication and the contentious battle for public opinion that exists within a world of competitive economics, aggressive politics and competing worldviews.

PUBLIC RELATIONS IN CLASSICAL ANTIQUITY

The antecedents of modern public relations practice lie in the ancient world.

We can begin in Mesopotamia, the land of contemporary Iraq. Archaeologists have discovered building inscriptions that are artifacts of a public relations campaign to boost the reputation of the kings. Clay tablets dating to 1,800 BCE served as *bulletins* and *brochures* that instructed farmers how to sow crops, irrigate fields and increase their harvests. What today we call *consumer affairs* was important to kings and other rulers, who knew that governmental stability depended on subjects who were well fed and prosperous.

Two of the oldest-known pieces of literature—The *Iliad* and The *Odyssey*, ascribed to the Greek poet Homer about 850 BCE—feature examples of effective *persuasive speeches*. Odysseus convinces the Cyclops not to eat him; Paris entreats Helen to leave her husband and go off with him; Hector and Achilles give stirring speeches to pump up their troops.

Earlier (though difficult to date) pieces of literature—the Pentateuch of the Hebrew Bible and the Sumerian epic of Gilgamesh—also have passages with strong persuasive rhetoric, again positioning advocacy as an important drive for both individuals and groups.

To enhance the *credibility* of communication, ancient Egyptian stories often were written as advice from a father to a son, generally implying that the wisdom had been handed down for many generations.

In China in the 4th century BCE, Confucius elevated the concept of *eloquence* in speech, persuasion based on the elegant use of language and expression of emotions. Chinese culture, as well as the related cultures of Korea and Japan, emphasize *interpersonal relationship* and the role of *personal influence* in the civic and professional spheres. Other aspects of Northeastern Asian rhetoric show the value of *silence* as a tool of communication.

In the 3rd century BCE in Athens, Socrates and Plato taught that effective communication should be *based on truth*. Plato's student Aristotle analyzed persuasive communication and taught others how to be effective speakers, specifically by developing *compelling and ethical arguments* that offer verbal proofs. Gorgias of Sicily taught that fostering skill in persuasive speaking was the primary job of a rhetorician.

PUBLIC RELATIONS IN GOVERNMENT

In antiquity, poems and stories often were written to bolster the reputation of kings and military leaders. The pharaohs of classical Egypt commissioned statues and built temples and pyramids to impress their people. Court advisers in Egypt 2,400 year ago told the pharaohs to *communicate truthfully* and *address audience interests*.

From the period of classical Greece, the antecedent Aristotle is still important today because he sought to equip his students with the persuasive skills to function effectively in a *democracy*. These skills have become increasingly useful as the world moves, meanders and, at times, marches toward giving all citizens a voice in their civic life.

In the 5th century BCE, the biblical Joseph (Yosef ben Yaakov in the Hebrew Bible, Yusuf ibn Ya'qub in the Quran) functioned in the role of *public relations adviser* in Egypt, analyzing trends and counseling the pharaoh as he developed a campaign to educate farmers about gathering food for a seven-year famine.

Philip of Macedonia and his son, Alexander the Great, used public relations as they extended Greek rule throughout Northern Africa and the Middle East into Central Asia and India. They employed tactics such as *public monuments, commemorative stamps* and *coins,* and *named buildings* and *stadiums.*

Elsewhere in the classical Mediterranean world, others also were studying communication. Corax of Syracuse wrote about *persuasive speaking.* Rome's most acclaimed orator, Marcus Tullius Cicero, developed the earlier Greek rhetorical methods for presenting *persuasive arguments* in public.

Julius Caesar wrote the first *campaign biography* to publicize his battlefield exploits as military governor of Gaul, successfully making the case that he was the best candidate to rule Rome. After maneuvering himself to be proclaimed "dictator in perpetuity," Caesar ordered the posting of the first public *newsletter* to keep his citizenry informed.

Later, the first Roman Emperor, Octavian Augustus Caesar (the adopted great-nephew of Julius), actively courted *public opinion,* realizing that he needed the support of the people in order to reign successfully. One of his tactics was to commission the poet Virgil to write an epic poem (The *Aneid*) depicting Caesar as being ordained by the gods to rebuild Rome. This gave *credibility* to the emperor as a legitimate ruler of his people as a successor to the Roman republic.

In pre-Islamic Arabia, poets played a role in news and public relations, often commissioned by tribal chiefs to create poetry and stories that influenced public opinion.

In 9th-century Persia (present-day Iran), caliph Harun al-Rashid (Aaron the Just) engaged in international *diplomacy,* sending emissaries to the European court of Charlemagne, the Chinese court of the Tang dynasty and the Pala empire of present-day Bangladesh. His internal public relations included what today would be called *constituent research* and *community relations.* The Arabian tales recount his practice of wandering among his subjects in disguise to learn how his government administrators were working for the benefit of his subjects.

Civil society and religion intersected in 1215, when the archbishop of Canterbury, Stephen Langton, used tactics of *lobbying* and *government relations* to persuade the influential English barons to join him in demanding that King John recognize the rights of both the barons and the church. The result of this successful persuasion was the Magna Carta, the document that laid the foundation for constitutional government not only in England but also, eventually, around the world.

Whereas Western rhetoric focused on persuasion, communication in Asia often valued *consensus*. Hindu philosophy developed the concept of *dialectics* particularly during the Gupta Empire around the 4th century. This is a form of *dialogue* and *conflict resolution* in which participants with different points of view discuss a topic not to persuade each other but together to reach a common understanding, which is very much in line with a contemporary approach to public relations. The message often had an underlying theme, such as supporting rulers and social elites.

India also had the experience of sutradhars, who had a role much like the more musical troubadours of medieval Europe. Both were traveling storytellers, narrators who interpreted the story, often with a message or moral with a bit of humor.

PUBLIC RELATIONS AND RELIGION

Much of the history of public relations, like so many other aspects of Western society, is connected with religion.

The Hebrew scriptures depict Aaron as a great public speaker who served as the *spokesman* for his brother Moses. In the Christian scriptures, John the Baptist was shown as the advance man in what became a new religion, *generating interest* and preparing the way for Jesus Christ. Jesus himself was a great storyteller who used *parables* and other *short stories* with strong, simple and easy-to-understand messages to teach moral lessons.

Indeed, all of the major religious scriptures associated with Judaism, Christianity and Islam as well as the texts of Hinduism and Buddhism all reveal the importance of *storytelling* as an essential ingredient in communication on religious, moral and spiritual topics.

In the mid-1st century, Shim'on bar-Yonah (known to history as St. Peter) and Saul of Tarsus (St. Paul) led the Christian apostles in using many persuasive techniques: *speeches, staged events, letters* and *oral teaching*. Their aim was to increase interest in Jesus, recruit for the new religious movement, and maintain morale and order among church members. Paul's letters in particular are examples of the *eloquence of the written word*.

The gospel writers Matthew, Mark, Luke and John used the strategies of *interpretation* and *audience segmentation*, each presenting the same story in four different versions to appeal to the interests, experiences and needs of four different audiences (Matthew writing for Jewish Christians, Mark for non-Jewish Greeks, Luke for non-Jewish Christians, and John for nonbelievers and later the network of Christian communities spreading throughout the Eastern Mediterranean).

The Roman Emperor Nero used the strategy of *orchestrating events* when he blamed the burning of Rome on the Christians, already the social scapegoats of his empire. It was a classic example of *framing*: telling one side of the story first so that any other versions are received as being different from what people already have heard.

The early Christian Church preserved and enhanced the concepts of *rhetoric*. In Roman Africa, the 5th-century philosopher-bishop Augustine of Hippo developed the art of preaching, insisting that *truth is the ultimate goal* of such public speaking. He had great influence in both civil and religious practice. Later in Northern Europe, the 8th-century Saxon theologian Alcuin reinterpreted Roman rhetorical teachings for the Emperor Charlemagne and his medieval court.

Use of public relations strategies and tactics was not limited to Christianity. In 6th-century Northern Africa, the prophet Mohammed sometimes retired to an out-of-the-way place to ponder problems facing his people, eventually to emerge with writings that he identified as the word of Allah. These writings, assembled as the Quran, thus received a *credibility* that encouraged acceptance by his followers.

In the Middle Ages, church leaders applied principles of *persuasive communication* in an effort to recapture the lands of Christian origin. Pope Urban II in 1095 sent his message throughout Europe using the only efficient communication system of the times—the network of monasteries and dioceses. He used a *sustained approach* that involved all the communication tactics of the times: *writing, public speaking, word of mouth, slogans* and *symbols*. The role of *opinion leaders* and the influence on *public opinion* was effective, attracting thousands of volunteers for the first in a series of crusades.

During the eclipse of Western civilization, the classical teaching of Aristotle had virtually been lost to European society. It was Muslim scholars, Christian Arabs and Arabic-speaking Jews who, during the 9th century, kept alive the study of Aristotle in the Middle East. One of the less-unfortunate consequences of the crusades was the subsequent introduction of this Arab scholarship to the West, such as the "science of eloquence" associated with the Persian scholar Abd al-Jurijani.

In the 15th century, Franciscan friar Bernardino of Siena overcame a speech impediment and became respected for his skills in *public speaking* and *preaching*, as well as the now-recognized public relations roles of *conflict resolution* and *reconciliation*. Bernardino became so well known that he successfully negotiated a peace settlement between warring factions in Italy and later participated in negotiations to reunite Greek and Roman branches of Christianity.

Soon the printing press made possible greater *literacy* and with it, an interest in reading the Bible. This laid the foundation for the Protestant Reformation and the subsequent Catholic Reformation. When friar Martin Luther tacked on the cathedral door his argument against various church practices, he was using a common technique for *public discussion* during that time in history.

That era led to the Catholic Church's establishments of the Congregatio de Propaganda Fide (Congregation for the Propagation of the Faith) to educate and support missionaries and advance the religion as Europeans pursued new openings in Asia, Africa and the Western Hemisphere.

The term "propaganda" comes from that organization, later applied to any group set up to spread a doctrine or promote a principle. In its original form, *propaganda* was the common word used to describe what today is public relations. Until the 1950s, both terms were used interchangeably, but propaganda increasingly took on negative connotations by its association with the propaganda ministry of the Nazi regime and other totalitarian governments. It came to indicate manipulative communication, hidden motives and half-truths. (With that in mind, American public relations pioneer Edward Bernays quipped that he practiced propaganda and not im-propaganda.)

Back to the field of religion, we find other aspects of public relations beyond Christianity. Some of these suggest additional approaches to communication and relationships.

As Buddhism extended throughout eastern Asia between the 6th and 12th centuries, it lifted up literature and poetry as elements of communication. Until recent times in Asia, imperial rule and social cohesion were the norm, and the Eastern social environment had little need for public discussion of issues and *persuasive discourse*. In Japan and China, Buddhism emphasized the unity of speaker and audience. Communication often was based on *relationships*. *Silence* and *nonverbals* often are more important than words.

Meanwhile, religious and cultural traditions for centuries intermingled in African society and among indigenous people of Australia and the Americas. These communities often emphasized the value of *storytelling*, the graceful use of language, the development of *consensus*, and the communicative value of *silence*.

All of these concepts of communication and social relationships have practical relevance for today's public relations practitioner, and they are finding their place within the strategic toolbox of the profession.

PUBLIC RELATIONS IN COLONIZATION

Public relations also played a role in European expansion and colonization of newly discovered lands.

In the 10th century, Vikings landed on an uninhabited island of ice and snow in the North Atlantic. Led by Erik "The Red" Thorvaldsson, they used creative *labeling*. The *Saga of Erik the Red* is explicit: "[which] he called Greenland, as he said people would be attracted there if it had a favorable name." Erik was successful, attracting 5,000 or so immigrants from Norway and Iceland (which, ironically, is warmer than Greenland). Pleasant labeling aside, it was the harsh climate change and unfriendly newcomers (the Inuits) that caused them to abandon the Greenland settlements five centuries later.

In the 16th century, Sir Walter Raleigh employed *positive messaging* when he sent glowing reports to England about Roanoke Island off present-day North Carolina. Compared to England, this new land had better soil, bigger trees and more plentiful harvests, as well as friendly Indians—so he said when recruiting settlers. *Promotional leaflets* with wild exaggerations attracted settlers and financial backers, but the claims didn't match reality. The island was largely swamp, food was scarce, sickness was prevalent, and harsh treatment by the colonists turned the native people hostile. The colony was abandoned after two years, giving evidence of another axiom of public relations: Mere words are ineffective when they do not reflect reality.

In other parts of the hemisphere, conquistadores sent similarly enthusiastic reports to Spain about cities of gold and fountains of youth. Neither were found, but the stories helped spur immigration to the Americas. In French Canada, public relations tactics were less exaggerated. Tactics included a *book* by Samuel de Champlain in order to "lure settlers," as well as a campaign to recruit young women from France as wives of the immigrants already in New France, most of them single men.

For more than 150 years, England had sent convicts and its Irish or Scottish prisoners of war as cheap labor to the American colonies. After the revolution, other destinations had to be found. At the same time, the war of 1776 displaced thousands of American loyalists, who found themselves no longer welcomed in the fledgling United States. Coincidentally, English explorers had recently claimed Australia, a potential haven for disaffected American colonists. At a time when reformers in England were demanding better conditions for prisoners, Australia also was a likely successor as a penal colony. A potential *win-win situation* was developing.

Again, *positive messaging* with romantic descriptions of Australia was sent back to England: fertile soil, mild climate, exquisite beauty and friendly Aboriginals—though the facts didn't always match the claims. (Where have we heard this before?) Shipping corporations encouraged immigration. *Newspaper ads* back in England promised free land and representative government.

In the 17th century, the first Europeans in Australia were convicts being resettled, but soon other immigrants came of their own will, lured by *publicity* and *advertising* promising land opportunities. Germans responding to similar *advertisements* went to Australia to escape religious conflict in Europe. Later, in the mid-1800s, looking for a cheap source of labor in the Northern Territories, Australia advertised in Chinese and Malaysian newspapers for immigrants.

This early aberration of public relations—exaggerated promises and unfounded claims—popped up once again in North America. The western expansion in the US brought a *glorified view* of life on the frontier. The *legend* of Davy Crockett and *stories* about Calamity Jane and Buffalo Bill Cody were among the persuasive messages developed to encourage expansion.

Corporations began using public relations to stimulate westward migration. The Southern Pacific Railroad, for example, hired a *publicity agent* to promote Southern California and *commissioned artists* to paint romanticized images of the Southwest. Land companies hired *promoters* to attract settlers, and the federal government hyped the California Gold Rush to foster *public opinion* for the war against Mexico. After the American Civil War, the Burlington Railroad promoted land grants for army veterans along its route in the northern plains. It even took out *newspaper ads* in Germany, Scandinavia and The Netherlands to attract European immigrants.

Who knows? Future generations may find similar exaggerations about undersea colonies or the first settlements on the moon.

PUBLIC RELATIONS IN REVOLUTION

The American Revolution stands as an example of the power of *public opinion* and the role that public relations can play.

Samuel Adams, the chief *strategist* for the independence movement, used many public relations strategies and tactics. He encouraged *organizing groups* such as the Caucus Club and the Committees of Correspondence. He created *activist organizations* such as the Sons of Liberty.

Adams organized *staged events*, most notably the Boston Tea Party, which was part of the resistance movement designed to satirize the British tea tax and symbolize colonial defiance. The in-your-face tactic shocked not only the British but also many colonists as well, and the propaganda machine went into high gear. *Sketches* and *pictures* were circulated depicting the fight with inaccurate details that inflamed the colonists. *Brochures* (many of them anonymous) were distributed in America and in England, describing—against the facts—an unprovoked attack on peaceful citizens.

In an example of *framing*, the colonists got their "official" version of the story of the Boston Tea Party across the Atlantic before pro-British loyalists could be heard. Benjamin Franklin, in residence in London, lost no time in being the first to circulate the revolutionary version of the event throughout the city.

Meanwhile, the rebel colonists were using persuasive messages including *songs* of protest and patriotism, *symbols* such as the Liberty Tree, and *slogans* ("Taxation without representation is tyranny").

They also became adept at *orchestrating the message*, such as their elaboration of the Boston Massacre—hardly a massacre, rather a riot caused by a drunken colonial mob. But *poems, essays* and *engravings* memorialized the event throughout the colonies (except in New York, where the story was suppressed by colonial leaders because of their continuing rivalry with Boston).

The colonists also built *alliances* with American Indians, though most tribes sided with the British because England recognized their lands and protected them from encroaching colonists.

The independence movement also had some of the darker elements that sometimes have been associated with public relations. It *demonized the opposition*, ridiculing King George and his representatives in the colonies. More seriously, it *ostracized sympathizers* of the opposition, such as in the *plays* and *poetry* of Mercy Otis Warren ridiculing loyalists in the colonies, and the Patriot Committee in each colony that harassed loyalists (real and suspected), including confiscation of their land, torture, even murder. Such actions caused most of the loyalist colonists to flee to Canada or relocate to Australia or elsewhere. (The term "lynching" derives from Judge Charles Lynch of Virginia, who, without trial, beat and jailed colonists accused of being loyal to their king back in London.)

Another negative strategy of the independence movement capitalized on people's *fears* and *bigotry*. The notable example of this was the anti-Catholic prejudice fanned in the colonies after England promulgated the Quebec Act. That law allowed Catholics in the former French colony of Quebec (recently conquered by the British) to practice their faith, something not permitted in most of the American colonies. The colonial leaders fueled the revolutionary sentiment against England by playing to anti-Catholic bigotry in what essentially were Protestant colonies.

Specific tactics employed during the American Revolution included:

- Anniversaries of events as news pegs for publicity
- Letters to opinion leaders
- Town and county meetings

- Petitions in colonial (later state) legislatures
- Leaks to the press
- Use of all existing communication tools (in today's terms, a multi-media campaign)
- Publications such as 85 Federalist papers
- More than 1,500 booklets and pamphlets in the 20 years of the independence movement
- Ghostwritten articles and letters (Samuel Adams wrote under 25 different aliases)
- Newspaper essays and editorials
- Speeches and sermons
- Personal correspondence
- Word-of-mouth planted by personal visits to taverns and other public gathering places
- Meetings
- Parades
- Posting of notices in public places

Consider the following observations showing the influence of public opinion and the power of public relations:

1 Despite the political rhetoric, colonists were not an oppressed people. In fact, they generally paid no taxes. Because of the distance from Mother England, they were already autonomous in most practical day-to-day matters.

2 Most of the colonists were not in favor of separation from England. Many families and even entire communities moved through New York and across the Niagara River into Canada or north through New England into the Maritime Provinces. About 100,000 colonists escaped to Canada, returned to England, or fled to the Bahamas, Australia or other British territories.

3 The colonies were not united. Indeed, there were serious and deep divisions and hostile suspicion among them. For example, the Boston Massacre was not reported in New York because of intra-colony feuding, and the issue of slavery nearly scuttled the ability to find common ground among the colonies.

4 The colonial experience had not been about freedom and equality for everyone, and the American Revolution did not

seek to change that. The very people who founded the colonies had introduced human trafficking and slavery, and many leaders of the independence movement owned slaves. The colonists confiscated Indian lands that had been protected under British rule. Most colonies excluded Jews and Catholics. Voting and other legal privileges were denied to women and to all men except white Protestant landowners, a very small percentage of the colonial population.

5   Yet the independence movement was successful, because *public opinion* ultimately is stronger than legal right or military might. And public relations lies at the heart of public opinion.

MODERN HISTORY OF PUBLIC RELATIONS

While history shows aspects of public relations as a constant element of human interaction, it has been only in relatively recent times that society had recognized and begun to practice what can be called the profession of public relations. Jobs have been created for public relations functions. Education has been developed to support this. Research has been undertaken to better understand the new discipline.

American scholar James Grunig is associated with a framework showing a four-phase evolution of modern public relations. These phases can be called the publicity era, information era, advocacy era and relationship era.

PUBLICITY ERA (1800S)

- Focus: Dissemination and attention-getting
- Nature of Communication: One-way
- Ethics: Full truth not considered important
- Research: Little
- Current Use: Entertainment, sports and marketing

Sometimes called the public-be-damned era, this is seen as the dawn of public relations as a contemporary profession. The focus was on *dissemination of information* and *gaining attention*. This **publicity model** is an aspect of public relations that exists today, particularly in entertainment, sports and marketing.

In the 1820s, Kentucky newspaper editor Amos Kendall became essentially the first presidential press secretary, though with more power and influence than is associated with that position today. Kendall assisted Andrew Jackson during his election campaign and his terms as president. He conducted *polls*, drafted *speeches*, wrote *news releases* and *editorials*, distributed favorable *reprints*, and advised Jackson on *image* and *strategy*.

As a member of the president's Kitchen Cabinet, Kendall helped Jackson play to populist elements and overcome his most controversial issue, his brutal and life-long campaign of ethnic cleansing against Native Americans. He also helped arrange for financial backers to make loans to editors and buy newspaper ads to guarantee *positive publicity*.

Meanwhile, Jackson's political opponents fought back. They raised up a backwoodsman Tennessee congressman with a larger-than-life *reputation*. Armed with *ghostwritten speeches* and even a *book* penned by someone in his name, Davy Crockett was elected to congress, where he unsuccessfully opposed Jackson's policies, particularly the Indian Removal Act. His public relations handlers and financial backers launched him into an unsuccessful re-election campaign.

After leaving Washington, Crockett went to Texas, later to gain fame by dying at the Alamo.

Once again, *propaganda* of the day wasn't constrained by facts. It was the Mexicans who were defending their country against the Texans seeking a breakaway territory where they could own slaves. In Disney's version of the story, Crockett died fighting, though weeks after the battle stories circulated that he and several other Texans had surrendered and were later executed.

As with Kendall, much of this early activity in public relations centered on individuals. William Seward, Lincoln's secretary of state, engaged in *media relations* by speaking frequently with newspaper editors. "They have a large audience and can repeat a thousand times what I want to impress on the public," he said.

Meanwhile in England Georgiana Cavendish, Duchess of Devonshire, was an influential socialite a century before women achieved the right to vote. She was well known as a sort of *publicist*, *lobbyist* and *campaigner* for Charles James Fox, a Whig statesman in the late 1800s.

The opening of the American West provided opportunities for *persuasive messages* to influence migration. Many of the tactics were taken from the playbook of promoters such as P.T. Barnum who successfully publicized circuses, concerts, museums, theaters and other entertainment venues.

Though exaggerated, many of the messages were effective. The legend of Daniel Boone and hyped stories of Buffalo Bill Cody, Wyatt Earp and Calamity Jane induced settlers to the territories west of the Mississippi. Railroads commissioned artists to paint romanticized pictures of the West, complete with peaceful-looking Indians and fertile lands.

As with the American experience, railroads became a prime business for doing public relations in other countries. The modern practice of the profession in India and Canada, for example, began with promotion of the railroads. The Great Indian Peninsular Railways developed a *communication campaign* directed toward England, then the occupying nation of the subcontinent. Attempting to attract tourists, the railroad's *publicity bureau* distributed *press releases* and purchased *advertising* in British newspapers. It introduced a traveling *film* for fairs and festivals.

Social reform in the second half of the 19th century also relied heavily on classic publicity techniques. Harriet Beecher Stowe *personalized* the issue of slavery with her influential novel *Uncle Tom's Cabin*, and Harriet Tubman gave face and voice to the abolitionist movement. Both were part of a massive public relations movement involving *opinion leaders, public meetings, lectures, sermons, religious tracts, petitions* and other tactics all loosely coordinated to end slavery.

The temperance movement to abolish liquor and the suffrage movement to gain women the right to vote were other successful social reform movements that relied heavily on public relations strategies and tactics.

It was during this formative period that the term "public relations" came into use. Dorman Eaton seems to have first used the term in 1882 when he addressed Yale Law School graduates on "The Public Relations and Duties of the Legal Profession." The Association of American Railroads apparently was the first organization to use the term in print, in the *1897 Yearbook of Railway Literature*.

Public relations played a role in the "War of the Currents" between Westinghouse and General Electric over the relative merits of alternating current and direct current as the better technology for making electricity available to the masses.

Thomas Edison and his General Electric business associates supported DC by conducting a *scare campaign* against exaggerated dangers of AC. Edison used *mudslinging* and *false advertising* as he *lobbied* lawmakers. He wrote *letters to the editor* attacking his opponents and hired false "experts" to speak on behalf of his DC cause. Attempting to shock audiences, Edison used AC to electrocute hundreds of animals, including dogs and horses. He even created a *special event* by arranging for the electrocution of a convicted murderer, a tactic that turned out so gruesome that it effectively lost the case Edison was trying to make.

Meanwhile, Westinghouse countered with calm, logic and appeals to reason, winning the argument with what is generally considered a more *strategic public relations campaign*. Today Westinghouse's AC is standard throughout the world. This war of the currents of the late 1880s and early 1890s is a prime example of the movement from the publicity model into the information era.

INFORMATION ERA (EARLY 1900S)

- Focus: Honest and accurate dissemination of information
- Nature of Communication: One-way
- Ethics: Accuracy and truth considered important
- Research: Readability and comprehension
- Current Use: Government, nonprofit organizations and business organizations

The transition from the public-be-damned era into a public-be-informed approach centered on a new standard of honest and accurate dissemination of *newsworthy information*. Truth telling became a public virtue. This **information model** is prevalent today in many business organizations, nonprofits and government agencies.

This time period saw a maturing of public relations to add a stronger *ethical base* to public relations tactics. *News releases* were now expected to be *accurate*, and speeches *truthful*.

As Europe was discovering with its nobility, America was seeing parallel truths about business potentates: The public matters. Ex-journalist Ivy Ledbetter Lee, often called the "father of public relations," bucked the prevailing business feeling associated with the empire builders and the Gilded Age, telling clients such as John D. Rockefeller, Walter Chrysler and George Westinghouse that the *public could no longer be ignored*.

Lee issued a Declaration of Principles calling for *honest communication* on behalf of clients and telling newspaper editors that he would offer them *newsworthy information* promptly, accurately and in the open. When one of his clients, the Pennsylvania Railroad, experienced a train crash, Lee advised the company to tell what had happened, bring reporters to the scene, and let them report the story first hand.

This era saw many "firsts": the first public relations agencies, first university publicity bureau, first employee newsletter, first public relations journal and the first public relations departments for groups as disparate as churches, military, unions, charities, nonprofit organizations and corporations.

Public relations saw parallel growth around the world. In Canada, public relations departments and agencies also were developing, beginning with Bell Canada. Railroads, banks and other companies hired publicity specialists to create effective *government relations* programs at the beginning of World War I.

Government agencies were created in the UK, France and the US during World War I to manage the flow of information, looking for citizen support for the military efforts.

The Indian government set up a publicity board during World War I as a link between the government and the press. In monitoring media criticism of the government, the board provided *feedback* to government strategists. The board later morphed into the Indian Ministry of Information and Broadcasting, which today coordinates public relations, publicity, advertising and film policy.

During the build-up to World War I, the German propaganda ministry produced *books* and *pamphlets, speeches* and even *children's books*. It established the German Information Bureau to influence Americans to remain neutral, a position supported by public opinion before April 1917, when the US entered the war.

One week after declaring war, President Wilson created the Committee on Public Information. The agency, headed by George Creel, sought to garner public opinion supporting a role for America in the war, *framing* it as a positive force for democracy.

Creel said that its purpose was to coordinate "not propaganda as the Germans defined it, but propaganda in the true sense of the word, meaning the 'propagation of faith'." The committee used all the tools at its disposal: *posters* and *newspapers, telegraph* and *radio, film* and *speeches.* Volunteers gave 7.5 million succinct four-minute speeches to audiences totaling 314 million people.

Meanwhile, England's theme was that it was a matter of duty to help France and Belgium threatened by Germany. *Posters* asked, "Daddy, what did you do in the Great War?" Recruiting *advertisements* asked women about their sons and husbands, "Is he to hang his head because you would not let him go?" Toward the war's end, the Ministry of Information pulled together the work of several different government agencies dealing with various aspects of media, news and public opinion.

In Australia, opponents to the government ban on drafting soldiers to fight in Europe, mounted a national referendum on the law as a sort of *public opinion.* The referendum was twice defeated, but publicity about the vote led 400,000 Australians to volunteer to help the Mother Country after England entered the war.

Not all public relations had good intentions. Two Atlanta publicists of this time, Edward Clarke and Bessie Tyler, gained a footnote in public relations history because of their immense success in *recruiting* and *fundraising.* They took a group from a few thousand members in 1920 to nearly 4 million in 1923. The group was the Ku Klux Klan, America's most notorious vigilante terrorist organization. This revival of the short-lived post-Civil War KKK reframed the klan as a patriotic nativist group and extended its traditional hostility toward blacks by adding Catholics, Jews and unions to its hate list.

Clarke and Tyler used many common public relations strategies and tactics: all kinds of *publications, speeches* and *symbols,* such as the burning cross. Most of the success was in the US, but the anti-Catholic message played in Canada as well.

The story of this second KKK shows the power of *negative strategy*, appeals to fear and hatred, and other divisive methods that can enjoy short-term success. But the story isn't complete without noting that this klan fizzled out and disbanded within 20 years, adding another lesson for public relations: Hate groups inevitably implode from their inability to sustain rabid negativity.

ADVOCACY ERA (MID-1900S)

- Focus: Modify attitudes and influence behavior
- Nature of Communication: Two-way
- Ethics: Transparent research and communication
- Research: Attitude and opinion
- Current Use: Competitive business organizations, causes and movements

By the mid-20th century, people were attempting to reconcile new facts on the international social consciousness: genocide in Armenia and popular German support for the Holocaust, along with behavioral theories such as conditioned reflex, cognitive dissonance and scapegoat theory. The thinking was: If people could be induced to do evil things, how can they be persuaded to do good?

The focus of this **advocacy model** was on *modifying attitudes* and *influencing behavior*. It introduced social research into the practice of public relations, establishing a role for *demographics* and developing techniques for *surveys* and *opinion polls* as well as *focus groups* and *content analysis*.

These are aspects of public relations still used today in competitive business organizations promoting products and services, as well as in advocacy causes and movements such as public health, welfare and human rights. Perhaps the largest field for this has been that of electoral politics and public policy issues.

This era is associated with Edward Bernays, with Ivy Lee the second founding figure for public relations. An Austrian-American and the nephew of Sigmund Freud, Bernays gave public relations a base in *social psychology* as he engaged the profession on behalf of an international list of clients.

Among his achievements were assisting President Wilson with the Creel Committee to encourage public support for American involvement in World War I. He later promoted water fluoridation as a public health issue and helped to introduce orange juice as a common breakfast beverage. One of his most noteworthy and controversial successes was a campaign on behalf of Lucky Strike cigarettes (which he labeled "torches of freedom") to make it socially acceptable for women to smoke in public, something he later came to regret as health literacy increased.

Bernays also wrote the first book on public relations (*Crystallizing Public Opinion*) and taught the first university course (at New York University) in the new discipline. It was Bernays who introduced the term "public relations counsel."

Bernays said public relations was about the "engineering of consent"—not by force or manipulation, but by carefully orchestrated strategies that were *based on theory* and *informed by research*, with a strong *ethical undertone*. Bernays remained a leading figure in public relations until he died in 1995 at the age of 103.

Doris Fleishman, Bernays' wife and professional colleague, used her public relations skills for feminist causes. She became the first married American woman to receive a passport in her maiden name.

Another key figure in public relations during this time period was Arthur Page. He became the first known in-house corporate public relations strategist when he accepted a job as vice president of AT&T, after negotiating that he would be a corporate adviser and decision maker rather than a publicity voice. Page insisted that his staff observe seven principles: Tell the truth; prove it with action; listen to the customer; manage for tomorrow; conduct public relations as if the whole company depends on it; realize a company's true character is expressed by its peoples; and remain calm, patient and good humored.

During the middle and latter parts of the 20th century, much of public relations (both research and practice) was built on the advocacy model. Organizations tried to influence the *attitudes and behaviors* of their publics. Governments around the world tried to nurture support for World War II, and *information as a weapon* (including *misinformation*; that is, lying and deception) became part of the Cold War, paralleling military might with communication-based campaigns to win the hearts and minds of people. Britain and the US used news and information to build support and later post-war propaganda campaigns. Other research was related to brainwashing and *social manipulation*.

Social reform movements continued to use public relations, attempting to change attitudes on issues such as child labor, worker rights, prostitution, food safety and regulation of big business.

Former journalist Elmer Davis headed the Office of War Information during World War II, coordinating public information from the military, mobilizing public support for the war effort and undermining enemy morale. Davis successfully campaigned against efforts to strip US-born Japanese-Americans of their citizenship and inter them in camps for the duration of the war. He urged President Roosevelt to allow Japanese-Americans to enlist for military service, even while their parents were forcibly removed from their homes and placed under military internment. Davis has been acclaimed as one of the "unsung forefathers" of the all-Japanese 442nd Regimental Combat Team that became the most decorated infantry regiment in American history. After the war, Davis returned to his career in radio, using that as a platform to campaign against Senator Joseph McCarthy's communist witch hunt.

It is interesting to note the language surrounding government and public relations. Totalitarian regimes often have used the *propaganda* label, such as Hitler's Ministry of Public Enlightenment and Propaganda, the Soviet Department for Agitation and Propaganda, and both the Office of Foreign Propaganda and the Communist Party Propaganda Department under China's Chairman Mao.

Democratic countries, on the other hand, have been more likely to use the *information* title, as with the Ministries of Information in Britain and Israel and the US Committee on Information and the US Information Agency. Today, most nations have abandoned the propaganda label for government agencies dealing with information, news and public relations.

RELATIONSHIP ERA (LATE 1900S)

- Focus: Mutual understanding and conflict resolution
- Nature of Communication: Two-way
- Ethics: Balance and symmetry in relationships
- Research: Perception and values
- Current Use: Regulated business, government, nonprofit organizations and social movements

In recent decades, public relations has assumed a focus toward programming aimed at mutual understanding, organizational adaptation and conflict resolution.

This **relationship model** today often is associated with social movements, as well as with nonprofit organizations, government agencies and corporations (especially regulated businesses which often interact with both government and social advocates).

Consumer-rights groups have drawn attention to a variety of health and safety issues, such as automobiles, airplane travel safety, clean water and children's sleepwear. Much of this activity has been spurred by social advocates such as Rachel Carson, a marine biologist whose book *Silent Spring* spurred a global environmental movement, and Ralph Nader, whose book *Unsafe at Any Speed* focused attention on auto safety in North America and beyond. In each of these cases, government and industry responded to *public opinion* supporting oversight and quality reform. Regulations were put in place as consumers adopted many pro-environment and pro-safety habits, often with government encouragement through public relations campaigns.

Meanwhile, speeches such as "I Have a Dream" and "I've Been to the Mountain Top" by Martin Luther King Jr. led not only to legal guarantees of civil rights but also to the personal transformation of many individuals toward celebration of racial and ethnic diversity. President Obama's second inaugural address referenced themes precious to marginalized groups, including his reference to the Stonewall riots (foreshadowing the gay rights movement) with parallel icons such as Seneca Falls (women's rights) and Selma (civil rights).

The relationship model, whether it involves advocacy groups or the companies and agencies dealing with their issues, drives public relations strategists toward helping their organizations listen to consumers and adapt their products and services to meet their needs.

Sometimes this means researching consumer interests or communicating more with publics. Often it also means making internal changes to deliver a better product or service. Organizations of all types have come to realize that, in order to be successful, they need to listen to consumers and adapt their products and services to meet their needs.

Thus the hallmark of the relationship model is *adaptation*, or at least the corporate willingness to respond to publics and make meaningful change to create a *mutually beneficial* environment for both the publics and the organization.

This new relationship model is built on the principles of *communication as listening* and is focused on *conflict resolution* and the search for *mutual benefits* for both organizations and their publics.

Internationally, this relationship approach has been seen in concepts such as *détente* and *rapprochement*. In the business environment, *public-private partnerships* and the courting of consumers are becoming common.

In the religious world, the *ecumenical movement* and *interreligious dialogue* are examples of the relationship model. The documents from the Catholic Church's Vatican Council II in the 1960s—particularly the statements on the church's relationship with other Christian denominations, with Jews, and with non-Christian religions—show the application of the relationship model to interreligious matters.

In all of these situations, public relations has become *research based*. It is more a function of the management and leadership of an organization, rather than simply the implementation of communication tactics. Meanwhile, new technologies associated with the Internet allow organizations to communicate directly with their publics and to offer *information-on-demand* in an interactive consumer-driven environment. These technologies, combined with the *fragmentation* of the so-called *mass media*, are creating new opportunities for public relations practitioners.

It is important to remember that the relationship model complements earlier visions of public relations focused on publicity, information and advocacy.

Consider an analogy with media technology. As a new advancement is introduced, it may change but rarely replaces an earlier technology. Books and newspapers have survived well into the broadcast era. Television didn't spell the end of radio, just a change in its content. Cable and satellite haven't replaced broadcast TV. The Internet isn't killing television, though it both expanded the potential delivery of television and to some extent has influenced its content. Tablets and smart phones are not replacing desk-top computers. Sirius and iPods are affecting radio but not supplanting it. And on it goes. The inevitable new communication technologies that will emerge undoubtedly will influence the existing tools, but we are likely always to have books and TV news networks and ever-smarter phones.

This also is true with the various approaches to public relations. Organizations will always need a publicity model for some of their public relations purposes, such as announcing new products and services and promoting upcoming events. Society will continue to use the information model that disseminates honest and reliable facts on which to base personal and civic decisions. The advocacy model will always be enshrouded as part of human nature, which frequently nudges us toward promoting a cause and fostering our beliefs. And the relationship model will continue to find favor wherever society values dialogue in an atmosphere of mutual respect toward win-win solutions that benefit everybody.

PUBLIC RELATIONS TODAY

Why the history lesson? Because it gives a background into the development of a profession that is still evolving.

As noted in Chapter 1, much of the misperception about public relations is based on incorrect or outdated information. With the understanding of the development as outlined here, we can better appreciate where public relations is today and where it seems to be heading in the upcoming decades.

At the beginning of the 21st century, public relations is evolving in several ways:

- from *manipulation* to *adaptation*
- from *program* to *process*
- from *Band-aid treatment* to *wellness programs*
- from *propaganda* to *information*
- from *external* to *internal*
- from *technician* to *manager*
- from *fire fighting* to *fire prevention*
- from *mass media* to *targeted media*
- from *isolation* to *integration*
- from *secret* to *transparent*
- from *closed* to *open*

When we look country-by-country, we see a clear link between social structure and public relations. The profession has an obvious connection with open government in which public opinion is needed for leaders to gain the consent of the citizenry, and with an economic system based on competitive markets and voluntary exchange between buyer and seller. That is, public relations operates best in democracy and capitalism.

While many of the activities that today we associate with public relations have become nearly universal, scholars and historians around the world agree that the conscious practice of public relations as a profession began in the United States. It quickly spread to other English-speaking democratic societies, particularly Canada, Australia and the United Kingdom, as noted in the previous section.

The discipline is so much rooted in North America that the English word "public relations" or direct translations ("relations publique," "relaciones públicas") are used almost universally rather than homegrown phrases. A German term "Öffentlichkeitsarbeit" sometimes translates as "publicity campaign" or "indoctrinated communication," but the English term is more commonly used in German-speaking settings. In Japan, the common term is "pee-ah-roo" or sometimes "paburikku rireshon."

Though the name may be the same, the role of public relations is not uniform throughout the world. The understanding presented here is consistent with professional practice and self-awareness in North America and in English-rooted cultures around the world.

In much of Europe, the focus is more on promotion and communication but less on strategic management issues, and the relationship between advertising and public relations remains unsettled. In many Asian cultures, public relations is focused on international companies trying to navigate domestic peculiarities in government and media. Arab culture sometimes equates public relations with social relations and hospitality.

Scholars have observed that public relations came late to totalitarian states, giving evidence to the observation by scholars that propaganda is a phase, a stepping-stone along the path toward open communication. In countries such as Poland, Chile and the Philippines—until recently associated with totalitarian governments—public relations still has not been completely severed from propaganda. This isn't surprising. The US has had more than two centuries of practice with democracy. Canada, Australia and the UK likewise have a long history with social and economic freedom. Yet even in these countries, there are remnants of deceptive propaganda.

Public relations by necessity requires literacy and higher levels of education. It is not surprising that countries with low literacy rates and education levels are ill equipped to generate a functional public relations profession. There is little opportunity to practice public relations in countries such as Mali, Ethiopia, South Sudan and several other African nations where less than 30 percent of adults are literate, or in Afghanistan where the literacy rate is only 38 percent.

Additionally, cultural differences come into play. In Japan, for example, it is considered impolite to ask questions at a press briefing; instead reporters hold their questions for follow-up one-on-one interviews. The International Communications Consultancy Organization has offered some observations on how public relations practitioners engage European journalists: Germans want small media briefings, but in the UK one-on-one interviews are preferred. Italian reporters like breakfast meetings, not too early. In Belgium, journalists prefer to get their news over lunch or dinner served with beer (well, who wouldn't?).

Here are some examples of the evolution and current status of public relations in other countries.

- **France**: Public relations has a long history in France. Cardinal Richelieu in the 17th century had a press department and a minister of information. King Louis XIV into the 18th century likewise had media and image advisers, promoting him through medals, statues and various print media. The *Declaration of the Rights of Man and Citizens* (1789) positioned the leaders of the French Revolution as supporting the right of citizens to express themselves and communicate freely. France established a propaganda ministry in 1792, which subsidized editors and supported efforts to create positive public opinion for the revolution. As in most other European countries, French public relations began as a profession following World War I and grew rapidly after World War II. In 1969, the government created the Ministry of Public Relations.

- **Japan**: Public relations was already being practiced in Japan before the post-war US occupation. When Japan created the South Manchuria Railroad Company in 1906, it established a public relations department to promote the railroad, impacting public opinion toward the eventual Japanese "encroachment" into China. Later the US occupation introduced public relations for corporate management. Today, public relations is an integral part of Japanese business and organizational life, though the Japanese cultural practice of not dealing publicly with controversial or negative information still exists. The main focus of Japanese public relations is media relations. Access to the media is gained through "press clubs" set up by each major industry and by government agencies, and it is the press club that decides whether to hold a news conference or issue news releases. Press clubs are generally not open to foreign reporters, and gift-giving practices sometimes conflict with ethical standards.

- **Middle East**: Public relations did not develop in the Middle East until the 1980s. In the decades following its independence from the British colony in 1971, the United Arab Emirates has become one of the wealthiest countries in the world. It also has become a center of public relations activity in the Middle East, home to local and international agencies. The International Public Relations Association has a Gulf States chapter with practitioners in Saudi Arabia, Kuwait, Qatar, Bahrain, Oman and the United Arab Emirates. The UAE-based Middle Eastern Public Relations Association (MEPRA) has chapters in cities throughout the Middle East and links with universities in Qatar, Egypt and the UAE. MEPRA sees public relations as marginalized in the Middle East, where it correlates with the degree of freedom, democracy and the role of public opinion in society. The organization has called on Arab governments to see public relations as an ethical element for the betterment of society rather than a tool for media manipulation and propaganda.

- **Finland**: Public relations in Finland and its Scandinavian neighbors began during the middle of the 20th century. The Finnish Association of Public Relations is the oldest in Europe, founded in 1947 (the same year that PRSA was created in the US). The organization was an outgrowth of Finnish efforts to promote the Olympics and handle propaganda tasks during World War II. One of the public relations successes of that time was the generation of international sympathy for Finland's David-and-Goliath resistance to Russia during the "Winter War" of 1939–40.

- **Vatican City**: In 1948, the Vatican created the forerunner of its Pontifical Council on Social Communications, which coordinates the press office's work with film, newspapers, television and social media. The commission also works with communication advisers for the Vatican secretariat of state and other Vatican agencies. Additionally, the Vatican has exercised the church's educational role by issuing commentaries on ethical aspects of the news and entertainment media, advertising, and social media.

- **Africa**: The African Public Relations Association includes 13 national groups in large nations such as South Africa and Egypt and smaller countries including Swaziland, Zimbabwe and Gambia. The Nigerian association alone has 7,000 members and 3,000 student members. More than 20 universities in South Africa teach public relations. Additionally, the Public Relations Institute of South Africa involves practitioners in South Africa and Zimbabwe.

- **India**: During World War I, the British government established a publicity board in India, and soon after its independence in 1947, India created a ministry of information and broadcasting. The Public Relations Society of India began in 1958 and was formalized eight years later. Since 1986, April 21 has been observed as National Public Relations Day. The purpose according to PRSI is "to focus attention on the public relations function and public relations professionals in India who have an increasingly important role in the development of the country." Much of that focus is on media relations, though international practitioners, and a growing number of universities with public relations programs, are expanding the concept of the discipline.

- **Russia**: When the Soviet Union existed, there was little need for public relations to promote goods or services to would-be consumers. The state provided both, generally only in one version, and consumer choice meant take it or leave it. There certainly wasn't a role for civic discussion or public opinion. It was only after the union collapsed in 1991 that public relations became a necessity with the social and economic reforms that occurred in Russia and the 14 other former Soviet republics.

  With the dissolution of the Soviet Union, public relations arrived in Russia as the new nation found that—in the economic and political environment, both inside and outside the country—public opinion would play a key role.

  Businesses introduced new products. Universities became more competitive by adding new areas of study, including public relations and strategic communication. Public relations agencies joined advertising and marketing agencies as newcomers to the Russian scene. The Russian Public Relations Society was founded, now with more than 600 members. In 2008, the Russian Communications Consultancies Association reported that, after only a 20-year history, the value of the Russian public relations market (the combined budgets of public relations agencies and in-house departments) had reached $2.5 billion (£1.6 billion, €2 billion).

One of the biggest growth areas for public relations in Russia has been in government. When he was president, Boris Yeltsin approached Western public relations agencies to promote his trips to other countries, his domestic programs and, later, his re-election campaign.

- **China**: In China, public relations had long been part of the economic scene in Hong Kong, which had been a Western enclave within China for nearly a century. Taiwan developed an effective public relations industry after it declared independence from mainland China.

  But for most of China, modern public relations began only after the political, economic and social reforms of the late 1970s. Hill & Knowlton was the first international agency to establish an office in Beijing, quickly followed by the first domestic agency, Global Public Relations.

  Today China has several thousand public relations agencies. More than 100 professional organizations have been created, including the China Public Relations Association and the China International Public Relations Association. More than 300 universities teach public relations, which is said to be one of the country's top five professions.

  Public relations in China began with basic publicity and media relations, later expanding into more strategic aspects of the profession, with a particular emphasis on government relations. Overall, public relations is a common element of business practice, especially as Chinese companies engage foreign markets.

  China has put its newfound public relations skills to the test in dealing with opposition to the government's plan for a high dam on the Yangtze River, the massive Sichuan earthquake and international attention during the Beijing Olympics.

- **Cuba**: Cuban public relations is still in its infancy. A few agencies are active as the country moves toward a market-oriented economy, working mainly in publicity, graphic design and similar nonstrategic areas. The government controls the news media and tries to suppress access to newer social media.

But the belief is that public relations has a brighter future in Cuba amid expectations that government controls will ease and conservative media policies become less restrictive.

TYPES OF PUBLIC RELATIONS

Public relations work is varied and diverse. This chapter gives you an overview of the various types or categories of public relations, along with some case studies of each.

Ask three people working in public relations what they do, and you are likely to hear about three very different jobs. That's because public relations is a wonderfully diverse discipline. All kinds of organizations practice public relations, which itself has many different subcategories, with much overlap among the various specialty areas. Here are some of these specialty areas of public relations.

- Strategic counseling
- Consumer relations
- Employee relations
- Community relations
- Relations with special publics
- Investor/donor relations
- Public affairs and government relations
- Special events and promotion
- Media relations
- Crisis communication

STRATEGIC COUNSELING

The top priority for every public relations practitioner should be strategic counseling. This involves proactive research, analysis, planning and evaluation. It is part of the management of every organization.

The term **issues management** often is used to describe this function. But the term **strategic counseling** suggests not only attention to issues but a major role for public relations at the highest levels of organizational decision-making. This counseling also is associated with **risk management** and **crisis communication**, two particular types of issues that call for close attention and readiness to act.

Public relations practitioners aim to advise others in organizational leadership, not simply to carry forth with tasks assigned to them by others who—by training, organizational role and/or personality—may not have the insight that practitioners themselves have to focus on the continuing and long-term relationship between the organization and its various publics.

This is an anticipatory practice that helps organizations detect areas and issues in which they potentially may be out of step with their publics. Ideally, they learn this early enough to do something to prevent or at least minimize any negative impact.

For example, fast-food companies such as Subway, McDonald's, Wimpy, MOS Burger and Burger King took note of public rhetoric about healthy food and introduced more salads, fruits and vegetables. That didn't spell the end of the Happy Meal, but it gave a choice to customers and a forum for the companies to promote their social responsibility.

Meanwhile an example of poor issues management has been the US auto industry, which insisted on making large cars while Americans were buying smaller imports from Germany and Japan, and which today lags behind other countries in hybrid auto technology.

US AIR FORCE

In 2009, when the US Defense Department announced an end to the 18-year ban on media coverage of the return to American soil of service members killed overseas, the Air Force public affairs office developed a strategic plan to honor the dead, respect their families and allow the media to report the solemn event.

The team surveyed nearly 1,300 active-duty airmen as well as veterans' organizations to gauge the opinion of the military. They analyzed media coverage of the policy change and took note of national polls indicating public support for the new policy. The research also identified potential areas of opposition.

The team developed a threefold strategy: focusing on grieving families and their privacy, facilitating transparency on the human cost of war, and providing media access when families approved.

Tactics included a media kit explaining the procedure and background on the transfer process as well as advisories to media when families approve coverage and individual briefings for media observers. They created a viewing area at the military mortuary at Dover Air Force Base modeled on Arlington National Cemetery, as well as a new family reception area away from the media. The team also developed procedures for providing its own videotaping of the ceremony for each family.

After less than a year, 81 percent of families were opting for media coverage of the ceremonial return. The Air Force public affairs team conducted follow-up research paralleling the initial surveys, as well as content analysis that found media coverage to be balanced and respectful.

CONSUMER RELATIONS

Every organization should have a program of **consumer relations** because every organization has consumers. These are the people who obtain and use the products or services of the organization. Consumers are the fans, patients, students, members, voters, parishioners, clients, shoppers and so on. Other important groups of consumers include former as well as long-term and consistent customers.

The relationship between these consumers and the organization is interdependent: consumers want or need the organization's products, services or ideas; and the organization depends on the consumers' money, time and support for its survival.

Thus consumer relations (also called **customer relations** or **consumer affairs**) warrants the careful and considered attention of the organization. Because it often is the front line dealing with customer fears and complaints, consumer relations should involve well-trained people who understand their mission to create and maintain the best possible relationship between the organization and its customers.

Research into consumers' knowledge, attitudes, opinions and behaviors is a major part of consumer relations. Tactics associated with consumer relations include advisory boards, brochures and other literature (both in print and online), informational video, direct mail, position papers, conferences, public relations advertising, and the usual array of media relations tactics.

Though interrelated, consumer relations differs from marketing in that it is focused primarily on people, with a mission to foster a mutually beneficial relationship based on understanding. Marketing is more about products and sales. But new concepts such as **relationship marketing** signal a conscious adoption by marketing of the public relations principles of long-term engagement, mutual benefits and transparency. Additionally, classic public relations is frequently used to launch new products, often under the name of **marketing public relations**.

PHILIPS NORELCO

The company's consumer relations team was dealing with a product relaunch, breathing new life into sales for its bodygrooming product for men. The previous launch campaign had successfully established the Bodygroom Pro as a basic tool for manscaping.

Now the company linked its product with an international environmental action campaign, based on research that showed that younger males were interested in the ecological theme. Called "Deforest Yourself, Reforest the World," the campaign pledged to plant a tree for every Bodygroom product sold, resulting in $75,000 (£47,800, €59,600) to the Arbor Day Foundation.

Based on research, the two-month campaign enlisted Carmen Electra, who drew a positive appeal for 85 percent of the intended audience (men 25–34). Her job was to attract media attention and present the message that excessive body hair is socially unacceptable. The campaign used a humorous and provocative message strategy, presented through its iconic website (shaveeverywhere.com) and its humorous ad that went viral on YouTube.

The result was 364,000 visitors to the website, with 40 percent of them crediting the public relations activity for leading them there. Social media counted 700 comments on Facebook, 700 "likes" for Carmen's posts, and 1.8 million Twitter impressions. Altogether, 138 million media impressions showed 100 percent positive or neutral coverage, and an 18 percent increase in sales.

EMPLOYEE RELATIONS

In many ways, employees are the first public of an organization. They are the people who make the product, perform the service, create the ideas and generate information that "sells" the organization to its various consumers and others. They are the people who ensure safety in the workplace and quality in the product.

The principle of **employee relations** (sometimes called **employee communication** or **internal relations**) is that the organization is likely to be successful when employees are informed, motivated and on board with its mission.

No organization will be successful without the cooperation and involvement of its employees—and by extension—its volunteers and often its retired employees and families of employees. Significant category distinctions among employees include union and management for some organizations; for others distinctions may center on tenure, line or staff function, length of service, rank and work shift.

In some organizations, groups such as boards of directors or trustees function both as employee publics and as extensions of the employer. Sometimes employers are only loosely connected with an organization, such as physicians who work at, but not for, a hospital.

Employee relations often involves internal communication programs—from high-tech interactive digital newsletters to no-tech bulletin boards—designed to motivate and educate employees. Other common tactics include e-mail, town-hall meetings, picnics and holiday parties, brochures, intranet sites and blogs. Research activities include focus groups, surveys and content analysis.

This specialization of public relations also involves recognition programs to reward employees for good work and encourage similar efforts from other employees. Employee relations often is a liaison between employers and workers and most organizations have a formalized policy that encourages open, honest, frequent, interactive and transparent job-related communication, supported by ongoing employee research and continuous assessment.

Employee volunteer programs are another important component of employee relations. Research shows that employees who are encouraged to participate in volunteer work, some of it on company time, ultimately are more productive and have lower turnover rates and fewer sick days, more than compensating the company for paid volunteer time.

DUKE ENERGY

When the Nuclear Regulatory Commission mandated limiting working hours with breaks and days off, Duke Energy wanted to ensure compliance by its 4,000 employees and contractors.

The company launched an employee communication project that began with interviews and surveys to identify key publics and areas of concern and potential resistance. Publics included not only employees at three nuclear sites and the general office in the Carolinas but also contractors, vendors and non-nuclear support staff.

The program included dissemination of information via fact sheets, e-mail and branded giveaways. It also involved hands-on opportunities for discussion and feedback, including work-group meetings and an intranet site.

Costing only $20,000 (£12,700, €15,900), the project resulted in an 85 percent awareness of the fatigue rule within a year, later extended to 98 percent. It also led to 96 percent understanding of the consequences of non-compliance. The intranet site was used by 90 percent of workers. Ultimately, the NRC found the company in compliance on the fatigue rule, which was the goal of the campaign.

COMMUNITY RELATIONS

Community relations is an organization's planned and ongoing engagement with people who live in the neighborhood or community in which it operates, to enhance its environment and foster a mutually beneficial relationship between the organization and the community. Like all aspects of public relations, community relations should be data driven and continually evaluated.

Community relations involves the civic role of an organization and its contribution to the quality of life in a community. It impacts other areas of public relations involving employees and volunteers, regulators and government agencies, donors and others.

Thus community relation projects might involve recycling, beautification, restoration and other environmental programs. It also plays out in sponsorships of academic teams, athletic sponsorships, children's activities, science competitions and other engagements with schools, as well as in cultural interaction such as visual and performing arts.

This specialty field also involves professional relationships gained by participating in business and civic groups such as Rotary, hosting meetings and events by outside groups, and buying locally.

Another aspect of community relations programs is **corporate philanthropy**, which involves financial, operational or administrative support for charity drives and scholarships. **Employee volunteer programs** also form part of an organization's community relations program, as well as part of employee relations as noted previously.

Why should organizations spend time and money for community relations? It serves as a type of insurance, building up goodwill for when a crisis occurs or when bad news attaches itself to the organization. It also can smooth the way when zoning variances or construction permits are needed and can help create an environment that is attractive to potential new employees.

BANK OF AMERICA

Bank of America's corporate social responsibility program supports local communities. Called the Neighborhood Excellence Initiative, the community relations program in the US and the UK has three components, operating in each of 45 cities.

First, in each city, Neighborhood Builders give leadership training and a $200,000 (£129,000, €160,000) grant for operating support and leadership training. Second, the Local Heroes program gives $5,000 (£3,200, €4,000) each to five people working to improve their communities. Third, the Student Leaders program provides leadership skills to students working to improve their communities

The program helps shore up the financial stability of high-performing local nonprofit organizations that revitalize neighborhoods. Since the program began in 2004, the bank has trained more than 1,200 leaders in 600 community-based organizations. The bank says the program is the largest philanthropic investment in nonprofit leadership development, more than twice the size of the next largest program by a competitor.

The Neighborhood Excellence Initiative has generated media coverage and earned several professional awards. The bank carefully monitors the program and assesses its outcomes, both to justify the expense to the bank and to enhance the program itself.

RELATIONS WITH SPECIAL PUBLICS

This is a catchall category indicating a unique public relations engagement with a particular public important to the organization's mission. The public might be defined in ethnic, religious, cultural or lifestyle terms. This is a type of community relations made more complex when the community is divided and the organization needs to foster a stronger relationship with a particular group within its community. For example, in communities with significant ethnic or religious divisions, organizations may find a need for particular outreach to each group.

In the US, for example, many organizations have special outreach to Hispanic or African American populations. Likewise organizations in the UK may try to build relationships with Indian and Pakistani communities. In Australia, special publics for many organizations may include Filipino or Vietnamese Australians.

Many government, business and nonprofit/nongovernmental organizations have a particular public relations engagement with indigenous peoples, such as Native Americans in the US, First

Nations and other aboriginal groups in Canada, the Maori of New Zealand, more than a dozen groups of Aboriginals in Australia, and hundreds of other groups of indigenous peoples around the world. In Australia, for example, 44 percent of community relations practitioners for the mining and minerals industry say they are developing relationships with indigenous peoples.

Sometimes the focus is on religious communities. Many nonprofit organizations, businesses and government agencies often have a program focusing on Muslin populations. This also occurs in countries divided along religious or ethnic lines, such as the Catholic-Protestant mix in Northern Ireland, the Arab-Israel divergence in the Middle East, or the Christian-Muslim relationships in Egypt or Lebanon.

Some religious denominations engage in public relations programs focused on other religions. Anglican/Episcopalian, Roman Catholic, Lutheran and other denominations engage in ecumenical relations, which are planned and managed engagements with other churches or with other religions, such as Judaism and Islam. True to its public relations link, such ethnic and ecumenical relations aim to develop mutual understanding and cooperation in an environment of respect and trust.

Organizations also may develop public relations engagements along lifestyle lines such as outreach to the gay community, programs for senior citizens and activities with ethnic groups such as Polish-Americans.

Such engagement usually is positive, with an emphasis on education, culture, development and other aspects of mutual benefits. Occasionally it is negative, such as Chevron's public relations campaign to discredit Amazon indigenous groups in a $27 billion (£17.2 billion, €21.5 billion) environmental lawsuit in Ecuador.

BEN & JERRY'S

Ben & Jerry's ignored possible criticism (but prepared for it) as research showed that key customers supported the company's commitment to social justice. The ice-cream maker had been one of the first American companies to extend health and employment benefits to domestic partners in both gay and straight relationships.

When same-sex marriage became legal in its home state of Vermont, Ben & Jerry's partnered with the Freedom to Marry organization to activate consumers to celebrate the milestone for marriage equality and to promote the cause elsewhere. The company wanted an effective campaign that would give it maximum exposure throughout the US and the 28 other nations in which it operates.

Ben & Jerry's promoted the campaign to bloggers as it mobilized a social-media plan using an e-mail newsletter, a website, Facebook and Twitter. It also sponsored an online marriage-equality resolution directed to other states.

At the same time, the company implemented an aggressive media relations program with established media, both mainstream and gay-oriented venues. Part of this included detailed talking points with both positive and negative responses in anticipation of opposition, which never materialized.

The biggest attention-getter was the renaming of its iconic "Chubby Hubby" ice cream as "Hubby Hubby" in its Vermont stores, with free samples to celebrate the legislation.

The campaign received nationwide media coverage (86 percent of this rated positive or neutral), reaching more than 433 million people in one month. The social media component led to nearly 3,300 Facebook likes, 35,000 Tweets, and 11,500 blog posts. The campaign also increased sales while most competitors were seeing decreases. In part, the campaign was responsible for a 720 percent increase in visitors to FreedomtoMarry.org.

Ben & Jerry's later had a similar promotion in the UK when parliament was debating marriage equality. The company launched a new flavor called "Apple-y Ever After." It used social media for a letter-writing campaign to members of parliament and created a Facebook app where people could "marry" their same-sex friends "because every-one is equal and deserves to live Apple-y Ever After."

INVESTOR/DONOR RELATIONS

Investor relations is a specialized area that requires expertise not only in public relations but also a focused knowledge of finance and economics, as well as the ability to follow detailed legal requirements associated with mergers, stock options, public disclosure and related matters.

Also called **financial public relations**, investor relations involves a planned communication program to help the organization interact with large-group investors such as pension programs, mutual funds and unions, and with individual investors who often have very different interests and needs. Business journalists and bloggers also are significant publics for this specialty.

People working in investor relations conduct research on attitudes toward the company and work on communication programs with shareholders, regulators, financial journalists and bloggers, investors, and both sell-side and buy-side analysts. Specifically, public relations practitioners help create presentations for these publics, write speeches, prepare print and digital information, and work with the financial media. They deal with information associated with mergers and acquisitions, both friendly and hostile.

Investor relations specialists oversee the company's annual (and sometimes more frequent) stockholder meetings. They prepare the annual report, which generally is a sophisticated print and online presentation of the company's financial situation and outlook.

Because investor relations executives sometimes deal with bad news, they are expected to embody the characteristics of accuracy, honesty and transparency, demonstrating a commitment to the long-term relationship between the organization and its financial stakeholders.

Investor relations also deals with **corporate social responsibility**, a relatively new commitment by many companies to contributing to the betterment of society while earning money for stockholders. The issue gained visibility in the 1980s, when universities sued corporations over investments in racially segregated South Africa and other social issues, and when orders of nuns with sometimes only token stock holdings sued giant corporations on their treatment of the poor, homeless and other marginalized people.

For nonprofit organizations, the financial field includes **donor relations**, often part of a wider fundraising and development program. This specialty area calls for tactics similar to those used for stockholders. Both are financial supporters, and both expect some kind of reward (financial for stockholders, philanthropic for donors).

DOW CHEMICAL

Dow is a global corporation that, in 2012, suffered a series of set-backs: loss of a $17 billion (£10.8 billion, €13.5 billion) project in Kuwait, an extended unsuccessful lawsuit to back out of a purchase agreement for the same amount with another US-based multi-national chemical company and decreased demand internationally throughout the chemical industry.

Investor relations was at a low point. In an effort to recover, Dow sought to relaunch itself as a leader in science and innovation.

Part of this rebuilding included a financial communication program aimed at various categories of stakeholders. Armed with research that showed a need to build confidence among analysts, Dow increased transparency, leveraged management time to interact with current investors and expanded international marketing efforts.

Tactics included a new digital newsletter, an enhanced investor relations website, and use of video both internally and externally on the company's Dow World News program. The company participated in 14 international road shows (compared with only one two years prior), with a major London-based meeting for sell-side analysts and a formal presentation with a European focus. Other events were held in Philadelphia and at corporate headquarters at Midland, Michigan.

The results of this campaign included positive coverage in major business publications and well-attended events. Follow-up research showed noticeable gains in perceptions around Dow as an invest-ment opportunity, leading to expanded investment and record-high stock prices.

PUBLIC AFFAIRS AND GOVERNMENT RELATIONS

Most organizations deal in some way with regulatory agencies and government entities. Corporations often have oversight groups looking at safety issues. Nonprofit organizations sometimes interact with legislators, and advocacy groups often focus on public policy issues.

Public affairs or **government relations** are umbrella terms for planned public relations activity involving organizations and gov-ernment agencies. The field sometimes is called **civic relations** or

cultural affairs (the latter term particularly when it is practiced by government agencies).

The tasks associated with public affairs include research and information-gathering, interactive activities such as conferences and meetings, and communication techniques including print and online materials, as well as the full round of media relations tools.

Lobbying often falls into this category of public relations, as organizations promote their causes and interests to lawmakers and government regulators, hoping to obtain favorably in votes or support. Increasingly both businesses and nonprofit organizations are involved in both nonpartisan issue advocacy and in the highly partisan electoral process, especially on the funding side.

Government agencies also practice **intergovernmental relations** as they engage their counterparts in other nations. This practice, sometimes called **public diplomacy**, differs from regular diplomacy in that the latter often is conducted in secret, whereas public diplomacy generally is more transparent and involves the use of news media and social media to foster positive relationships between nations.

The term **public affairs** can be misleading, because many government agencies use this term for their entire public relations program. At one time, congress refused to fund public relations activities, fearing that other branches of government would try to manipulate public opinion. But it does fund **public information** by agencies and the military, through press secretaries, public information officers and well-trained public affairs staffs.

Practitioners in this field hold news conferences, maintain pressrooms, produce videos, seek publicity, and recruit and perform all the other tactics associated with public relations. During the Iraq War, coalition forces (led by the US and including the UK, Italy, Poland and several other nations) launched a YouTube channel where videos showing aspects of the military operation attracted more than 9 million views.

Despite their occasional need for secrecy and tact, government and public relations practitioners generally try to be seen as open and transparent.

Over the years, governments have created commissions on public information and supported the use of information as a strategic element of defense and diplomacy. The Australian Army Public

Relations Service, for example, provides support for strategic communication objectives. In Britain, the Royal Air Force includes active journalists in its reserve units, many working in the Public Relation squadron that, among other things, provides media training.

In the US, congress occasionally has been critical of certain public relations practices, such as the second Bush administration's payment for placing favorable stories in Iraqi newspapers.

RENEWABLE ENERGY

The importance of performance and adaptation as the foundation for effective public relations can be seen in the international public affairs campaign to select a world headquarters for the International Renewable Energy Agency.

The agency's 130-plus members had to agree on a location for the headquarters. Denmark, Germany and Austria pushed their status as recognized leaders in renewable energy. But a public relations plan on behalf of the United Arab Emirates helped shape the outcome.

UAE is a leading producer of oil, but the agency also focuses on renewable energy—a seemingly improbable pairing. For several years UAE had been making a commitment to renewable energy. It was building the city of Masdar as the world's first carbon-neutral, zero-waste city with sustainable technology.

After public relations showcased UAE's forward-looking energy policy, the renewable energy agency voted to establish its international headquarters in Masdar, affirming that UAE's performance on clean energy had matched its words—the ultimate test of effective public relations.

SPECIAL EVENTS AND PROMOTION

All kinds of organizations engage in **special events**, dramatized activities designed to generate publicity, increase understanding and generate support for the organization's services, products or causes. Special events are associated with other categories of public relations activities. Organizations may hold an open house or stage a grand opening as part of a consumer relations program, hold picnics and recognition dinners for employees, or sponsor appreciation events for donors and other supporters.

Such events should be potentially newsworthy, cost-effective and linked to the organization's mission. For this reason, newspapers and libraries hold spelling bees, men's clothing stores sponsor golf tournaments, health-care organizations support marathons and museums recreate historical events. Cities bid to host the Olympics, Stanley Cup and other international events to promote tourism and trade. Resorts and restaurants often have large staffs to help plan special events for guests.

The International Special Events Society estimates that each year worldwide, spending on special events totals more than $500 billion (£323 billion, €399 billion).

The work of special events involves not only strategic planning to ensure the right fit between the organization and event, but also much attention to detail. In corporations, special events may include organizing the logistics of annual stockholder meetings: creating print and digital materials, organizing food and hospitality, assisting with tours, and accommodating the news media. It involves mundane considerations, such as ensuring that enough parking and toilets are available, that menus consider people who are vegans and those with food allergies.

SNAUSAGES

A publicity-focused special event raised money for animal charities and promoted Snausages, a brand of doggie treats made by Del Monte Foods. Faced with competitors outspending it in advertising, Snausages turned to public relations to pull it out of its slump.

The Iditarod is a well-known dogsled race, with teams of huskies pulling drivers more than 1,000 miles across Alaska. Snausages turned the tables and garnered international publicity, including ESPN, with a "man sled" race.

Teams of men pulled canine mushers, dogs that had previously pulled in the Iditarod. An Associated Press photo of the event was the most e-mailed photo on Yahoo News for three days running. The brand mascot, Snocrates, refereed the race, ensuring the Snausages visibility in photos and video footage. Donations went to animal charities recommended by each human participant in the race, upping the publicity factor.

The event increased traffic by 30 percent at the Snausages website and led to a rise in customer demand.

GANDER MOUNTAIN

Sometimes organizations can use special events to create new public activities to support their strategic goals. Outdoors retailer Gander Mountain wanted to reach out more proactively to outdoor and hunting enthusiasts during the holiday season.

Consumers in North America (and, increasingly, around the world) were used to Black Friday (the day after Thanksgiving and the busiest shopping day of the year) and Cyber Monday (the following Monday and the busiest online shopping day).

In that fashion, Gander Mountain created Camo Thursday as a new unofficial holiday, co-opting Thanksgiving Day itself for online shoppers. This even stretched for several weeks, and on every Thursday between Thanksgiving and Christmas the retailer featured online sales promotions.

The idea attracted the attention of both print and broadcast news media. The company strategically used Facebook and Twitter support, generating much attention through social media. The result was a record-setting sales season.

MEDIA RELATIONS

An organization's engagement with news media is the best-known part of public relations. Indeed, many people think only of this instead of the wider array of public relations environments and activities.

Media relations involves gaining support for an organization through the news media. Those media include the established print forum, such as newspapers and magazines, as well as broadcast and cable media including television and radio, both in their traditional form and in newer satellite and online environments. The media also include a growing array of digital venues, including blogs and websites, social media such as Facebook and LinkedIn, and digital sharing sites such as YouTube and Flickr.

One premise of effective media relations is the mutual relationship between organizations and media. Organizations rely on media to help them communicate with their publics. The media rely on organizations to provide information that they find newsworthy enough to share with their audiences. Thus both sides need each other.

Research for media relations involves knowing media audiences as well as media **gatekeepers**, who are the decision makers on producing or publishing a story.

Commonly used tactics for media relations are **fact sheets** with newsworthy bullets and **news releases** with fuller journalistic presentations of the same information. Both may be disseminated by mail and e-mail and posted online for journalists and others.

There are many variations on news releases. They can be general or local, depending on the organization, its publics and the news being presented. They may include photos for print media or they may be directed to broadcast media with audio or video news releases, supported by voice actualities or video B-rolls. They may have a multi-media focus or interactive features of social media releases (for example, visit the Multi-Vu PR Newswire website. http://www.prnewswire.com/news-releases/videos/).

Feature releases, meanwhile, can focus on individuals with a biography or an interview, or on an organization with a history or product overview. They may be service articles telling readers how to accomplish a certain task. Thus a food company might provide a recipe for healthy-yet-affordable meals, and a human service organization may give advice on how to deal with depression or help a friend in an abusive relationship. Feature releases may be written as a narrative or as a series of questions and answers or action steps.

Media relations also provides an outlet for organizational opinion. Some opinion statements are imbedded as quotes in news and feature releases. Others are presented more formally as **position papers** or as **letters to the editor** or **guest editorials**. Blogs and other websites also provide a venue for presenting organizational opinion.

Increasingly, organizations are gathering their media relations materials at web-based **media pages** or **online newsrooms**. Here are a few examples of effective media pages: entertainer Jack Johnson news/press section, Toronto Maple Leafs hockey team, the press section of the Louvre museum, and the Holy See Press Office of the Vatican. For examples of good online newsrooms, check out these organizations: IBM, Pepsi, Anhauser-Busch, United Nations, Australian Department of Immigration and Citizenship, US Navy or the Diamond Jubilee of Queen Elizabeth.

Inviting and responding to requests for one-on-one interviews are part of tasks for media relations. So is organizing **news conferences**, which are group interviews in which an organizational spokesperson makes a newsworthy announcement and reporters ask follow-up questions. But journalists are very competitive with each other and do not favor news conferences, instead preferring to question news sources in private.

---

12 principles of effective media relations

1 A relationship is both inevitable and necessary between an organization and the media. The actions of the organization will determine if this relationship is good or bad.

2 The organization should publicly speak with one voice by designating and preparing a single spokesperson (or multiple spokes people with a coordinated message).

3 The person closest to the situation should be the designated spokesperson or at least be in close communication with the spokesperson.

4 "No comment" is never an option. Every bona fide question should be addressed.

5 The organization should look upon reporters as allies in reaching various publics rather than as intruders or enemies.

6 The organization should consider itself accountable to all of its various publics, internal as well as external. This includes customers, employees/volunteers, stockholders/donors, supporters and the community. Further, it should view the news media as one of the vehicles available for communicating with these constituencies.

7   The organization should not expect to control the media's agenda or their assessment of what is newsworthy. But it can help add issues to that agenda.

8   The public/media relations office should always be "in the loop" in all newsworthy situations, especially those with negative potential.

9   Reporters should be accommodated with professional assistance such as parking permits, access and a functioning media room.

10 The organization should expect that it occasionally will "take a hit" in the media. Its response should be to accept this, try to understand it and get over it as quickly as possible.

11 Media skepticism and scrutiny can be more bearable when the organization interacts with reporters in a timely manner and with openness, accuracy and candor.

12 Media coverage is considerably more credible than advertising. The effective use of the news media gives an organization a believable voice in the community.

DUBLIN ZOO

With a decline in visitors during an economic recession and less government funding, Ireland's Dublin Zoo used media relations to attract more visitors at full-price admissions.

Providing media training to zookeepers, the campaign reached out to journalists with a series of media-friendly events such as a mock "zoo elections" to select the most popular animal (an orangutan named Sibu). It facilitated media coverage of the births of a hippo, giraffe, elephant, rhinoceros, bongo, gorilla and a pair of pandas. It created special events such as Orangutan Awareness Week with a strong television presence with messages of conservation and endangered animals.

The zoo also used the news media for several high-profile incidents, including the theft of a penguin that was subsequently returned unharmed. It produced a behind-the-scenes TV series called "The Zoo" that attracted about 300,000 viewers.

Beyond established news media, the campaign created social media opportunities with an interactive website and a new 15,000 Facebook fans and Twitter followers. It gave exclusive early-morning access for 20 of Ireland's leading bloggers and photo bloggers.

The result was the highest media profile ever for the zoo, and the highest annual paid attendance—963,053—in its 180-year history. The benefits continued as the zoo attracted more than a million visitors the following year and raised enough money to open a new Gorilla Rainforest.

CRISIS COMMUNICATION

A **crisis** is a major, negative, public, sudden and unpredicted event that can seriously disrupt an organization's activity and potentially hurts its bottom line or mission.

Because crises can and eventually do affect every type of organization, **crisis communications** programs are a standard component of the wider public relations agenda. Because a crisis occurs in a public environment, even private businesses and nonprofit organizations cannot shield themselves from the expectation of being accountable to their publics.

By its nature, a crisis invites outside scrutiny and jeopardizes the organization's reputation. An organization can find itself in the role of either culprit or victim in a crisis situation. Regardless of the cause, if a crisis is handled properly, it offers the organization an opportunity to create a positive impression with its key publics.

Public relations people engage in crisis communication in various stages. The **pre-crisis** time is one of anticipation and prevention. Effective practitioners look for warning signs, undergo media training, and develop response plans for worst-case scenarios—all to be ready for events they hope will never occur.

The **acute stage** is when the crisis breaks forth on the public stage. It is a time to contain the problem, work with regulators and the media, and begin investigating the cause. In the **post-crisis stage**, the focus is on recovering: returning to normal, assessing the extent of both physical and reputational damage, and planning to prevent a recurrence of the crisis.

The court of public opinion is a common reference with public relations, and a new subspecialty of crisis communication merges this concept with actual legal courts. The media historically have covered lawsuits primarily with information from law enforcement and prosecutors. **Litigation public relations** provides a tool for defense attorneys to manage communication before and during legal disputes in an effort to impact the outcome of the case.

Generally, this area focuses on pre-trial publicity, which makes sense because most lawsuits are settled before trial. Specifically, it involves seeking balanced media coverage, counteracting negative publicity, strategically releasing information or inviting the media to give voice to a client's viewpoint, wordsmithing legal language for maximum impact with publics, and helping the media and their audiences understand legal complexities. It sometimes is able to influence the prosecution to bring a lesser charge.

Litigation public relations also is related to **reputation management**. In this role, it also may be directed toward protecting the client's reputation.

Practitioners are careful to protect the integrity of both the legal and communication processes, particularly because pre-trial publicity involves both factual and emotional messages. Litigation public relations generally enjoys the attorney-client privilege of confidential interaction and thus has some specific regulations.

Tactics associated with litigation public relations include courthouse news conferences, attorney participation in talk shows, and daily media briefings by the prosecution. But it also involves behind-the-scenes activity.

Some observers have noted that this area is growing, particularly in the US and the UK, where the media are increasingly covering legal cases. Because the legal process is adversarial and creates a win-lose situation, the public information and advocacy models of public relations are most in play in the litigation area.

Seven principles of crisis communication

Principle of Existing Relationships. Communicate with employees, volunteers, stockholders, donors and other constituent groups. Keep them informed, because their continued support will be important in rebuilding after the crisis.

Principle of Media-as-Ally. Organizations in crisis should treat the news media as allies that provide opportunities to communicate with their key publics. If the media are intrusive and/or hostile, it may be because the organization has not been forthcoming in providing legitimate information to the media and, through them, to the organization's other publics.

Principle of Reputational Priority. After safety issues, the top priority is to shore up the organization's reputation. Focus on doing what's best for all publics—not only managers and stockholders, but also employees, customers, neighbors and others. Set objectives that deal with maintaining credibility. Use the crisis as an opportunity to enhance the organization's reputation for social responsibility.

Principle of Quick Response. There's a one-hour rule: Within one hour of learning about a crisis, the organization should have its first message available to its publics, particularly the media. Details about injury or death should be delayed until families are notified.

Principle of One Voice. A single spokesperson should be designated to speak for the organization. If multiple spokespersons are needed, each should be aware of what the others are saying, and all should present a coordinated message and work from the same set of facts.

Principle of Disclosure. Without admitting fault, organizations in crisis should work from the premise that they should share everything they know with their publics, subject to specific legal or other strategic justification for not releasing certain information.

Principle of Message Framing. Managing the agenda means that the organization maintains some level of control over how the story unfolds. This can be accomplished by seizing an opportunity early in a crisis by being accessible and providing information that sets the tone for subsequent reporting. The premise is that, if the organization does not tell its own story, that story will be told by others who probably have less knowledge of the facts and certainly less interest in the organization and its reputation.

CHILEAN MINE RESCUE

The world watched as 33 men were trapped half a mile underground in a copper-gold mine in Chile. The government estimated that it would take four months to rescue them.

Two days' worth of emergency food rations stretched to more than two weeks before a lifeline could be dropped to provide the miners with fresh air and more food. As the story unfolded in real time, both the company and the government were transparent and forthcoming with information.

The trapped miners were in radio contact with rescuers above ground. Deep underground, one miner organized an exercise program to help his colleagues lose weight so they could fit through the small rescue shaft being drilled. Another monitored the health of his fellow miners. One man set up a chapel and led daily prayers, with rosaries sent by Pope Benedict. Another hosted video journals sent to the surface from a mini-camera dropped through the emergency shaft.

Shortly before the rescue, the miners were prepped for their encounter with reporters, helping them deal with the media attention that was inevitable when they were rescued. The director of the government rescue program, a former radio journalist, trained the miners as they neared the end of their entrapment. The message: Be yourself. Speak from your heart. Use journalists as a way to communicate a positive message to the general public. Help the journalists tell your story. Don't become unnerved by a barrage of questions; pick the ones you want to answer.

After 69 days, far sooner than anticipated, the rescue shaft was completed. As the world watched in real time, the rescue went flawlessly.

PRACTICING PUBLIC RELATIONS

Public relations includes different types of work calling for a variety of skills and perspectives. This chapter focuses on three of the most needed elements for success: good writing, effective research techniques and a practical base in communication theory.

As should be clear from the previous chapters, public relations is a serious profession. It's nice to have a bubbly personality, good to be a "people person" who enjoys others. But certainly, neither is a career requirement. If public relations were mainly about hosting parties and posing for photos, a fabulous wardrobe and movie-star looks would probably be assets. But it's not, and they aren't.

As a serious profession, however, public relations does call for some special skills. All of these can be learned. Generally the learning comes through both increasing knowledge (translate that as: reading books and professional articles, and studying public relations at university level) and experience (getting into the trenches and actually doing the work).

In truth, some skills such as effective writing require a lifetime of learning and practice. Others call for a mindset of curiosity and appreciation for explanations of why things are what they are, whether they are what they seem to be and what might be under a particular set of circumstances. That's where research and communication theory come into play.

Career counselors can help people match their personal attributes and practical skills with various aspects of the public relations profession. But it is important for people considering careers in public relations to know what will be expected of them.

This chapter will explore each of these necessary ingredients for a successful career in public relations. Let's look first at writing.

WRITING SKILLS

Topping the list of absolutely crucial skills is good writing. Public relations deals with language: clarity, brevity and accuracy. It calls for subtlety, understanding the nuance in choosing not just an OK word but the exact right word. Writing deals with strategy, knowing why you are sitting in front of a blank computer screen or a blank sheet of paper. It involves determining what you want to accomplish, whom you are writing for and what that person wants and needs, and what impact you hope to make.

Is it necessary to love writing? Probably. It may be possible to be a good writer without enjoying it, though that's hard to imagine. Most people who are successful in public relations genuinely like to write. They enjoy the process as much as the outcome. They like being able to research a topic and then strategically craft the relevant information into a piece that is persuasive, newsworthy or otherwise effective in achieving a certain purpose.

Let's briefly review some of the various types and formats of public relations writing. These formats (presented alphabetically) are among the writing tools that public relations practitioners are skilled in using on behalf of their organization or cause.

Actuality: Recorded **sound bite** imbedded within a news release for distribution to radio stations.

Advocacy Letter: Public relations format for direct-mail, Internet or publicity release promoting a cause or supporting an issue.

Annual Report: Press report written by an organization required of stock-issuing companies and voluntarily produced by many other companies and nonprofit organizations.

Announcement Release: Type of news release that announces an upcoming activity or a new program or product.

Appeal Letter: Central part of a direct-mail package that presents the persuasive message to the reader.

Audio News Release (ANR): Public relations information packaged as a completed broadcast report for radio, featuring a news release written for radio use and accompanied by an actuality.

B-Roll Package: Public relations presentation of **video B-rolls** without a written news release; intended for background information.

Background Fact Sheet: Type of **fact sheet** that presents information about an organization or issues it deals with; sometimes called a **factoid** or a **breaker box**; compare with **news fact sheet.**

Backgrounder: Type of public relations release that provides factual information to give a context to an organization or an issue.

Biographical Release (Bio): Type of public relations release that provides a narrative or feature article about a person significant to an organization.

Blog: Type of website featuring short articles called **blog posts** and reader comments.

Blue Paper: Type of **position statement** with lengthy and detailed information, often accompanied by a **white paper** serving as an executive summary.

Broadcast News Release: Version of a **news release** prepared specifically for radio and television, usually briefer than releases for print media, more conversational in tone, and incorporating broadcast writing style and **pronouncers.**

Brochure: Printed form or organizational media, usually folded sheets meant to be read as a booklet and providing information meant to be relevant over an extended period of time; also called **leaflet, folder, pamphlet, booklet, tract** and **bulletin**; compare with **flier.**

Case Study: Consumer-interest release that narrates how a particular organization identified and addressed a problem or issue; also called a **case history.**

Contingency Statement: Type of position statement prepared in different versions to accommodate various potential situations or outcomes; also called a **stand-by statement.**

E-Mail Release: Public relations communication delivered via e-mail; in format, it is briefer and more concise than a printed release.

E-Newsletter: Online electronic newsletter.

E-Zine: Online electronic magazine; also called a **cyberzine.**

Elevator Pitch: One-minute persuasive message to present an idea or advocate a cause.

Event Listing: Writing format that provides basic information for use in calendars and other listings of upcoming activities.

Fact Sheet: Bulleted series of information items about an activity or program; usually including who, what, when, where, why, how and contact information, sometimes with background and quotes.

Feature Release: Type of public relations release that emphasizes personalities and human-interest angles rather than hard news.

Feature Reprint: Public relations practice of reprinting and selectively disseminating, sometimes with a brief commentary, a published article that includes positive information about an organization.

Flier: Printed form of organizational media, usually unfolded sheets meant to be read as single units and providing time-specific information; also called a **circular, broadside** and **handbill**; compare with **brochure.**

Follow-Up Release: Type of **news release** in which the organization responds or adds to prior news reporting.

Green Paper: Type of **position statement** with background information but no proposals.

Guest Editorial: Opinion piece published as a solicited or approved editorial presenting the view of a person or organization not affiliated with the publication; similar to an op-ed commentary.

Handout: Inappropriate slang term for **news release.**

House Organ: Generic term for a publication written by an organization for public relations purposes, such as newsletters and employee or consumer magazines.

How-To Article: Consumer-interest release that provides step-by-step instructions in addressing a problem or issue; also called a **service article.**

Info-Action Statement: Part of a **news release** that clearly presents information on how audiences can take action or obtain additional information.

Information Digest: Consumer-focused publication that presents information based on technical reports in language for non-technical readers

Internet News Release (INR): Adaptation of video news releases that could be transmitted over the Internet.

Interview Notes: Type of public relations release that provides reporters with an unedited transcript of an interview they can use to develop a story.

Lead: Beginning paragraph of a news release, written to gain the attention of the audience.

Lead-In: Transition in a broadcast news release introducing a sound bite or **actuality**; also called a **throw.**

Letter to the Editor: Journalistic opportunity sometimes used by public relations practitioners for publicity or advocacy purposes.

Magapaper: Type of newsletter that is a hybrid with a newspaper; also called a **minimag** and **maganews.**

Media Advisory: Memo written by public relations practitioner notifying reporters about an upcoming activity; also called **media alert**.

Multimedia News Release: Repackaging of print, audio and video message with web links for a comprehensive presentation of an organization's public relations information.

News Brief: Opening paragraphs of a news release including the summary lead and the benefit statement, written either to stand alone or to provide the beginning of a lengthier release.

News Fact Sheet: Type of fact sheet that provides information about a newsworthy activity; compare with **background fact sheet.**

News Release: Common format used by organizations to provide information to the news media and other publics.

Newsletter: Printed form of organizational media, usually multipage serialized publications prepared for particular publics such as employees or customers.

Official Statement: Type of position statement that focuses on a brief proclamation of a timely issue.

Op-Ed Commentary: Opinion piece presenting the view of an individual or organization not affiliated with the publication; similar to **guest editorial** but not necessarily solicited by the publication.

Organizational History: Type of public relations release that provides a feature article based on the background of an organization.

Organizational Profile: Type of public relations release that provides information about the structure and mission of an organization; often used in tandem with an organizational history.

Petition: Hybrid of an advocacy letter and a proclamation, providing a common statement with numerous signers.

Pitch Letter: Promotional letter to media gatekeepers to persuade them to report on some aspect or activity of an organization.

Position Statement: Public relations format presenting the formal and public position of an organization on a particular topic; also called **white paper**; categories include a **position paper** and **position paragraph** depending on the length of the statement.

Press Release: Inappropriate and outdated term for **news release** which implies news for all media, not just the written press.

Proclamation: Formal statement issued by an organization or public authority commemorating an event.

Pronouncer: Phonetic tip included in news release, scripts and other public relations vehicles to help readers correctly pronounce unfamiliar words, usually names of people and places; also called **pronunciation guide.**

Public Advisory: Announcement notifying media audiences about an important matter, usually one with potential harm.

Public Relations Advertising: Category of commercial and noncommercial advertising focusing on advocacy and image rather than on the marketing of products and services.

Public Service Advertising: Type of public relations advertising in which media donate time or space to nonprofit organizations to promote messages that the media consider to be in the public interest.

Question–Answer Piece (Q&A): Consumer-interest release that uses a format of brief questions posed directly to readers and responses to each question.

Short-Form Q&A: Type of question-answer format that has only a few questions with brief answers, presented in a non-narrative Q&A format.

Social Media Release (SMR): Packaging of print text with audio and video messages, photos, and web links and interactive features for a comprehensive presentation of an organization's public relations information.

Sound Bite: Brief, memorable quote used by a news source, especially for radio and television reports; compare with **actuality.**

Story Idea Memo: Memo to interest the media in reporting on a person or program, usually involving soft news or feature possibilities.

Talk Paper: Type of internal position statement used by organizations to provide common messages for spokespersons; also called talking points.

Video B-Roll: Type of video news release that provides unedited videotaped pieces for reporters' use.

Video News Release (VNR): Public relations information packaged as a partial or completed broadcast report for television.

Wiki: Type of website that serves as a forum for team writing and editing.

Seeing a list such as this, there's little wonder why many people inside the profession say that excellent writing skills is the one indispensible requirement. Most practitioners are excellent in written communication, not only because they bring strong writing skills to their job, but also because most of them write every day in their work.

All the other skills associated with the profession can be learned or enhanced on the job. But nobody succeeds in public relations without being a good writer, and it's mindboggling to think that anyone could be a good writer without first enjoying writing.

It is far beyond the scope of this book to provide a comprehensive focus on the specific specialty of public relations writing. Entire books are available on this topic alone. But it is helpful to understand the nature of news and how to prepare a news release.

Despite fewer opportunities via newspapers to use news releases, this format nevertheless remains the versatile foundation in virtually all public relations writing. It serves as the basis in writing for print and broadcast media, social media, and other online venues such as blogs and e-mail. Using the principles of effective news releases enhances even advocacy and fundraising pieces.

WHAT IS NEWS?

What are some of the principles of good news releases?

We begin with **news**, which is information that is important, previously unreported and dealing with a topic having significant impact for potentially large numbers of people. Journalism books often have lengthy lists of attributes of news. They identify elements such as action, change, conflict, consequence, controversy, fame, personality and proximity, along with many others. Here's a simpler list from a public relations perspective. News is information that is significant, local, balanced and timely, with two value-added characteristics involving unusualness and fame. Let's simplify things with the acronym **SiLoBaTi + UnFa.** This convenient way to remember the main ingredients of news is made up of the first two letters of each of the elements: significance, localness, balance and timeliness, plus unusualness and fame.

- **Significance**. First, news is information of importance and significance. It has meaning to many people, even those beyond the organization. It is information of consequence and magnitude. It overcomes the "So What?" question that meets information of lesser importance.
- **Local**. News deals with information relevant to the local area, as defined by the coverage area of the news medium featuring the information, or to the special interests of an audience. Local might be defined geographically for a community newspaper or focused on the interests of a particular audience such as a Hispanic newspaper or a college alumni blog.
- **Balance**. News is information presented with objectivity and balance. While the public relations practitioner uses information to promote the organization or client, it should not be packaged merely in a promotional manner. Rather, it should be presented with the air of detachment and neutrality that is associated with credible news venues. It is not hyped or exaggerated.
- **Timeliness**. The final key ingredient in news is that it is current and timely, being connected with contemporary issues, especially those high on public and media agendas.

In addition to these four key elements, newsworthiness is magnified by two other factors, which strategists in public relations strive for.

- **Unusualness**. News interest is enhanced when the information deals with unusual situations. This is what writers call human interest, that hard-to-define quality involving rarity, novelty, uniqueness, milestones or slightly offbeat occurrences.

- **Fame.** News interest also is enhanced when the information involves fame. "Names make news" isn't idle chatter. Well-known or important people can add interest to a newsworthy situation. Sometimes their involvement can take an otherwise routine event and elevate it to the status of news.

Public relations people are aware that there are different types of news. **Hard news** is information that deals with momentous events: accidents, crime, death, disaster, scandals and activities with immediate results such as elections, trials and sporting events. **Breaking news** is hard news that is happening even as the media are covering it. Both hard and breaking news often throw public relations practitioners into the area of crisis communication in a reactive mode.

Two other categories of news lend themselves more to proactive public relations. **Soft news** is lighter information dealing with upcoming events and new programs, developments without major consequences, and activities and trends with more distant results. **Specialized news** deals with information of importance to particular publics and particular segments of the media. This includes news about business, religion, sports, the arts, agriculture, science, health, home, fashion and other interest areas.

Sometimes, news spontaneously occurs within organizations, usually in crisis scenarios. But in a more proactive way, public relations practitioners know how to generate newsworthy information that will interest both their publics and the media. Sometimes this involves a **news peg**, linking the organization's message to something already being reported by the media. For example, if a celebrity goes forward in dealing with mental illness, health advocacy organizations may be quick to engage reporters on news and feature stories about how to identify the illness in friends or loved ones, the kinds of treatments available and so on.

Some other ways that organizations can generate news include giving an award, holding a contest, announcing personnel changes, addressing a local need, issuing a report or localizing a wider existing report, launching a campaign, giving a speech, involving a celebrity and addressing a public issue.

NEWS RELEASE: THE BASIC TOOL

There has been much speculation about the importance of news releases in the practice of public relations. The news release is dead, proclaim some observers. They base that declaration on the fact that fewer people read newspapers and that newspapers have less news and therefore use fewer news releases than they once did.

But public relations writing is rooted in journalistic writing. News and advocacy based on newsworthy issues lie at the center of all public relations writing. The news release, in its various forms, remains a staple. They serve the obvious purpose of providing information to help newspapers report on an organization. But news releases also can be written to serve the format needs of both the broadcast media and social media.

Knowing how to write effective news releases also helps public relations practitioners write advocacy and fundraising letters, position statements and annual reports. It also assists with less formal writing associated with blogs and other interactive forms of media.

Here are the basic components of a news release:

- The **lead** (pronounced LEED) is the most important paragraph. It is the gateway to the entire story, the basis on which editors will decide to print the release and readers will decide whether to read it. The most common type is a **summary news lead** that provides a one- or two-sentence report of the most interesting facts. Details such as names and dates will come later, but the summary lead announces that corporate profits are up, that a new executive director has been selected, or that a new program or product will be available soon.

- The **benefit statement** is the biggest difference between a news release and a journalistic report. The former always includes information indicating how this newsworthy information will be useful to people. The benefit statement clearly indicates the advantage or opportunity the organization is offering to its key publics. One of the smoothest ways to highlight the benefit statement is to develop it as a quote or narrative explaining the advantage.

- Another feature found in news releases, but not necessarily included in journalistic reports, is the **information/action**

statement. This is a way to mobilize readers and viewers. It gives the audience how-to instructions on obtaining more information or acting on the information provided in the release, such as buying a product, visiting a museum, calling for more information, casting a vote, volunteering for a project, making a donation and so on. This may highlight a website, phone number or public meeting.

- **Secondary details** amplify information in the lead. For example, the lead may note that a biology teacher with 20 years of service to the local school district has been appointed assistant superintendent for science education. Later in the release would be biographical information about the teacher and organizational information about how science is taught throughout the district. It might also include information about the selection process.
- **Background information** provides context for the report. In the education scenario noted above, background information might deal with a statewide report on science education or with published reports about the outlook for science-related jobs in the near future.
- Some news releases include an optional section with **organizational identification**. This is a paragraph with standard wording that routinely is dropped into a news release, usually at the end. It often deals with corporate structure, such as by identifying a company as a subsidiary of a larger corporation and noting the industry ranking or the business. Organizational IDs are seldom published, but they alert reporters to perhaps useful information. They also become part of the report when the news release is posted on the organization's website.

Within this structure, public relations writers follow the basic journalistic guidelines for proper news reporting. Foremost among these: focusing on objective presentation of newsworthy information. Other standards for news writing include using short sentences with simple language, and attributing quotes and all paraphrases that deal with opinion to a news source. Releases for newspapers generally are one or two pages long.

Like reporters, public relations writers follow a journalistic stylebook such as the *Associated Press Stylebook* in the US, the *Canadian Press Stylebook* and *Reuters Handbook of Journalism* used in many other

English-speaking parts of the world. These stylebooks outline standard ways to use names and titles, abbreviations, capitalization, punctuation, governmental and military references, numbers and other details of writing.

Public relations practitioners know that journalists often do not use news releases verbatim. But the information they contain often becomes part of the story produced by reporters. Additionally, practitioners routinely archive news releases at an online newsroom or media page at their organizational website.

BROADCAST NEWS RELEASE

With this basic structure as the starting point, public relations writers can adapt the news release for many purposes. Releases tailored for broadcast media are more conversational, writing that is professionally casual, with contractions, "you" references, and short sentences written for the ear rather than the eye.

Broadcast releases generally use stylebook variations developed specifically for radio and television. Generally, this means omitting middle initials, avoiding leads with names unfamiliar to audiences, avoiding courtesy titles (Mr, Mrs, Ms), using long titles only after names, and using attribution at the beginning of a quote or paraphrase rather than at the end.

Broadcast releases also assist reporters with pronunciation. They include pronouncers for unusual names such as mah-MOOD ah-mah-dih-nee-ZHAHD and OO-goh chah-vehs and place names such as La Jolla, Calif., (lah-HOY-uh); Hjo, Sweden (YOU); Drogheda, Ireland (DRAW-heh-deh); and Wauchope, Australia (WAR-hope).

Broadcast style also has special guidelines for abbreviations. For example, the Food and Agriculture Organization of the United Nations is abbreviated to FAO for print releases; broadcast releases would use F-A-O, indicating that each letter should be pronounced separately. But the United Nation's Educational, Scientific and Cultural Organization would use UNESCO for print releases and Unesco (or perhaps you-NESS-koh) for broadcast releases, indicating that the acronym should be pronounced as a word rather than a series of letters.

Actualities often are imbedded in broadcast releases. These are sound bites provided by the public relations writer with eyewitness reports, explanations by experts, or comments with an organization's viewpoints.

Broadcast releases are sometimes repackaged as ready-to-air packages as audio news releases or video news releases. Meanwhile, video B-rolls provide unedited video to TV stations to use in their reporting of information included in news releases.

SOCIAL MEDIA NEWS RELEASE

Another adaptation of the basic news release is an e-mail release. Its contents follow the same pattern and guidelines as other releases, but the e-mail release has the advantage of providing attachments of photos, supplemental text and links. Generally the subject line indicates that they are news releases from a particular organization, with the topic part of the subject line (making it easy to locate archived copies).

A more complete social media release expands on the basic written release. It may include text, audio, video and digital photos, charts and maps, as well as links to sites with related information or background information on complex scientific or health-related topics. Often the narrative is paralleled by a fact sheet bulleting the same information.

Writing for digital and social media also has some unique standards for public relations practitioners. Web writing should be short and concise, generally fit for a single screen. It should be scanable, which means it features short paragraphs, bullets, and boldfaced, or otherwise highlighted, text to make it easy for readers to scan through a piece rather than read every word. It also includes links and navigation tools.

Writing for blogs and other types of social media should be professionally casual; that is, writing that is conversational, friendly, less formal than other news releases but not chatty. The same kind of writing that produces good news leads can cut to the chase with blog items, online newsletters, web pages and related media. As with all public relations writing, accurate information as well as correct grammar and spelling are important.

Specialized stylebooks also have tips for writing for blogs and other venues of social media. These include acceptable uses for terms such as "app," "click-through," "LOL" and "unfriend," as well as advice against retweeting without full disclosure and confirming sources found on blogs.

FEATURE RELEASE

Feature writing goes behind the news with information about people, organizations and issues that touch on a news peg. Public relations writers thus develop releases such as biographical narratives, profiles and interviews about organizational people; histories, profiles and backgrounders about the organizations themselves; and how-to articles, Q&As, case histories and information digests dealing with issues related to the organization.

Such releases are lighter in tone than news releases. They may not follow the inverted-pyramid style but instead may read more like a magazine article.

Feature leads seldom summarize the story. Rather, they set up a short anecdote, ask a question or provide description. Some feature leads directly address readers. Others may focus on a pun. The intention of such a lead is to captivate readers, to entice them into continuing with the story.

Feature leaders are followed by a **nut graph** (short for **nutshell paragraph**; as in, here's the key point of this story in a nutshell). Essentially the nut graph is the news lead that doesn't begin the story. It provides a transition into the heart of the story and tells readers how the story is timely and important.

Because feature writing has fewer of the stylistic conventions associated with news writing, many public relations writers enjoy the flexibility and creativity that this type of writing offers. Increasingly organizations are finding a ready outlet for such articles in their websites.

OPINION WRITING

It might seem that news releases have little to do with advocacy and opinion writing, but the same principles apply. Information should be newsworthy; opinions should be attributed (either individually to a person, or corporately to an organization). The usual news release issues of audience interest and strategic significance to the organization apply equally to opinion writing. The entire process is informed by an issues-management perspective as outlined in Chapter 3.

Public relations people often have a role in advocating for an organization or for causes and issues associated with it. After careful research and strategic decision-making, organizations often wish to communicate their position to employees, customers, professional colleagues, legislators and government regulators, stockholders and donors, and other publics that they might influence.

Vehicles for this include position statements, letters, op-ed pieces, lobbying material, speeches and organizational advertising. Often a news release announces the release of an important organizational statement on matters of public interest.

The key vehicle for organizational advocacy is a position statement, which may be made public or may serve internally as a source document for speeches, letters and other communication vehicles. Either way, a position paper generally has a few standard elements:

- An issue backgrounder identifies the topic, explains its significance to the key publics, provides relevant history and context, indicates the current situation and projects likely developments.
- The position itself gives a clear statement of the organization's official stance, along with a justification for this policy. The justification usually includes supporting arguments and pre-emptively refutes any arguments that opponents are likely to make.
- The conclusion makes recommendations and sometimes includes formal citations that document information included in the statement.

With the position statement as the foundation, organizations often amplify their opinions and policy recommendations through other vehicles. **Talk papers** or **talking points** encourage consistency among organizational spokespersons and supporters. **Letters to the editor** allow the organization to present its opinion to newspaper readers. **Commentary** and **op-ed pieces** in newspapers and other publications (both print and digital) offer another venue for organizational policy recommendations.

Proclamations and **petitions** also can emerge from position statements. Proclamations are formal advocacy messages made by some authority. Petitions are requests for action circulated among supporters and signed by many people, often urging governmental

or other officials to act in some way. Online petitions can generate
millions of signatures.

FUNDRAISING AND ADVOCACY APPEALS

Appeals to donors and support for social causes may seem far
removed from the standard protocols for writing news releases.

But here again, the principles of newsworthiness, audience
interest and organizational strategy are always important. These
same principles come into play when organizations ask for financial
support, seek new members or volunteers, appeal directly—or
through constituents—for government support, or invite political
action on behalf of a cause.

Writing such appeals calls for careful planning, especially with
research into the interests of would-be recipients of the appeal
message. The benefit statement associated with news releases is a
key ingredient in such appeals, because the focus always should be
on how the requested involvement will help the public rather than
what it will do for the organization.

Because people are altruistic, the what's-in-it-for-me? question
may involve helping others. Pet lovers want to prevent animal
cruelty. Outdoorsmen care about the environment. Churchgoers
may be interested in missionary work or community services. Other
people may find their personal benefit by feeding the hungry, supporting a political goal, supporting research for a particular disease
or any number of other advantages that can come about through
their positive response to an organization's advocacy campaign.

Like feature writing, practitioners often enjoy the challenge and
creativity associated with advocacy writing. When they personally
believe in the cause they are promoting, their work can become a
true labor of love.

SPEECHWRITING

The basic news release process even informs speechwriting. Good
speeches generally present news of some kind, telling audience
members something that they didn't know before. They also
address audience interests and clearly present a benefit. These qualities stem from research on the audience to find out what its
members already know and what they care about.

Writing the draft of a speech pulls together elements that public relations practitioners use for broadcast releases, such as a conversational tone and a professionally casual approach. It also includes the use of pronouncers to help the speaker. Additionally, crafting a speech includes much of the flexibility and creativity of approach that practitioners find in writing feature releases.

Speechwriting also involves making effective use of the strategy that is so much of a public relations practitioner's repertoire. Speeches generally revolve around a **proposition**, a single main idea. A **factual proposition** asserts the existence of something, such as an increase in acid rain pollution in Eastern forests, or a plan to change a university's foreign language requirements. A **value proposition** argues the worthiness or virtue of something (the joy of writing, the merits of international banking reform). A **policy proposition** identifies a course of action and encourages its adoption, such as advocacy for requiring a license to practice public relations, or a proposal to make parent-education classes a requirement for a high school diploma.

Propositions are only as good as the arguments that support them. Generally a proposition should have several **subordinate points** that are strong and convincing. Effective writers are careful not to weaken the argument with over-generalized statements, drawing unwarranted conclusions, building on false facts, launching personal criticism, or otherwise presenting logical flaws that make it easy for audiences to refute the proposition.

An effective conclusion to the speech often summarizes the proposition and offers recommendations.

Speeches that are followed by a question-answer session sometimes are accompanied by talking points to help the speaker remain on track. Forums for this include news conferences, testimony before government agencies, town meetings and other face-to-face encounters with journalists or with other publics (employees, stockholders and so on).

ONLINE NEWSROOM

Most organizations have media newsrooms that archive news releases and virtually all of the writing produced for public consumption. This includes releases for print and broadcast media, social media releases, and both color and black-and-white photographs as JPEG or GIF files (often presented as thumbnails that can be downloaded in varying levels of resolution).

Online newsrooms also post feature releases, organizational media kits, and information with biographies, organizational histories, and other information about the organization and its products, services or cause. These sites also highlight audio and video material, both packaged for media use as well as background interviews and video footage that media and other users can edit into their own pieces. Often, these sites post organizational documents such as annual reports, speeches and official statements by organizational executives, and sometimes brochures and other material produced by the public relations team.

Many online newsrooms include readership aids such as information on how journalists and others can sign up for RSS feeds and opt-in e-mail notices, along with subscribe buttons inviting readers to join the organization's Facebook page, blog site and Twitter feed.

Generally, online newsrooms can be accessed not only by reporters but also by customers, donors, shareholders, industry analysts, and both professional colleagues and competitors. They often include links to social media sites, as well as sharing features so readers can easily pass along the information to their friends (real or virtual).

RESEARCH TECHNIQUES

Good public relations programming is data-driven and research-based. It is founded not on hopes or hunches but on evidence derived through careful and impartial investigation of facts. Thus the ability to conduct and manage nonbiased research is a key element in the practice of public relations.

Don't be put off by the concept of this. **Research** is nothing more than the systematic, objective and unbiased gathering of information.

Let's look at four common types of research areas that are part of public relations: interviews, focus groups, surveys and content analysis.

INTERVIEWS

One important aspect of this research is the **interview**, the same kind of question-answer engagement that journalists practice with their news sources. Whatever you need to know, chances are that someone already knows it. You just need to find that person and interview him or her. Public relations practitioners interview experts and information sources within their organizations to help transfer their knowledge and insight into news releases, letters to the editor, blog entries, web pages, brochures, position papers and many other public relations venues.

In-person interviews generally are best, but interviews also can be conducted by phone, e-mail, Internet chat or voice protocols such as Skype. Here are some tips for preparing interview questions.

- Always plan the interview. Identify the topic, decide whom to interview.
- Build on what you already know. It's a waste of time to ask experts common information that you can easily get from secondary sources, so learn as much as you can beforehand.
- Write out questions, and take good notes (or complement some minimal note-taking with a recorded back-up).
- Build rapport with your interview expert by showing an interest in the person and the topic. Explain how the information will be used. Point out that, unlike a journalistic interview, your purpose is to help both the interviewee and the organization communicate in a positive way with your publics.
- Distinguish between knowledge and opinion questions. Both are valid, but be prepared to ask both "What is ... ?" and "What do you think about ... ?"
- Don't rush into a sensitive area. Ease into it slowly.
- Nudge for additional information, and probe for underlying meanings.
- At the end of the interview, invite additional information. By this time your interviewee knows that you are interested in the topic. Being an expert, he or she may have additional relevant information to suggest.

FOCUS GROUP

A **focus group** is a kind of small-group discussion or interview, in which a researcher guides a conversation about a particular issue. The result is an interactive discussion that can generate ideas, comments and anecdotes. Public relations people use focus groups to test ideas and message strategies, to get feedback on potential communication vehicles such as videos or ads, and to learn what people representative of their publics know or feel about the organization or issues affecting it.

A focus group moderator is a neutral facilitator who invites comments on the topic and keeps the discussion moving among the 8–12 participants in the group, without interjecting personal opinion. The moderator works from a discussion guide, which is a list of predetermined questions and discussion starters. Commonly these begin with "Tell me about … " or "What do you think about … " The moderator needs to remain flexible, sometimes introducing a topic with "Does anybody have any other views about … " Other probing questions may begin with "Can you give me an example of … " or "Why do you think that is so?"

The focus group yields a written report that summarizes participant's comments, quotes key phrases and sentences, and provides insight into the conversation by noting, for example, if a comment was widespread or if it evoked a spirited response. The report may include recommendations to the organization.

Whereas focus groups answer the questions of "why" and "how," surveys generate information about "how much." Focus groups can give insight into what people know about an organization or issue, while surveys can reveal specifics such as percentages of how much people know about this or whether they support that.

SURVEY

A **survey** is one of the most common research tools of public relations practitioners. Surveys (or **polls**) can be applied to large or small groups. Done well and with an appropriate sample, surveys can be quite accurate, with the added advantage of being able to be extrapolated to large numbers. National political polls with only a few thousand respondents, for example, can predict voter sentiment with a high degree of accuracy.

Here are a few aspects of surveys:

- **Sampling** involves selecting relatively few respondents to stand in for the wider population. The key to effective sampling is probability. A **nonprobability sample** is one that is haphazard: a **convenience sample** in which the researcher goes to a location such as a mall where it's easy to find a lot of people, or a **volunteer sample** that invites people to participate if they feel strongly about an issue. A better approach is the probability sample such as a true lottery-style **random sample** in which everyone has an equal opportunity to be selected, or a **systematic sample** that involves selecting, say, every 10th name on a list. Some more sophisticated techniques are a **weighted sample**, **stratified sample** and **cluster sample**.

- **Sampling error** is a measurement of the extent to which the sample does not perfectly correspond with the target population. Basically the larger the sample, the smaller the margin of error. Many researchers are comfortable with 3–6 percent sample error.
- The ideal **sample size** is not a specific percentage of the population. Many researchers use 384 as the ideal sample size for a 5 percent margin of error for any size of population of 50,000 or larger. Most polling aims for a sample of 2,000–3,000 to allow for analysis of subcategories (such as by geographic area, race, age, political affiliation and so on).

Beyond careful selection of a proportional sample, the main ingredient for a quality survey is a good **questionnaire**. This is the list of items given to respondents. Here are some guidelines for creating effective questionnaires.

- Keep items short and clear.
- Be specific, and avoid ambiguous words that could be open to different interpretations.
- Ask only questions relevant to the research topic.
- Use positive constructions. For example, ask "Do you participate in a fitness program" rather than "Do you avoid fitness programs?"
- Avoid "double-barreled" items that ask two questions but provide only one answer.
- Use neutral, nonpartisan words. And don't signal a bias with a question such as "Do you prefer reading good literature or just popular novels?"
- Avoid a prestige bias by associating a statement with an authority figure. "Do you agree with the mayor that property taxes are too high?"

- Don't ask for an opinion on something that is a matter of fact.
- Avoid hypothetical questions. "Would you prefer to move to a colony under the sea or in outer space?"
- Make sure questions can be reasonably answered. Don't ask how many hours of television a person watched in the last six months. Rather, ask how many hours of TV watching they do in an average weekday.

There also are some suggestions for presenting response categories.

- Give ranges for responses dealing with income and age.
- Allow "other" categories when these might reasonably occur, such as when asking a person's racial or ethnic background.
- Make sure that multiple-choice responses are both comprehensive (offering every possible response) and mutually exclusive (only one possible response for each respondent).
- Use checklist items to allow for more than one response, such as types of music or food that a respondent likes.
- Use forced-choice items to lead a respondent to indicate agreement with one of two or three statements.
- Rather than a simple yes/no, use a rating scale such as 1–5 to learn about the intensity of a respondent's feelings. Or use the Likert scale with four or five points between agree and disagree.

CONTENT ANALYSIS

Content analysis is another type of research that public relations practitioners find useful. This is an objective and nonintrusive type of research that looks at existing communication artifacts (such as news items, letters to the editor, advertisements and so on). It is after-the-fact research that can shed light on the messages of communication, assess the image of a group or organization, and make comparisons between media and reality.

Let's say an insurance agency has a new policy covering sports cars. It wants to know what radio stations sports-car drivers listen to. A survey would be unwieldy. But using content analysis, the agency might contact top maintenance and repair shops specializing in sports cars and ask them to note the radio station that the radios are tuned to when the cars are brought in.

A public relations practitioner might be reminded at a "meet the editors" event that local news media prefer local content. The practitioner could use content analysis to evaluate the content of an organization's past news releases to compare the amount of strong local content with the exposure that the releases received through the media for the past several years.

Doing content analysis can be a simple task. Identify the "population" (perhaps news releases or blog entries). Then identify the units of analysis, which are the elements to be counted and compared. This might be the local news emphasis in a news release lead, or the topics of blog entries. Units of analysis might be headlines or photos, types of communication (direct mail, television, e-mail and so on), or message content (theme, spokesperson, etc.). Select the units of analysis, then develop a coding sheet, and track how each unit of analysis is presented through each population sample

Count data in each of the categories and compare.

COMMUNICATION SAVVY

Another "must" for the effective practice of public relations is a commanding understanding of communication. This involves a theory base that informs us about how communication operates in both personal and organizational settings and, more usefully, what public relations practitioners can learn from these theories.

Don't be afraid of the idea of **communication theory**. It simply is the field of study that tries to make sense of how people communicate, in part by explaining the effects of mass communication and to suggest ways to use the media effectively. It may deal with **interpersonal communication**, involving how individual people as well as groups and organizations use both words and non-verbal forms of communication. It also gives insight into how culture and social context support or interfere with effective communication.

Communication theory also involves the role of media in its various forms: advertising, broadcast, digital, print, recordings and social media.

One broad-based way of looking at communication theory is to see the evolution of research and the conclusions drawn from this. Since communication research began in earnest in the mid-20th century, the studies have yielded three successive paradigms about how the media affect audiences. Together they are called media effects models.

Growing from stimulus-response research (remember Pavlov and his slobbering dogs?), early research suggested that the media have direct, immediate and powerful effects on their audiences. It was called the **powerful-effects model**, and metaphors of this model such as the **hypodermic needle theory** and the **magic bullet theory** reflected the concern of the 1940s and 1950s about Hitler's successful use of the media during the Holocaust and World War II and continuing propaganda surrounding the Cold War. The idea was that, if media generate irresistible messages to influence people to do bad things, could they also employ messages and symbols that would induce people for socially positive outcomes?

In either situation, people were seen as pawns to be moved around, incapable of resisting the powerful effects of the media. But the powerful-effects model had many flaws, not the least of which was that further tests showed it not to be true. Research shows that the media simply do not consistently and single-handedly exert a strong impact on audiences.

Researchers then shifted their attention to a paradigm of a **limited-effects model** in which the media were seen as being rather impotent in affecting people's attitudes, opinions and behaviors. Many people simply do not believe information they obtain through the media. More important is the influence of family, friends and respected experts and their own psychological reinterpretation of media messages.

But this limited-effects model also has flaws in that it doesn't explain the observations that, in many situations, the media do seem to play a significant role in what people think, say and do.

More recently, the topic has re-centered on a **moderate-effects model**. This model acknowledges that, over time, the media have a cumulative effect on people. Many studies have focused on violence, social tolerance and sexual issues as they are depicted by the media. While no single media message exerts enough power to control audiences, they do seem to be instrumental over time in affecting audiences on issues such as sex and violence and on topics such as social tolerance and acceptance of racial minorities, gay people, and people of various religious affiliations and ethnic backgrounds in participating in society.

Through each of the paradigm models and the many theories associated with them, it has become clear to communication researchers that people are so wonderfully complex that it is difficult to predict how they will be impacted by the media. What works for one audience may be counterproductive for another.

Among the many variables that shape how the media will affect people are sex, age, educational achievement, self-esteem, media-use habits, group involvement and their own sense of identity as it relates to culture, religion, lifestyle, ethnicity and race.

Here are some selected examples of public relations theories and other communication models (presented alphabetically) that can be useful for public relations:

Accounts. Using communication to manage relationships in the wake of rebuke or criticism is the focus of the **theory of accounts** associated with Michael Cody and Margaret McLaughlin. An account is the language (verbal and nonverbal) that explains why a person or organization took a particular action. It is a narrative that is particularly important in public relations crisis situations and is useful in conflict resolution, whether interpersonal or organizational.

Agenda-Setting. The **agenda-setting model** deals with the influence of the media, particularly the news media, and their ability to tell audiences what issues are important. Researchers Max McCombs and Donald Shaw developed the notion that the media don't tell us what to think but rather tell us what to think *about*. The issue has been studied in many contexts, most often in relation to government and voting. Two assumptions are that the news media do not reflect society but instead help shape it by raising up certain issues as being important. A criticism of this is the **herd mentality** of the media, whereby a newspaper or TV network feels compelled to report on something just because its competitors are focusing on the same topic. And by concentrating reporting on a topic, the public is left to think that the issue really is important because coverage seems to be everywhere.

Apologia. Keith Hearit presents an **apologia approach** in terms of crisis management. An apologia is a formal defense of an organization's actions (not to be confused with an apology). Hearit outlines a threefold approach to persuasive accounts that

has no legs, as they say. But if a vicious attack on a homeless man occurs in your community, the situation changes. The attack becomes the news peg that is likely to heighten media attention to the message of the advocacy group.

Image Repair. Bill Benoit has introduced the **image restoration theory** to help organizations understand and emerge from crisis situations. Benoit's model suggests several options, including denial, evasion of responsibility, reduction of offensiveness and corrective action. Many of the lessons of this theory emerge in the Public Relations Planning section of this book in Step 5, in which organizations consider their various options for dealing with outside criticism.

Inoculation. The **inoculation theory** proposed by William McGuire and Demetrios Papageorgis suggests that unchallenged beliefs and attitudes can be swayed with persuasive information, while attitudes that have been tested are more resistant to change. This latter aspect is particularly useful to strategic communicators seeking to create resistance to potentially opposing arguments.

Models of Public Relations. James Grunig provided a matrix of four different approaches to public relations, each with different purposes and characteristics. These loosely translate as the publicity, public information, advocacy and relationship models that were presented in Chapter 2 of this book.

Multi-Step Flow of Communication. Originally the **two-step flow model** presented by Paul Lazarsfeld and Elihu Katz, this has expanded into a **multi-step flow model**. This theoretical model focuses on decision-making and how information affects people's choices. The notion is that the media present information to **opinion leaders**, who in turn interpret that information within their own context and then extend it to others within their sphere of influence. Thus the model connects personal influence and media influence, bringing together two different aspects of communication research. This concept can be useful to public relations practitioners, especially as they identify opinion leaders among their various publics.

Rhetoric. The classical rhetorical theory associated with Aristotle continues to offer insight into the practice of public relations. The threefold outline of ethos, logos and pathos still stands. Public relations practitioners focus on the message source, selecting a spokesperson on the basis of credibility, charisma and control or influence of the audience. It deals with the logical aspect of an argument, gathering and presenting facts and sound reasoning. And it looks to the emotional impact of messages and the nonverbal communication used to express them. Much contemporary research is conducted concerning these, particularly source credibility.

Situation. James Grunig's **situational theory** looks at publics as being active or passive. It also observes that some publics are active on all issues, others on only single issues. The value of this insight to public relations practitioners is that it avoids a one-size-fits-all approach and instead helps them engage their publics in an effective way, drawing on the interests and span of the publics themselves.

Sleeper Effect. Researchers have observed that sometimes the persuasive impact of communication increases as time elapses. Carl Hovland and Walter Weiss identified this sleeper effect. What people may have initially received from a source with low credibility can eventually become separated from the source, leading to an increase in message credibility. Conversely, what people initially considered a highly persuasive message may fade over time.

Social Judgment. The **social judgment theory** put forward by Muzafer Sherif and Carl Hovland observes that individuals accept or reject messages to the extent that they perceive the messages as corresponding to their internal anchors (attitudes and beliefs) and as affecting the person's self-concept.

Spiral of Silence. In an attempt to explain the formation of public opinion that gave social power to the Nazis, Elisabett Noelle-Neumann articulated the **spiral of silence theory**. This explains that people learn through media reporting and other social impressions what appears to be the majority opinion. People holding minority viewpoints often silence themselves, preferring not to express their opinion and thus not "rock the boat." Public relations practitioners, especially those advocating for what appears to be a minority opinion, have found that they can "unsilence" people by showing that other people, too, have opinions that run counter to the majority, or even that the presumed majority opinion isn't as common as it is thought to be.

Systems. The interdisciplinary **systems theory** often deals with biology, engineering and technology, but it also sheds light on some organizational aspects of social psychology, particularly with its associated concepts of feedback and mid-course adjustment. Public relations practitioners have found it useful in understanding how organizations relate to their various publics. The concept of **linkages** is especially useful, helping practitioners identify various categories of publics. This forms the basis for part of Step 3 in the strategic planning process outlined in the second half of this book.

Uses and Gratifications. This theory, associated with Jay Blumler and Denis McQuail looks at why audiences use the media and what they get out of it. This approach sees audiences as taking a proactive role in the information-exchange process. This theory helps public relations practitioners attempt to satisfy the interests of people who actively seek their information, which has become more common through the development of information-on-demand venues such as websites. It often is helpful for practitioners to realize if audiences are seeking information for entertainment, news-surveillance purposes, personal identity or any number of other reasons.

Part II

Public Relations Planning

Effective public relations calls for a strategic planning process. This section of the book outlines a four-phase, nine-step planning model that can work for every kind of organization—corporate or nonprofit, large or small, well resourced or penniless.

Part II is presented as a how-to workshop. This approach presumes that you, the reader, are personally and actively engaged in creating a public relations plan for an organization in which you are involved. Thus the writing style in this section is more direct, more "you" centered. It offers a series of steps that unfold into a comprehensive public relations plan.

Here is an overview of this process that will be fleshed out over four chapters.

PHASE 1: FORMATIVE RESEARCH

The focus during the first of the four phases is on the preliminary work of communication planning, which calls for gathering information and analyzing the situation. In three steps, the planner draws on existing information available to the organization and, at the same time, creates a research program for gaining additional information needed to drive the decisions that will come later in the planning process.

Step 1: Analyzing the situation. Your analysis of the situation is the crucial beginning to the process. Everyone involved—planner, clients, supervisors, key colleagues and the ultimate decision makers—should be in solid agreement about the nature of the opportunity or obstacle to be addressed in this program.

Step 2: Analyzing the Organization. This step involves a careful and candid look at three aspects of the organization: (1) its internal environment (mission, performance and resources), (2) its public perception (visibility and reputation) and (3) its external environment (competitors and opponents, as well as supporters).

Step 3: Analyzing the Publics. In this step you identify and analyze your key publics—the various groups of people who interact with your organization on the issue at hand. You also will analyze each public in terms of its wants, interests, needs and expectations concerning the topic of this plan; each public's relationship to the organization; its involvement in communication and with various media; and a variety of social, economic, political, cultural and technological trends that may affect it.

PHASE 2: STRATEGY

The second phase of the planning process deals with the heart of planning: making decisions dealing with the hoped-for impact of the communication on the key publics, as well as the nature of the communication itself.

Step 4: Establishing Goals and Objectives. In this step, you will focus on the ultimate position and the associated goals sought for the organization and for the product or service. This will help you develop clear, specific and measurable objectives for each key public.

Step 5: Formulating Action and Response Strategies. A range of possible actions is available to the organization, and in this step you consider what you might do in various situations. It includes both public relations initiatives and responses to outside influences.

Step 6: Developing the Message Strategy. This step deals with the various decisions about the message, such as the spokesperson presenting the message to the key publics, the content of the message, its tone and style, verbal and nonverbal cues, and related issues.

PHASE 3: TACTICS

During the third phase, you will consider various communication tools, and you will create the visible elements of the communication plan.

Step 7: Selecting Communication Tactics. This inventory deals with the full range of communication options. Specifically, you will consider four categories: (1) face-to-face communication and opportunities for personal involvement, (2) organizational media (sometimes called controlled media), (3) news media (uncontrolled media) and (4) advertising and promotional media (another form of controlled media).

Step 8: Implementing the Strategic Plan. With this step, you turn the raw ingredients identified in the previous step into a recipe for a successful public relations plan, packaging those tactics into a cohesive communication program. You also will develop budgets and schedules and otherwise prepare to implement the communication program.

PHASE 4: EVALUATIVE RESEARCH

The final phase of strategic planning deals with evaluation and assessment. This enables you to determine the degree to which the stated objectives have been met. On that basis, you can decide about modifying or continuing the communication activities.

Step 9: Evaluating the Strategic Plan. This is the final planning element, indicating specific methods for measuring the effectiveness of each recommended tactic in meeting the stated objectives.

[For more information on this process, see another book by this author, *Strategic Planning for Public Relations*, 4th edition, 2013, Routledge/Taylor and Francis.]

5

PUBLIC RELATIONS PLANNING
PHASE 1: RESEARCH

This chapter begins a step-by-step approach to planning a public relations campaign or project. It is the first of four such chapters that will walk you through each phase of creating an effective communication program.

Let's look at the first phase of strategic planning for public relations, research.

You've heard the phrase "shooting in the dark." It means trying to hit a target you don't see. That's what public relations without research would be. Research provides the foundation for strategic communication planning. Without research, you'd be sending messages of little value to your organization and little interest to your publics (who probably won't be listening anyway). Research keeps you rooted in reality and prevents creativity from becoming merely bizarre.

The most common type of public relations research is **formative research**, the kind of fact gathering that precedes and shapes a campaign or project. It's part of every good public relations activity.

Even during crises when reaction time is short, most practitioners make time to do some research to get a quick read on public opinion or to pull from relevant existing research. There are two types of formative research: strategic and tactical.

- **Strategic research** is data that provides insight into issues and publics, and guides decisions on what an organization might do to address a situation.
- **Tactical research** is information that guides the production and dissemination of messages.

During this research phase, you will conduct a situation analysis to gather information in three key areas: (1) the situation you are facing, (2) your organization or client and (3) your intended publics.

Don't let the idea of research scare you. Research begins with informal and often simple methods of gathering relevant information. You probably are already familiar with some of these techniques.

- **Casual research** informally collects what is already known. You "pick the brains" of clients, colleagues and others, interview colleagues with experience and other people with expertise, and brainstorm with other planners.
- **Secondary research** looks at information that already exists. Why spend time and resources to study what already has been studied? Instead, you can review what others have already learned and apply this to your research topic. Common sources of secondary research are organizational files, studies by trade and professional organizations, and government reports. Information also is available in libraries and online (but be wary about the validity of what you find on the Internet).
- **Primary research** is the gathering of new information. This often includes more formal research methodologies. Three specific techniques—focus groups, surveys and content analyses—are frequent elements of public relations programs.

STEP 1: ANALYZING THE SITUATION

The first step in public relations planning is to identify the **situation**, which is a set of circumstances facing an organization.

A situation for a football team might be the loyalty of fans. For a hospital, the situation could be knowledge (or lack thereof) of preventive medicine among would-be patients. For an auto manufacturer, the availability of side air bags. For a counseling organization, misunderstanding about mental illness.

Note that situations are presented as nouns—loyalty of fans, knowledge about health care, availability of air bags, misunderstanding about illness.

Make your research as wide reaching as possible. For example, if you are helping the football team focus on fan loyalty, start by learning what you can about how other teams maximize the allegiance of their fans.

Fan loyalty is a general concept, so don't limit your research merely to football. Explore how baseball teams, hockey leagues and wrestling alliances interact with their fans. Study golf tournaments and racecar competitions, as well as international events such as the Olympics or the World Cup. Consider sports with small-but-loyal fan bases such as boxing and sumo, curling and polo. The point is, investigate many different examples of how sports-related organizations promote a supportive and ongoing relationship with their fans.

OBSTACLE OR OPPORTUNITY

In classic terms, a situation refers to a **problem**. Don't think of this as something necessarily negative. Rather, a problem is a question to be considered and answered, something that calls for our attention. (Knowing the derivation of the word might help. The word "problem" comes from ancient Greek and Latin words meaning "a thing put forward"; thus when we address a problem, we put forward a possible course of action.)

A public relations problem (the situation) can be positive or negative. Make sure there is agreement within your organization on these, because what one person may call an obstacle, another might see as an opportunity. Here's a useful distinction.

- An **opportunity** provides an opening with a potential advantage to the organization. It is a problem in the sense that it offers an opportunity and a benefit. Examples of this might be fan loyalty or the introduction of an air-bag feature on new car models, both positives that can enhance the organization and the publics.

- An **obstacle** is a roadblock to be overcome, something that can limit the organization in achieving its mission. This type of problem needs to be addressed to prevent disruption or unrealized potential. Examples might include the misunderstanding about mental illness or the lack of knowledge about preventing disease.

Consider the spiritual principle of zen, which values harmony. A problem is not something negative but rather something lacking harmony, a point of yet-unrealized potential. An obstacle is at a crossroads, allowing us to go this way or that.

The ultimate public relations problem is a **crisis**. Yet even that word gives us philosophical pause. Interestingly, the Chinese term *wei ji* and the parallel Japanese word *kiki,* both of which translate as "crisis," are made up of two characters—one meaning "danger," the other meaning "opportunity." A crisis is a decision point where choices point to consequences.

Here are some real-world examples of good public relations that turn obstacles into opportunities.

GOLD'N PLUMP POULTRY

Because of consumer fears about industry-wide health risks such as avian flu, salmonella and arsenic in animal feed, sales were tanking for Gold'n Plump Poultry, the largest chicken company in Midwestern America. The company needed to address such consumer fears, attempting to turn an obstacle into an opportunity.

To accomplish this, Gold'n Plump spent $150,000 (£95,800, €119,000) on a six-month "Takin' Names Tour," driving an old farm truck to towns and villages in Minnesota and Wisconsin, asking residents to sign their names on the vehicle. For every signature, the company donated four meals to rural food shelves to help families in danger of losing their small farms.

The project generated media attention, reversed its sales decline, and rebuilt brand loyalty.

DOVE SOAP

Traditional marketing of beauty products uses idealized (and unrealizable) portrayals of women. Unilever, the British-Dutch consumer goods corporation, commissioned an international study on women's attitudes toward beauty that became the basis for the Dove "Campaign for Real Beauty" by one of its companies.

Using mainly public relations tactics with strategic advertising support, the project focused on "real women with real bodies and real curves," a departure from the supermodel approach taken by most competitors in the beauty-products industry. The campaign earned local and international news coverage and attracted millions of visitors to its website.

Ultimately the campaign not only sold beauty products but also sparked an international discussion about women and beauty. It also led to the Dove Movement for Self-Esteem, an international project of mentoring and education directed toward younger girls, with a goal of reaching 15 million girls around the world.

Even in crisis situations, obstacles can be approached as opportunities, if the problem has not been self-inflicted. Public attention generated by a crisis can help an organization explains its values and demonstrate its quality.

Whether the issue is viewed as an opportunity, an obstacle or simply an unrealized potential, the communications team and the leaders of the organization or client need a common understanding of the issue before it can be adequately addressed. Ideally, it means trying to turn an obstacle into an opportunity.

Fast-food chains such as McDonald's, Arby's and Burger King, for example, could have ignored growing international concerns about obesity, particularly long-term effects on young people. Instead these companies anticipated a growing concern and introduced healthier low-calorie menu items.

Public relations practitioners call this **issues management**, a process by which an organization tries to anticipate emerging issues and respond to them before they get out of hand. This involves monitoring and evaluating information, potentially leading to change. The name for this is **adaptation**, the ability of an organization to make changes on the basis of what its publics want and need.

Early identification of important issues can give an organization time to study them and develop an appropriate and effective response. This is one reason that research skills are so important for public relations practitioners.

Why is all this important? To be effective, all organizations must be prepared to act as circumstances change. As consumers weigh health-care choices and as regulatory agencies impact the cost of health care, organizations such as insurance companies, hospitals, pharmaceuticals and medical providers try to predict trends within the health-care industry and, in some way, to influence its future.

Some organizations use a **best practice** approach by studying and potentially imitating a leader in the field. A hospital wishing to site an off-campus methadone clinic might see how a hospital in another city was successful in a similar project. The hospital might even look to the failure of similar efforts in other cities, learning from their mistakes.

Issues management helps the organization interact with its publics. It may help an organization settle the issue early or divert it, or perhaps even prevent its emergence in the first place. More likely, however, the organization will have to adjust itself to the issue in some way, trying to maximize the benefits or at least minimize the negative impact. Public relations often drives this early-warning system within an organization.

Closely related to issues management is **risk management**—the process of identifying, controlling and minimizing the impact of uncertain events on an organization. Public relations people often have early access to criticism from various publics, which is especially important if others inside the organization fail to observe signs of unrest.

DUKE UNIVERSITY

Risk management involves a careful assessment of the potential impact on both the organization and its publics. Often this means taking into consideration the emotional elements that may be in play.

An example of this is the "perfect storm" effect of the Duke University rape case in 2006, what a British newspaper called a "gourmet feast, a deluxe news-hook omelette."

The ingredients in that dish catapulted the case into a major public relations crisis: race, sex, class and privilege, credibility, firings, legal reversals, politics, police collusion, media scrutiny, cause advocates, athletic suspensions and premature campus reaction.

Eventually the legal charges were dismissed, but not before Duke and its athletic program were drawn into extended international negative publicity—much of which might have been minimized if the school had a carefully drawn crisis communication or risk management plan.

NESTLÉ INTERNATIONAL

Nestlé saw itself as a nurturing company, failing to recognize the intensity of criticism over its marketing of infant formula.

As international opposition mounted, the resulting boycott and related protests involved more than 100 countries, beginning in the late 1970s and continuing 3½ decades later. The opposition and the negative publicity it inspired cost the Swiss-based corporation millions in bad publicity, lost customers, legal fees and a weakened reputation.

Despite the opposition, Nestlé remains the world's largest nutrition company worth about $200 billion (£128 billion, €58 billion).

Yet it undoubtedly would be even stronger if the protests had not spurred bans on Nestlé products in schools and colleges, government bans on some of the company's products, links to deforestation as Nestlé companies destroy forests to create palm oil plantations for beauty products, accusations of child labor on Nestlé-supported cocoa plantations, and a continuing (and seemingly growing) list of complaints and criticisms, many with long-term legal and economic impact.

DOW CORNING

Another classic case study in crisis communication involved silicone breast implants. Dow Corning saw itself as a conscientious company and believed that science was on its side, so it aggressively countered criticism and public concern about the safety of its breast implants.

When class-action lawsuits began to be filed, the company failed to take quick action. It didn't think any response was needed. Instead, the corporation followed common (and bad) legal advice to say nothing sympathetic about women who claimed they were harmed by the company's product. Dow was prepping the case for the legal courts while ignoring the court of public opinion, where reputations are made and broken.

The case yielded record settlements: $5.4 million (£3.4 million, €4.2 million) to one woman, $7.3 million (£4.7 million, €5.8 million) to another, $27.9 million (£17.8 million, €22 million) to three women. Dow Corning ended up in bankruptcy for nine years, emerging only in 2004, two decades after the problem began.

The irony is that Dow Corning's science eventually was vindicated. Multiple studies have since concluded that there is no connection between the implants and breast cancer. But the fact remains that the company's public relations fiasco has become a textbook case of how to mismanage a crisis.

EXXON

This oil giant was another company that refused to take the critics seriously, apparently having little interest in risk management. As a result, the company suffered in the long term for mishandling the Alaska oil spill caused by its freighter *Valdez* in 1989.

Eleven years later, a jury ordered the oil company to pay $3.5 billion (£2.2 billion, €2.8 billion) for defrauding Alabama on royalties involving oil wells in the Gulf of Mexico. That verdict was set aside, and in a new trial three years later, the jury awarded even higher damages to the state: $11.9 billion (£7.6 billion, €9.4 billion).

Jurors said one reason for the high penalties was that the Alaska situation showed them that Exxon was a company that could not be trusted and deserved to be punished.

Appeals and counterclaims continue, costing ExxonMobil millions in legal fees. The Alaska spill is still cited in other unrelated lawsuits in the US and elsewhere, such as in Venezuela where Exxon received less than $750 million (£478 million, 594 million) in 2012, little more than 6 percent of the $12 billion (£7.7 billion, €9.5 billion) it had been seeking for five years since when Venezuela nationalized Exxon's operations there.

The purpose of issues management is to deal with issues before they get out of hand. When that happens, the issue becomes a crisis. **Crisis management** is the process by which an organization deals with out-of-control issues.

Consider this analogy: Issues management is like sailing. You run with the wind when it's blowing in the direction you want to go. You tack to make some progress against the wind. Sometimes you stall when there is no wind. But always, you adapt to an ever-changing environment.

In a crisis situation, you try to ride out a storm. Often that means you drop sail, hang on, and hope the vessel is strong enough to survive without too much damage. Issues management deals with preparation for dealing with potential events; risk management is about implied threats; and crisis management focuses on reactive responses to actual occurrences.

An organization committed to the concept of strategic communication is probably engaged in an ongoing issues management program that identifies crises in their early stages. Less nimble organizations may be caught off guard by a crisis.

Reality sometimes slaps you in the face and forces you to think the unthinkable. It happened at Virginia Tech and Columbine High School, at the movie theater in Aurora, Colo., and at the youth camp at Buskerud, Norway. It happened with the Al Qaeda attack on the World Trade Center and the Boko Haram attacks on churches and businesses in Nigeria. The unthinkable also burst onto the scene with the earthquake/tsunami/radiation leak at Fukushima and when the Costa *Concordia* cruise ship grounded and sank off Italy.

Forward-thinking organizations prepare for the unthinkable and plan for unexpected disasters.

TYLENOL

What happened in Chicago in 1982 remains an example of how companies should face the unthinkable. Johnson & Johnson woke up in crisis when somebody laced Tylenol capsules with cyanide, killing seven Chicago-area residents. That's an unthinkable tragedy for a pharmaceutical company.

As the country panicked, Johnson & Johnson pulled 31 million bottles of Tylenol from store shelves. The company used satellite news conferences to reintroduce Tylenol the over-the-counter medicine with a triple-seal tamper-resistant package that soon became an industry standard. Johnson & Johnson also offered customer incentives such as free replacements and discount coupons.

The company saw a quick recovery of its 35 percent market share and in the process fostered an ongoing customer loyalty. Because of its good reputation and its responsible handling of the still-unsolved murders, the company emerged from the crisis with even more consumer respect and confidence.

More than 30 years later, the legacy of Johnson & Johnson is a case study in good crisis communication and solid public relations, a morality tale that shows the value of a corporate conscientiousness that places its customers first and keeps its promise of safety.

Considering subsequent scandals involving Blackwater, Enron, WorldCom and Arthur Andersen, obviously some companies didn't get the point. But those that did noted the value of proactive management and quick communication in crisis situations. Forward-looking companies realized that preparedness is the key to effective issues management, particularly in crisis situations.

Some experts have banded together as a kind of self-help group to guide each other in risk and crisis situations. One such coalition is the British-based Crisis Communications Network (CCN), a register of business and communications people with experience in managing crises that is associated with the Institute for Public Relations. The CCN network offers several tips for issues management:

- Develop active dialogue with various stakeholders.
- Make sure an issue is worth trying to manage.
- Nurture expert contacts that can provide third-party research and endorsement when necessary.

- Form a coalition with organizations similar to yours.
- Create a risk-management plan and review it regularly, updating and modifying it as necessary.
- Include senior management on this team.

One thing to remember is that crises may be sudden and unpredicted, but they seldom are unpredictable. Crises are more like volcanoes that smolder for a while before they erupt. Warning signs abound, if a trained eye is watching.

Studies by the Institute for Crisis Management (crisisexperts.com) consistently find that only about 40 percent of companies' crises burst suddenly onto the scene, while 60 percent have been smoldering situations that eventually ignited. The biggest crisis categories involve white-collar crime, followed by facility damage, accidents, workplace violence, labor disputes and mismanagement. The institute finds that about half of all crises are caused by management, one-third by employees and the remaining few by outside influences.

Even crises triggered by natural disasters such as floods and earthquakes often are linked to human error or unprepared management. The nuclear disaster at Fukushima—radiation leakage triggered by a tsunami caused by an ocean earthquake—was worsened because of poor communication, lack of preparation and low government standards.

DEEPWATER HORIZON

The Deepwater Horizon oil spill in the Gulf of Mexico, in 2010, has been called the worst environmental disaster in North American history. It also was a public relations debacle for British Petroleum.

The events are well known: A deep-sea explosion off the Louisiana coast killed 11 oil-rig workers and led to the release of nearly 200 million gallons of oil that polluted an area of 3,900 square miles.

The out-of-control spill and efforts to cap the well led the news for weeks. The economic impact was severe: $2.5 billion (£1.6 billion, €2 billion) in immediate damages to the fishing industry and $24 billion (£15.3 billion, €18.9 billion) to tourism, with predictions of decades-long effects. BP estimated the cleanup costs would mount to nearly $40 billion (£25 billion, €32 billion), and more than two years after the disaster, BP was still haggling with the federal government and the states of Louisiana and Mississippi over its share of the costs.

BP, once considered the greenest oil company in America, was blamed for the disaster and criticized for how it handled the tragedy. For the early weeks of the spill, its British CEO, Tony Hayward, was the face of BP. He had a reputation in Britain as being a knowledgeable and trusted corporate leader. But the confusion surrounding the facts in the crisis wore on him. Then he was photographed sailing in a yacht race at the height of the crisis, followed by an outburst about "wanting his life back." Hayward resigned several weeks after the explosion.

How did BP handle its crisis communications? First it tried to blame others: drillers it had hired, owners of the rig and government regulators. This violated one of the tenets of good crisis communication: Accept responsibility for fixing the problem, and don't lay blame.

Rather quickly, BP's public relations strategy turned toward the future: how the company would contain the spill and compensate the victims. BP set up a $20 billion (£12.7 billion, €15.8) fund to reimburse victims for their economic loss. It was a good move, though one later threatened by charges that BP mismanaged the fund.

Critics observed that BP lost public confidence by ceding to the media the task of providing public education about deep-water drilling. It let others tell its story. BP eventually created an educational component to its website, but the details were too technical and confusing for most visitors.

A year and a half after the spill, BP engaged in some heavy-duty image repair with advertisements reporting that the gulf ecology had not been as severely damaged as it originally seemed to be and that the fishing industry was then showing signs of economic recovery. BP hired chefs Emeril Lagasse and John Besh to promote gulf seafood, and it gave away fish tacos and seafood jambalaya at Sugar Bowl parties in New Orleans.

Inevitably, the Deepwater Horizon spill drew parallels with the rupture of the Exxon *Valdez* 21 years earlier, the classic example of bad crisis communications. What are the public relations lessons of the two disasters?

Both companies made public relations blunders in appearing to emphasize technology over people. Both seemed to minimize the environmental consequences, and the emotional reaction to oil-slicked birds and oil-drenched shorelines. But BP was quicker to compensate fishermen and other victims, and it cooperated with government regulators more than Exxon did.

Another difference concerns fault. The *Valdez* spill was caused because the ship's captain was not at the helm, and the cleanup was delayed because the company had removed cleanup equipment from the area prior to the accident as part of a corporate strategy to de-emphasize the risk of such a spill. The public concluded that the Exxon spill was the fault of Exxon. On the other hand, the gulf explosion resulted from the failure of safety equipment on a rig owned and operated by another company.

Both companies were accused of minimizing the extent of the spill and the environmental consequences. BP's fault was more that it tried to remain optimistic that things were moving faster toward containing the spill. It low-balled estimates of how much oil was being discharged, though some of this was based on what BP itself knew at the time.

Neither company appears to have had a workable crisis communications plan to address a worst-case scenario. Not only were the disasters unanticipated, but also the companies seemed not to know how to act once they occurred.

But there are some significant differences that lead to the conclusion that BP handled the situation better than Exxon did. For the most part, BP's corporate leaders were seen as part of the potential solution, rather than as avoiding responsibility and ducking public exposure as was the case in the *Valdez* spill. BP produced fewer contradictory statements.

WORKSHEET FOR STEP 1: ANALYZE THE PUBLIC RELATIONS SITUATION

The focus in Step 1 has been on identifying and analyzing the nature of the issue you are addressing. It may be a routine activity in the life of an organization or it may be a crisis situation. Your purpose in Step 1 is to make strategic decisions about the nature of the issue that later will guide you in addressing it.

Specifically, answer these four basic questions:

1   What is the situation facing the organization?
2   Do you consider this situation an obstacle or an opportunity?
3   What is the significance or importance of the situation?
4   How might the situation be addressed for the mutual benefit of everyone involved?

You may also flesh out these basic questions by considering whether the situation is new or ongoing, how it is linked to the organization's mission, what trends may be associated with it, and the extent to which it is a priority for the organization.

PLANNING EXAMPLE FOR STEP 1

This is the first of an evolving example of the planning steps in action. It focuses on the hypothetical G^X (Global Exchange), a nonprofit advocacy organization that supports a variety of international engagements between young adults in professional environments. The organization works with several professional organizations to support international internship opportunities and university exchange programs. To make this scenario easier to understand, we'll focus on a local chapter of this organization in a mid-sized city.

The situation that G^X is dealing with involves the *value of international engagement* among young professionals. Overall, G^X considers this to be an *opportunity*, though it also involves some *obstacles* to be overcome.

G^X believes that there are several *advantages* to global engagement on a personal professional level. Among these are practical enhancements for an individual's career, networking opportunities, expansion of job skills, strengthened communication and interpersonal skills, and personal development. Opportunities also are present for businesses and nonprofit organizations, which benefit from employees with these qualities, as well as potential business connections that can result from international engagement.

Research by G^X also reveals some *impediments* to this, including the cost in time and money, ignorance of the professional benefits of this engagement, a feeling of being insufficiently prepared and a sense of cultural superiority.

The significance of the issue is that valuing international engagement is central to the mission and vision of success for G^X.

In considering this situation, G^X is researching organizations such as university exchange programs, international business internship programs and international service organizations. It also has investigated several discipline-specific programs involving journalists in Canada, Mexico and the US; engineers in the UK and Australia; British, French and American chefs; and other global exchange programs for accountants, lawyers, nurses, teachers and business executives.

Ideally, the situation will be handled in such as a way as to address the benefits of international professional engagement as well as to deal realistically with the obstacles.

STEP 2: ANALYZING THE ORGANIZATION

Effective communication involves self-awareness. This calls for a close look at the organization: its performance, reputation and structure. The process is the same for all types of corporations: small family businesses, multinational or transnational corporations, regional companies and so on. Likewise noncommercial enterprises such as schools and hospitals, government, membership associations, nongovernmental organizations, and cultural and religious organizations all require the same measure of self-awareness.

What follows is a breakdown focusing on internal environment, public perception and external environment.

INTERNAL ENVIRONMENT

Public relations involves more than words, and an audit of an organization's strengths and limitations begins with a candid understanding of what the organization is and does. Here are some areas you will need to assess as you enter Step 2 of the strategic planning process.

- **Performance**. This is the most important aspect of an organization's internal environment. It involves the quality of the goods and services provided by the organization, as well as the causes and ideas it espouses.
- **Niche**. This focuses on the organization's specialty, the function or role that makes it different from other organizations.
- **Structure**. The audit considers how the public relations operation functions within the organization. This includes both the

mission of public relations (for example, whether it sits at the management table where decisions are made) and the financial, equipment and personnel resources it has for conducting public relations.

- **Ethical Base**. Public relations has been called the conscience of an organization, giving it moral grounding. In analyzing the internal environment, give thought to this ethical base, and identify the values and operating principles that are important to the organization.

- **Internal Impediments**. End your analysis of the internal environment with a look at the impediments or obstacles within the organization that might impede the public relations program. Remember that impediments are merely temporary roadblocks to be circumvented, rather than permanent blockages.

PUBLIC PERCEPTION

The next task in preparing your public relations audit is to consider what people know and think about the organization.

- **Visibility**. Examine the extent to which the organization is known, and the accuracy of the information people have.

- **Reputation**. This deals with perception, what people think about the organization based on what they know. Reputation is part of the social capital of an organization; arguably it's the most important public relations asset. Reputation is based on what the organization says but more so on what it does, and on what others (including the media) say about it.

EXTERNAL ENVIRONMENT

This part of the analysis looks at how outsiders might impact an organization.

- **Supporters**. Every organization has a group of people who currently or potentially can help the organization achieve its objectives. Make sure you know whom they are.

- **Competitors**. Likewise, most organizations have people or groups who are producing similar goods, performing similar services, or espousing similar ideals. In highly competitive environments, it is important for public relations to understand the role of others in the field.

- **Opponents**. Many organizations also have groups who act in some way to counter the organization. These groups may be advocates of an opposing cause, dissidents who oppose you because of your stance, activists organized to foster change at odds with your organization's products or services, or any number of other types of opponents.
- **External Impediments**. Other political, social or economic factors may limit the effectiveness of an organization.

WORKSHEET FOR STEP 2: ANALYZE THE ORGANIZATION

Step 2 has focused your attention on the organization itself. It calls for introspection and candor.

Here are some questions dealing with the organization's internal environment:

1 What is the quality of the organization's performance?
2 What communication resources exist?
3 How supportive is the organization of public relations activity?

Here are questions about the public perception of the organization:

4 How well known is the organization?
5 What is its reputation?

Finally, some questions on the external environment:

6 What is the major competition?
7 Does any significant opposition exist?
8 Is anything happening in the external environment that can limit the effectiveness of the organization?

PLANNING EXAMPLE FOR STEP 2

The *internal environment* of G^X is strong and open. It has strong support with a small number of organizations, particularly environmental nonprofit organizations and businesses with engineering and technological focuses. G^X leaders are on record as seeing a potential for expanding into other sectors.

The *quality* of G^X services is high; the cost of those services are relatively low, due in part to some past grants by the state Business Development Council, though there is no certainty of receiving future grants from this agency.

Communication resources for G^X include a part-time staff member with experience in media relations, and several volunteers with interest and skills in social media. In the past, the organization often worked directly with business associates and did not have a media plan. New board direction is pushing the need for a more proactive strategic approach to communication.

In terms of its *public perception*, G^X is known by some organizational executives, but it has a low *visibility* among rank-and-file employees and in the general community. Where it is known, its *reputation* is generally positive. Past partner companies have described G^X as being well organized, reliable and cost-effective.

The *external environment* seems not to involve any organized opposition, nor are there other organizations with a parallel mission. Some service clubs do small projects involving international business exchange, and the state Economic Development Council occasionally organizes short-term discipline-specific visits to other countries.

Overall, G^X has been hurt by a weak economy, but this is changing as local companies emerge from the economic slump and once again are looking toward long-term interests of building a productive workforce in increasingly competitive circumstances. Financial belt-tightening has caused the largest local university to cut staff in its international exchange program, creating a potential void that G^X might fill.

STEP 3: ANALYZING THE PUBLICS

A **public** is a group of people that shares a common interest vis-à-vis an organization, recognizes its significance, and sets out to do something about it. Members of publics are homogeneous in that they are similar in their interests and characteristics. They usually are aware of the public relations situation and their relationship with the organization. They think the issue is relevant, and they are at least potentially organized or energized to act on the issue.

A public is like your family. You don't pick them; they just are—generous Cousin Ezekiel and crazy Aunt Bertha. Publics may be helpful or annoying, friendly or not, but an organization must deal with them regardless. They exist because they share an environment and interact with the organization.

Note some important differences among publics and related groupings. If a public is like your family, a **market** is more like your friends. You pick them; they pick you. Organizations identify markets by determining those that might be interested in buying their products or using their services.

An **audience**, meanwhile, is merely a group of people who pay attention to a particular medium of communication—people who read the same blog, watch the same TV program, or follow the same person on Twitter. Audiences are important for public relations only to the extent that they include members of an organization's public.

A final category, **stakeholder**, is a bit fuzzy because it has different meanings. Some see stakeholders as groups of people relating to an organization on the basis of its mission and objectives, as compared to publics that relate on the basis of the organization's message on a particular topic. Others suggest that stakeholders care about an organization, whereas publics may or may not care. So far, there is no consensus among public relations practitioners that stakeholders are in any way significantly different from publics. This book treats stakeholders as synonymous with publics.

CHARACTERISTICS OF PUBLICS

When you identify publics, you can look for five distinguishing characteristics.

- **Distinguishable**. A public is a recognizable grouping of individuals, though not necessarily a formal group. For example, a public for a jewelry company might include people getting engaged or people celebrating significant birthdays or anniversaries. Not formal groups, but groupings of people with common interests with whom you can communicate.

- **Homogeneous**. A public's members share common traits and features. They may not know each other, but they have enough in common for you to treat them as a group.
- **Important**. Not every identifiable group is worth your attention. A public has a potentially significant impact on the organization, and vice versa.
- **Large Enough**. A public should be large enough to warrant the organization's time and resources. Generally, a handful of people would not be considered a public but rather could be dealt with in personal ways.
- **Accessible**. A public is a group with which you can interact and communicate. A community college might find it relatively easy to interact with potential students because they all live in a small geographic area. But an internationally renowned university would have a much harder time connecting with potential students thinly scattered throughout the world. The difference might mean that the community college could push messages out, but the university would have to more passively respond to inquiring potential students.

CATEGORIES OF PUBLICS

It becomes a bit easier to identify publics if they are subdivided into four categories. This is based on the concept of linkages, the study of how organizations and groups are interrelated.

- **Customer**. The most obvious type of public is the customer. These are people who receive the products or services of an organization. They may be purchasers, clients, students, fans, patients, patrons, shoppers, parishioners, members and so on. They may be current, past or potential customers.
- **Producer.** These are the publics that provide input to the organization. They include employees and volunteers, unions and management, vendors and suppliers, and donors and investors.
- **Enabler.** One useful category of linkages involves enablers, groups that help organizations exist and prosper. These include regulators, professional standard setters, opinion leaders, colleagues and the media.
- **Limiter.** On the other hand, there may be groups that inhibit organization, such as competitors, opponents and hostile forces.

While the media should first be considered enablers, public relations practitioners have learned that some (such as an antagonistic blogger or an unfriendly TV network) occasional become limiters.

Publics in these categories generally are in direct relationships with the organization. However, there are some other publics that are more distantly linked.

Public relations identifies a **secondary customer** as the customer of your customers. Examples are businesses that might hire a university's graduates or a graduate school that might attract applicants to them for advanced education.

An **intercessory public** bridges the organization and its publics. In everyday life, we often ask a friend or colleague to intercede for us, put in a good word as we look for a job, go for a loan, or seek a date with the new staffer who works in another department. In professional terms, organizations may direct attention to groups that are already in contact with a key public. For example, a university might communicate with high school careers counselors, asking them to mention the university to their students. In this step of the planning process, identify such potential associates for networking possibilities later on.

In addition to intercessory publics, we sometimes deal with intercessory individuals. An **opinion leader** is a person with a particular influence on an organization's publics. Research shows that the media often influence opinion leaders such as business leaders, political figures, teachers, clergy, celebrities, media commentators and others who in turn influence an organization's publics. Opinion leaders often generate word-of-mouth support for an organization or its products, services or causes.

Where are opinion leaders located? Everywhere, it seems, depending on the issue involved. A study at Shih Tsin University in Taiwan asked more than 2,000 people around the world where they get information on energy and technology. The finding reported that 68 percent of respondents get their day-to-day info online (from personal, professional, organizational and media sites), 11 percent from magazines, 6 percent from television, 6 percent from newspapers, 2 percent from radio and 7 percent from other sources.

COCA-COLA IN EGYPT

Opinion leaders can be especially important when practicing public relations in an international context.

Pepsi has always been the soft-drink standard in Egypt and in most other Arab countries. To its cultural detriment, Coca-Cola has been linked with non-Arab Western interests and with American consumerism. An old saying in Egypt, laden with cultural implications, is that Pepsi is for Arabs and Coke is for Jews.

A rumor circulated in 2000 that Coca-Cola was anti-Islam, "proof" of which was that when the Coke logo was viewed upside-down in a mirror, it read as "No Mohamed. No Mecca." Or not. Regardless, Coke sales plummeted 20 percent. Protests erupted. Some areas of the country banned Coke advertising and signage.

Coca-Cola Egypt decided to move quickly, with a particular emphasis on the concept of opinion leader. The company requested a meeting with the grand mufti, the country's top religious leader, asking his advice. It also asked a panel of Islamic scholars to consider the matter. Both the grand mufti and the scholarly panel ruled that the rumor was unsubstantiated.

In a public statement, the religious leader scolded those who disseminated the false rumor for risking the jobs of thousands of fellow Muslims employed by Coca-Cola. He also later said in interviews that he himself enjoyed a daily Coke.

Besides relying on news coverage of the intervention, the company highly advertised the grand mufti's statement and gave copies to its drivers, distributors and sales people. Within weeks, sales returned to pre-crisis levels where Coke, though still a distant second in the cola wars, was playing in a more even cultural environment.

Today, marketing reports suggest that Coke accounts for about one-quarter of the youth market in Egypt, still trailing Pepsi, which remains the No. 1 soft drink throughout most of the Middle East.

KEY PUBLIC

Every organization has many publics, but no public relations plan will be successful if it tries to engage everyone. Instead, practitioners prioritize the various publics and select a few **key publics**, also called **strategic publics**. (Note that some sources call these "target publics," though that term implies one-way communication that fails to focus on mutual engagement.)

Once the key public is identified, the planning process focuses on analyzing each. Much of the needed information will come from informal research such as interviews and brainstorming; some of it may require formal techniques such as focus groups and surveys. Here are some things to look at in analyzing each key public.

- **Public Relations Situation**. Assess the public's wants, interests, needs and expectations related to the issue, as well as what it does not want or need. Consider relevant attitudes of the public.
- **Organization**. Consider each key public's relationship with the organization—how your organization impacts the public and vice versa. Consider the extent to which the public understands this relationship and knows about the issue at hand. Also consider the visibility and reputation of your organization with this public.
- **Communication Behavior**. Study the public's communication habits, such as the media or communication channels it uses. Identify opinion leaders and others who might be credible message sources. Indicate whether the public is seeking information on the issue. (This assessment will have a major impact later when you choose your communication tools, because information seekers are likely to initiate communication or make use of tactics that require their direct involvement.)
- **Demographics**. Identify demographic traits such as age, income, gender, socioeconomic status or other relevant information about this public.

Conclude your analysis of the key publics with a **benefit statement**. Clearly articulate the benefit or advantage your product or service can offer this public, or the way you can help satisfy its need or solve its problems.

For example, the benefit a community foundation might offer its donors could be stated as follows: "The Equity Foundation offers donors the opportunity to pool their money with the donations of others, thereby compounding small donations into larger, more effective grants with a greater impact on the community."

In more of a marketing vein, the benefit an online bookstore might offer college and university students could be written as this: "Cyber Booksellers can assure university students that it can provide class textbooks at discount prices with immediate delivery."

CULTURAL CONTEXT

Publics don't exist in a vacuum. Understanding their cultural context is crucial in this research phase of the strategic planning process. Public relations practitioners who give a priority to learning the nuances of the culture in which the publics exist are likely to develop campaigns that can be successful.

This is particularly important in the international arena. What works in one culture may not be appropriate for another.

Even basic communication can be hampered in international contexts. Language itself can be a barrier to communication. This is particularly true in Africa. South Africa, for example, has 11 different national languages. Nigeria has about 500 languages and dialects, with English as the official language used mainly in cities, making it very difficult to mount any countrywide communication program.

Technological differences can add to the problem. Social media and mobile media, so common in Western societies, are not present enough in some parts of Africa to make them useful tools for public relations, though this is changing rapidly as many countries are experiencing sustained growth in cellular technology. Social media may be banned or censored in some countries.

Outsiders do themselves and their public relations interests a disservice when they fail to understand the diversity that exists within a culture. In the US, for example, public relations practitioners should understand that there are major differences within the Hispanic community. For example, mistakenly thinking that Puerto Ricans, Cuban-Americans and Hispanics from the Dominican Republic all have the same cultural perspectives can create embarrassment for organizations and counterproductive responses from publics. Likewise Mexican, Panamanian, Columbian and other Latin American cultures may share a common language base, but from a public relations perspective they may have more differences than similarities.

Likewise with Asian Americans from very different national and cultural backgrounds. About the only thing they have in common is that non-Asian Americans tend to see them as all being the same.

Situations can get even more complicated when applied to other countries. Some nations such as Mexico, Canada, Australia and Japan—as well as the US—have historic tensions between indigenous peoples and the dominant culture. Others experience significant differences, even hostility, based on language (such as Canada and Ukraine), religion (Uganda, India, and sporadically, Northern Ireland), race (South Africa) or tribal background (Rwanda).

Gender roles and socially acceptable relations among men and women also vary greatly, as do social attitudes toward people who are gay, aged, disabled or otherwise different from the social norm.

WORKSHEET FOR STEP 3: ANALYZE KEY PUBLICS

In Step 3 you have focused on your key publics—who they are, what they are like. Most importantly, you have looked at ways to identify the interests and aspirations of each key public, which is the needed foundation for eventually formulating an appeal to each.

Here are four basic questions to be addressed in Step 3:

1 What are the major publics for your organization on this issue (the key publics)?
2 What is the nature of each key public?
3 What are the major wants, interests, needs and expectations of each key public?
4 What benefits can you offer each public?

You can build on these questions with more probing information about the awareness of each public toward these potential interests, whether the public is seeking information on the topic, and who might be influential opinion leaders.

PLANNING EXAMPLE FOR STEP 3

Here is a listing of publics for G^X:

- *Customers* include local organizations with international counterparts and young professionals (up to age 35). Potential customers include university seniors and graduate students in professional programs.

- *Producers* include G^X staff (2 full-time, 3 part-time); volunteer workshop presenters (approximately 14); 9-person board of directors of the local chapter. Producers also consist of the donors including individuals, foundations, corporations, and grant-giving agencies and organizations.
- *Enablers* include the news media (general, business-oriented, cultural and university-based); social media with professional or global interest; professional and business organizations with an international perspective; and cultural organizations with a global/intercultural agenda. Opinion leaders include university faculty in professional programs. Enablers also include approximately 35 current and past participants in the G^X international programs, as well as their employers and professional mentors/ colleagues. Another category of enablers includes groups and individuals associated with trade organizations, foreign consulates and (at a greater distance) foreign embassies.
- *Limiters* include banks that are cutting back on loans. There are no apparent opponent groups.

After due consideration, three key publics for this campaign are identified:

1 Young business professionals, and university seniors and graduate students in professional programs.
2 Companies, nonprofit groups and professional organizations with global perspective.
3 News media (particularly business-oriented media) and associated social media.

Here is an analysis of each key public:

1 Young business professionals and university students want an opportunity to be successful in their careers, especially by pulling ahead of others competing for the same jobs. They use various media, particularly social media, though they are likely to pay attention to professional media that addresses their career interests. By definition, this public is young. It has better-than-average

education and reflects the general ethnic, racial, lifestyle and religious demographics of university graduates living in this area. This public is likely to be open to mobility, travel and inter-cultural/international engagement. Collectively these are wants and interests, though perhaps this public would not identify them as needs.

2. Companies, nonprofits and professional organizations want and need opportunities to be more competitive and more effective in their work. An interest is to have a workforce of people who are open, creative, resourceful, motivated, and committed to both customers and the company.

3. News media want and need information that is newsworthy, available and relevant to their audiences.

Here is the benefit statement: G^X can provide information to each of these key publics that will interest them and will satisfy their wants and needs.

6

PUBLIC RELATIONS PLANNING
PHASE 2: STRATEGY

> Strategy deals with planning that focuses on the desired outcomes and
> the conceptual ways of achieving them. It's not about specific tools
> of communication but rather deciding where to go and how to get there.

Strategy is the organization's overall plan. Building on the research
from Phase 1, this strategy section sets out the organization's decision
on what it wants to achieve and how it wants to achieve it. Strategy
focuses on being both proactive and responsive, according to the
needs of the situation. It also deals with the content and presentation
of the organization's messages.

This phase is interrelated and interdependent. Goals guide the
development of objectives. These in turn help drive decisions about
what persuasive approaches to use and who can best present the message.

Later, in the next phase, the decisions made here will guide the
various tactics that will present the organization's message to its publics.

STEP 4: ESTABLISHING GOALS AND OBJECTIVES

The purpose of this step is to clearly indicate the direction you are
heading toward addressing the key publics about the situation. This
involves articulating both the general direction and the specific

marks of success. Here are short definitions of key concepts used in this step.

- A **positioning statement** is a general expression of how an organization wants it publics to distinguish it vis-à-vis its competition.
- A **goal** is a global indication of how an issue should be resolved.
- An **objective** is a statement of a specific outcome expected for a public, indicating a way to more precisely conceptualize the goal.

POSITIONING

As you spell out the desired interaction with your publics, focus first on positioning. This means asking yourself a simple question: What do we want the key public to think about us?

Positioning is the process of managing how an organization distinguishes itself with a unique meaning in the mind of its publics— that is, how it wants to be seen and known by its publics. This usually means an implicit comparison with the organization's competitors. A **position statement** is the articulation of this desired positioning.

Most organizations are known for their distinctiveness: the large public university, the small church-affiliated college, the high-priced two-year private school, the community college with open access, the mid-sized public institution that began as a teachers college and so on.

Make sure your desired position is realistic. Who wouldn't want to be known as "the best in (whatever)"? But there can be only one best, and public relations is not about pretense or stretching beyond possibility. Here are some reasonable positioning statements:

- Great value, reflecting low cost and high quality.
- The most economical.
- The hospital preferred by women.
- The family-friendly restaurant.
- The eco-friendly garden center.

GOAL

With the positioning statement as a guidepost, turn your attention to the **goal**. This is a short, simple statement rooted in the organization's mission that indicates the desired outcome for the situation. A goal is stated in general terms, lacking measures (these will come later in the objectives).

Think in terms of three types of goals focused on reputation, relationships and tasks.

1 **Reputation-management goals** deal with the identity and perception of the organization. Here are some examples of this:

- Improve the university's reputation for science education.
- Reinforce the museum's image with potential donors.
- Enhance the hospital's reputation for cancer treatment.

2 **Relationship-management goals** focus on how the organization connects with its publics.

- Reduce opposition to the building of a wind farm near an affluent community.
- Enhance the relationship between the store and its customers.
- Maintain a favorable relationship with season-ticket holders.

3 **Task-management goals** are concerned with getting certain things done.

- Influence motorists to refrain from texting while driving.
- Attract a sell-out crowd for the concert.
- Foster continued growth in the number of new customers.

OBJECTIVE

In public relations, an **objective** is a statement giving detail about the goal and providing markers for measuring progress toward achieving that goal. Here are some elements of an objective:

- **Goal rooted**—growing from and giving detail to the goals.
- **Public focused**—linked firmly to a specific key public.
- **Impact oriented**—defining the effect you hope to make on the public by focusing on intended achievements rather than tools to reach these.
- **Research based**—consistent with the data obtained in the first phase of the strategic planning process.

- **Explicit**—offering a concrete and precise indication of the intended outcome.
- **Measurable**—with metrics indicating quantifiable performance indicators.
- **Time definite**—with a clear timeframe for achieving the results.
- **Singular**—focusing on only one desired response for each objective.
- **Challenging**—offering the organization something to stretch toward.
- **Attainable**—yet also able to be achieved.
- **Acceptable**—earning the buy-in of the organization's managers.

Objectives are presented in a logical progression through three stages of persuasion: awareness, acceptance and action.

Awareness objectives deal with what people know about the organization. This is the cognitive (informational) component of a message. It deals both with visibility and reputation, allowing an organization to build on accurate and positive awareness or to attempt to counter misinformation.

These awareness objectives often are used for transmitting functional information, for communicating on noncontroversial issues and for the early stages of any communication campaign.

Acceptance objectives focus on the interest in and attitudes of the publics based on what they know. These objectives deal with the affective (feeling) part of the message. They indicate the level of interest or the kind of attitude an organization hopes to generate in its publics.

These objectives are useful in forming interests and attitudes where none existed before, reinforcing existing interests and attitudes, and changing existing positive or negative attitudes.

Action objectives articulate how we want the publics to act, based on what they think or feel about what they know. They offer two types of action: opinion (verbal action) and behavior (physical action).

These action objectives may attempt to create new behaviors or change existing ones, positively or negatively.

Generally a goal should have at least one of each of these three types of objective. Here is a scenario to help you understand how these fit together. Let's say they are for a task management goal of obtaining volunteers among university students for a program called MMS, Mentors in Math and Science.

- To *create awareness* of the MMS program among students, specifically to have 40 percent of the 25,000 students (10,000) at three area colleges and universities understand the program and the benefits of volunteering, within six months.
- To *create acceptance* among these students, specifically generating interest among 5 percent of the student population (1,250 students), within six months.
- To *generate action* among the students, specifically to achieve an action rate of 1 percent, achieving 250 volunteers after a six-month campaign.

Notice how each level grows from the previous one. Notice also that there will be no guessing about whether success is achieved. The outcomes of measures and timeframes are identified clearly.

TOYOTA

The world's largest automaker Toyota has shown the importance of reputation goals, which are particularly significant in crisis situations.

With auto recalls in 2009 and 2010, Toyota endured what was initially called the worst handled auto recall in history, with predictions that the reputation of the Toyota brand would be damaged for years. Faulty accelerators were linked to 19 deaths, and consumers were reaching near-panic levels. The company that had built its reputation on quality and safety recalled 9 million vehicles, shaking consumer confidence and causing stock prices to fall by 15 percent.

Toyota's confidence in its own reputation may have caused the company to fumble its public relations in the early stage of the recall crisis. Some critics accused the company of corporate arrogance: withholding internal test reports, hiding the problem from unsuspecting customers, and paying off lawsuits behind closed doors without remedying the problems.

Supporters countered that the company acted quickly when information became available. It took full-page newspaper ads alerting consumers of the recall, and it temporarily halted sales and shut down production. American and Japanese officials gave television interviews presenting the company's message of reassurance.

The strategy seemed to work. Within a year, Toyota stock prices were even higher than before the recall and the Toyota reputation was once again an asset to the international corporation. Toyota continued as the No. 1 automaker in the world.

Polls show that Toyota had fewer complaints than American, and most other imported, automakers, another testimony to the importance of keeping reputation as a top goal of any organization. Also, in the aftermath of the crisis, Toyota set a renewed priority on customer responsiveness.

WORKSHEET FOR STEP 4: ESTABLISH GOALS AND OBJECTIVES

Step 4 turned the gaze both inward and outward, focusing on the organization's anticipated outcome. It's all about what the organization wants people to know and feel and how it expects them to act on these factors.

Here are the basic questions for this step:

1 What position do you seek?
2 What are the goals to achieve this positioning?
3 What are the specific objectives (awareness, acceptance and action) for each public and each goal?

As necessary, flesh out these questions with additional information about the viability and practicality of the position and goals, the level of support for the position and goals, and the consistency of each objective with previous decisions about the organization's publics.

CONSENSUS CHECK

At this point, meet with your planning colleagues and with your boss or client. Make sure that agreement and harmony exists within the organization about the recommended objectives, because what is formulated here will be the basis for subsequent strategies and tactics.

If there is agreement and buy-in, proceed to Step 5. If not, consider the value and/or possibility of achieving consensus before proceeding.

PLANNING EXAMPLE FOR STEP 4

As a *position statement*, G^X wants to be the go-to source for international professional engagements.

Two *goals* are associated with this:

- A *reputation-management goal* to promote the visibility and reputation of G^X among young business professionals and the companies or organizations that employ them.
- A *task-management goal* of increasing the number of participants in its engagement and exchange programs.

Objectives for Public #1 (individual professionals):

1   To have an effect on the *awareness* of young professionals about G^X, specifically to increase their understanding of the advantages that G^X offers by 50 percent within one year.
2   To have an effect on their *acceptance*, specifically to increase their interest in the engagement/exchange programs by 25 percent within one year.
3   To have an effect on their *action*, specifically to generate 10 applicants for long-term exchange programs and 40 for short-term engagement programs within one year.

Objectives for Public #2 (organizations):

1   To have an effect on *acceptance*, specifically to increase the awareness of corporate executives and human resources staff about the G^X program opportunities (50 percent of identified organizations within one year).
2   To have an effect on their *acceptance*, specifically to generate feedback and inquiries from these organizations (15 percent within one year).

3   To have an effect on their *action*, specifically to generate invitations for G^X to meet with organizational leaders (25 organizations within one year).

Objectives for Public #3 (news media):

1   To have an effect on their *awareness*, specifically to increase their knowledge about the G^X programs (journalists at 50 percent of identified news media and news blogs within one year).
2   To have an effect on their *acceptance*, specifically to generate inquiries from these journalists (25 percent of identified news venues within one year).
3   To have an effect on their *action*, specifically to see publication/broadcast of positive/neutral pieces by 10 percent of identified news venues within one year.

STEP 5: FORMULATING ACTION AND RESPONSE STRATEGIES

Actions speak louder than words, and effective public relations involves the ability of an organization to perform services and provide goods that reflect benefits to users. Public relations strategists have several options, which generally fit into one of two categories: proactive or reactive.

Proactive strategies come into play at the organization's initiative, such as when it launches a campaign or initiates contact with the news media to publicize a new product or service. Typical proactive elements involve generating publicity, presenting newsworthy information and developing a transparent communication process.

Reactive strategies are those through which an organization responds to influences and opportunities from its environment, including hostile pressures from the outside.

PROACTIVE STRATEGY 1: ACTION

The first category of proactive public relations involves tangible deeds undertaken by the organization to achieve its objectives.

Organizational performance is a key type of proactive action. It involves assessing and, when necessary, changing the output of an organization. This process is known as **adaptation**, in which an organization changes itself to better interact with its environment.

A publicity campaign on behalf of a restaurant that serves mediocre food won't be very successful until the food improves. A politician who fails to address the interests of voters isn't going to attract much support.

Review Steps 2 and 3 of this strategic planning process. Compare the output of the organization with the wants, interests, needs and expectations of the publics. Then address any differences between the two.

Audience engagement is another important proactive strategy. This involves using two-way communication to understand and address audience interests. If possible, build in opportunities for your publics to participate in the program.

For example, Bosque de Chapultepec in Mexico City, the hemisphere's oldest urban park, invited thousands of volunteers to pick up trash as part of a wider effort to encourage its 15 million visitors to use sanitary facilities. The involvement of these volunteers spurred the campaign and created thousands of environmental ambassadors who continued to look after park sanitation and cleanliness long after their volunteer cleanup ended. Audience engagement also involves creating feedback opportunities, such as online surveys and interactive websites

Organizations sometimes sponsor a **staged event** to generate audience participation. These are activities created by the organization as a focal point for public involvement and potential media attention. Staged events can involve positive activities such as tree-planting ceremonies, recitals, competitions such as sporting events or essay contests, parades and anniversary events. They also could feature more confrontational approaches such as rallies, demonstrations and other activist events.

Organizations with a common goal sometimes join together in **alliances and coalitions**, a strength-in-numbers approach that compounds their influence and often generates media attention as it works toward organizational goals. For example, the North Carolina Health Literacy Council put together a coalition of health centers, public health agencies, religious groups, insurance companies, school groups and medical research centers—all with the goal of helping people become more knowledgeable about health issues.

Related to alliances are **sponsorships**, through which an organization provides financial, personnel and other resources to support a community project. The relationship should be a strategic one with mutual benefits. For example, a technology company might sponsor a science fair, or a newspaper might support a literacy program.

Some sponsorships are based on existing marketing relationships. For example, Lexus sponsors polo championships because enthusiasts of that sport reflect the luxury car's customer base. So too with Budweiser's sponsorship of the Super Bowl and Emirates Airlines as official airline of the 2014 FIFA world cup and the 2015 World Cricket Cup.

Activism is another proactive strategy, a confrontational approach focused on persuasive communication and advocacy. It's a strong strategy with pros and cons, and because it can generate opposition as well as support, organizations are cautious about engaging in activism. But this strategy can be very successful, especially for cause-related organizations and movements dealing with social issues, environmental matters, political concerns and so on.

Some of the tactics associated with this strategy include boycotts, marches, petitions, pickets, rallies, sit-ins, strikes, vigils and outright civil disobedience.

Sometimes activism takes the form of street theater, such as when Amnesty International coordinated a protest in 83 cities around the world, mostly near military bases or embassies. Protestors dressed in orange jumpsuits and black hoods, courting media attention to protest the lack of due process for suspected terrorists detained for years by the US military at Guantanamo Bay.

Some activism is in-your-face, literally, as pie-throwing became a publicity tactic to protest designer use of fur (pieing Oscar de la Renta), euro currency (Dutch finance minister Gerrit Zalm), endangered sea turtles (Renato Ruggiero, director general of the World Trade Organization), seal hunting (Canadian oceans minister Gail Shea) and the faces associated with many other causes.

ONLINE ACTIVISM

With the mushrooming of the Internet globally, many organizations have embraced **online activism**. Also called **cyberactivism**, this strategy harnesses the power of the Internet for social engagement. It erases geographical boundaries, circumvents local media interests, and allows organizations to engage their publics directly and frequently.

The Internet thus extends an organization's reach beyond traditional media. Additionally, sites such as Facebook are making e-activist tools available to their users, making it easy for supporters to volunteer, donate and share the organization's message to their own list of online friends.

Cyberactivism has been a catalyst for social protests such as the Arab Spring, the Greek economic protests and the Occupy movement. As a tool of social engagement for public relations purposes, cyberactivism can involve advocacy, mobilization and action/reaction, making it useful in fundraising, lobbying and community building.

Groups such as Amnesty International and Greenpeace have embraced online activism in a big way. Such organizations long have encouraged volunteers to sign petitions and contact government leaders and corporate executives on behalf of various causes. Now visitors can go to the organizations' websites to learn about current campaigns and to sign up to receive information on topics of particular interest.

On Amnesty's website (amnesty.org), for example, members and supporters can help pressure the UN to protect civilians in Sudan or urge governments to free political prisoners, end disappearances and abductions, and otherwise protect human rights. They can join others in advocating for free expression, international justice, support for refugees, and fair treatment of gays, women and other oppressed people.

The advantages of cyberactivism fit neatly into the game plan of Greenpeace, which uses its website (greenpeace.org) to update visitors on various environmental issues and campaigns around the world. With a simple mouse click, visitors to the website can add their name to petitions and mail campaigns directed toward government officials and corporate executives on a range of issues: global warming, forests and oceans, endangered animals, green energy production and sustainable fishing.

Friends of the Earth (foe.co.uk) offers online petitions and social media support for clean air, bees, sanitation, biodiversity and support for a green economy.

People for the Ethical Treatment of Animals (peta.org) invites online visitors to contact lawmakers and advertisers and to spread the word via its own Facebook page, Twitter and other social media networking.

Cyberactivism sometimes co-opts the Internet in more direct ways. For example, Greenpeace used GPS technology and the Internet to help the indigenous Deni people of the Amazon protect their land from logging by monitoring the movements of illegal loggers.

PROACTIVE STRATEGY 2: COMMUNICATION

Another category of proactive public relations strategies deals with communication, specifically the various options an organization has to communicate with its publics.

At some time, every organization seeks **publicity** to gain attention through the news media. The value of this is that information reported by newspapers, blogs and TV broadcasts has both credibility and potentially a wide audience. A limitation is that the information must be considered newsworthy, a decision that is made by media **gatekeepers** (editors and news directors who determine what gets reported).

To attract media interest, news and publicity also should have a strong **visual element**. Stand-up commentators or talking heads don't make it on most TV news reports. Audiences demand active, even entertaining, visual presentation of their news.

This is where the strategy of staged events mentioned above can come into play. For example, the Nuns on the Bus information tour during the 2012 US presidential campaign had plenty of visual appeal. A group of Catholic nuns traveled through eight states in a brightly painted bus. With backdrops of homeless shelters and soup kitchens along the way, as well as legislative offices, the nuns focused international media attention and much local awareness as they lobbied legislators and otherwise provided a platform to speak out on social justice. This was in opposition to budget-cutting proposals in congress that they said would unduly hurt the poor.

For publicity efforts to be successful, organizations must have newsworthy information. Sometimes this happens spontaneously, although unexpected news often is bad news (accidents, fires, hostile takeovers and so on).

But public relations strategists know how to generate news that can be more favorable for their organizations. Here's a short list of some ways to create news.

1 Give an award to draw attention to values and issues.
2 Hold a contest to involve others in your values and issues.
3 Select personnel to head a new program or begin a new project.
4 Comment on a local need or problem.
5 Conduct research and issue a report about a local need or problem.
6 Launch a campaign to accomplish something.
7 Give a speech to a significant audience and tell the media about it.
8 Involve a celebrity visiting and/or addressing your organization on a topic of concern to you.
9 Tie into an issue already high on the public or media agenda or link your organization to the top news of the day.
10 Localize a general report.

[For more on how to generate news, see another textbook by this author, *Becoming a Public Relations Writer*, 4th edition, 2012, Routledge/Taylor and Francis.]

Regardless of its genesis, information coming from organizations must be **newsworthy**. A lot of information is important to an organization but not news as media gatekeepers would see it. For example, the fact that an organization is planning a major fundraising dinner and needs advance meal reservations may be important, but the news media are not going to report it three weeks early just so the caterer can get a head count. The organization would have to find other ways of reaching its key publics. Look back to Chapter 4 for the section "What Is News?" Recall that we define news as *significant information relevant to a local media audience, presented with balance and objectivity and in a timely manner.*

Strategic public relations planners try to find those topics associated with all three groups (media, publics and the organization) involved in the dissemination of newsworthy information. At the intersection of these three groups is a **news peg**—a topic on which the media are already reporting that interests audiences and publics and also touches in some way on the organization.

For example, if the media are reporting on a national story involving an international crisis in Asia, a local Asian-based cultural organization may contact the media and offer an informed local perspective on events half a world away. Or if a high-profile celebrity goes public with a diagnosis of depression, a mental-health clinic might move quickly to offer media interviews on how to identify and deal with the illness.

Here are two real-world examples of effective public relations use of news pegs.

DAWN DETERGENT

Every time there is an environmental disaster involving oil-covered birds, Proctor and Gamble gets the opportunity to note that its Dawn detergent is THE cleaning agent of choice for groups such as the International Bird Rescue Research Center and the US Fish and Wildlife Service.

The company generates news releases, promotes interviews, and uses internal and social media to communicate directly with its consumers—all ways to enhance Dawn's positioning as a skin-friendly but high-powered cleaner.

OAKLEY SUNGLASSES

When the world watched as 35 miners were rescued in Chile after being trapped underground for 69 days, Oakley donated sunglasses to help the miners' eyes return to normal after so much time without sunlight.

At a retail cost of $180 (£115, €142) for each pair of sunglasses, the company turned an investment of $6,400 (£4,075, €5,000) into international media exposure estimated to be worth $41 million (£26.1 million, €32.4 million).

Proactive public relations also calls for **transparent communication**, which moves an organization beyond the just-trust-us model and openly makes the case to its publics.

Several years ago, the CIA was asked to investigate the crash of TWA flight 800 off Long Island. The report not only detailed what the investigators found, but it also included a thorough discussion of the investigation process that led to the conclusion. "Report goes beyond being 'open,'" wrote the late Pat Jackson in *PR Reporter*. "Open implies something else is closed, which raises questions. CIA's report is transparent—everything is laid on the line. Its thoroughness leaves no questions."

Organizations engage in transparent communication when they lay out for their publics the issues, background, influences and options. If financial pressures are pushing your organization to curtail services, let your publics know about the financial problems and the various options before announcing a service cutback. Nobody likes bad surprises, especially when it suggests that the organization has been hiding information from key publics.

REACTIVE STRATEGY 1: PRE-EMPTIVE ACTION

A pre-emptive strike is one taken before an opponent launches its first charge against the organization. From a public relations perspective, it's a **prebuttal** (a play on the word *rebuttal*). An organization may present advance information defending itself when bad news is inevitable, or it may announce opposition to something not yet formally introduced.

POLITICAL OPPOSITION

It was pre-emptive action when congressional Republican leaders criticized President Obama's health-care bill, Iraq policy and jobs proposal even before the president had issued any of these. They anticipated what he would propose and registered their opposition first.

Similarly, it was a prebuttal when Obama responded to the shooting of school children and their teachers in Newtown, Conn. His plan was to reduce gun violence while at the same time respecting the Second Amendment—a move toward minimizing the impact of expected opposition from the National Rifle Association.

Obama even co-opted several NRA proposals: improving school safety, tightening mental-health screens and enforcing existing gun laws with increased vigor.

The concept underlying a prebuttal—the benefit it offers—is the notion that the first one to tell the story sets the tone, against which all alternative versions must compete.

REACTIVE STRATEGY 2: OFFENSIVE RESPONSE

Public relations planners sometimes try to operate from a position of strength in the face of opposition. For example, they may use the **attack** strategy, claiming that an accusation of wrongdoing is motivated by an accuser who is negligent or malicious.

Another offensive strategy is **embarrassment**, in which an organization tries to lessen an opponent's influence by using shame or humiliation. In 2003, the Liberian Women's Peace Movement held street demonstrations to embarrass the government into ending a violent civil war. They locked down a conference hall until a peace accord was signed. Soon after, the UN charged Liberia's president with crimes against humanity. The president resigned; he was exiled and replaced—by a woman.

Embarrassment sometimes takes a turn toward alarm, with attempts to **shock** people with information.

Sometimes organizations use **threat** as an offensive strategy, promising that harm will come to the accuser or the purveyor of bad news.

PETA

People for the Ethical Treatment of Animals has built a reputation for outrageous strategies in its animal-rights campaigns. PETA used shock strategy to force McDonald's to agree to more humane practices in chicken coops and slaughterhouses.

For example, PETA distributed "Son of Ron Unhappy Meal" boxes with a plastic cow in bloodstained hay, a plastic butchered pig, and a Ronald McDonald figure wearing a blood-spattered butcher's apron and wielding a meat cleaver. Some parents complained that PETA was upsetting their children, though the group said more people expressed disgust with how McDonalds treated animals.

REACTIVE STRATEGY 3: DEFENSIVE RESPONSE

Another set of strategies involves a more overt defensive approach by the organization. One such strategy is **denial**, in which an organization tries not to accept a problem by claiming that the problem doesn't exist. The explanation may be one of innocence ("We didn't do it"), mistaken identity ("You have us confused with someone else") or blame shifting ("So-and-so did it").

Another common defensive strategy is **excuse**, through which the organization tries to mitigate wrongdoing. This may be based on provocation ("We didn't have a choice"), lack of control ("The problem was caused at a higher level"), accident ("We were at the whim of natural causes beyond our control"), victimization ("A culprit outside our organization caused this") or mere association ("We inherited this problem").

Justification is a related defensive response, with the organization admitting to the deed but explaining that it did so for a good reason. One type of justification is based on good intention ("We were trying to avoid worse harm"), context ("Look at this from our side"), idealism ("We are following higher principles") or mitigation ("We did this, but it was the result of impairment/illness/coercion/etc.").

Another defensive response strategy is **reversal**, in which an organization under criticism tries to gain the upper hand.

PEPSI

The cola giant faced an accusation in 1993 that medical syringes had been found in cans of diet soft drink. After the news media reported the first case in Tacoma, Washington, similar claims popped up throughout the US.

Pepsi used defensive strategies by saying that it was an innocent victim and by denying that any crisis even existed. It supported this denial with video news releases showing how its production process made it impossible to contaminate the product before it left the plant.

The company also used offensive strategies by claiming that the accusers had planted the objects and by vowing to pursue legal action against people making false claims. Pepsi later produced video news releases showing the arrest of a tamperer, and the circulated convenience store surveillance videos of the tampering incident.

It quickly became clear that there was no basis to the claims, and thus no continuing crisis. Pepsi concluded with a campaign to thank loyal customers, with advertising headlines that read: "Pepsi is pleased to announce ... nothing."

REACTIVE STRATEGY 4: DIVERSIONARY RESPONSE

Sometimes an organization tries to divert attention away from itself and the problem it is associated with. One way to do this is through **concession** ("We can't fix this problem, but we can do something else that you will like"). An organization may give an aggrieved public something that both value, drawing attention away from the problem that remains.

Related to this is **ingratiation** ("Let's try to divert them by tossing a bone"). This approach, which raises ethical questions, involves giving a public something insignificant under the pretense that it has value.

Disassociation ("We've just fired the people who caused this problem") is another diversionary response in which an organization tries to distance itself from the wrongdoing associated with it. Sometimes this involves firing employees who violated organizational policy, for example when groups such as schools and youth organizations move quickly to get rid of employees or volunteers accused of abusing children.

An associated strategy is **relabeling** ("We'll change the name so people won't think of us concerning this problem"). This has led Al Qaeda in Yemen to change its name to Ansar al Sharia, Philip Morris tobacco corporation calling itself Altria Group and Exxon successively changing the name of the notorious tanker *Valdez* to *Sea River Mediterranean*, later sold and renamed *Dong Fang Ocean* and most recently *Oriental Nicety*.

CALIFORNIA PRUNE BOARD

Which would you rather eat: Chinese gooseberry or kiwi? Dolphin fish or mahi mahi? Rapeseed oil or Canola? Toothfish or Chilean sea bass? Slimehead or orange roughy? You get the idea: Labels matter.

That was the concept facing prune farmers in California, who grow 60 percent of the world's prunes and supply all of the US market. In parts of Europe, prunes are popular fruits. But in the US, prunes were known primarily as laxatives to help old people with their bowel movements.

With support from California legislators, the Food and Drug Administration gave permission for a relabeling. The California Prune Board began a $10 million (£6.4 million, €8 million) rebranding effort involving public relations, advertising, sales promotion and education. For American consumers, prunes became dried plums. Same fruit. Same taste. But a much more appealing name.

Surveys by the newly renamed California Dried Plum Board found that most Americans didn't realize that what they knew as prunes are, by definition, dried plums. Research showed that 70 percent of consumers preferred the new name. Taste tests gave a 9:1 edge for "dried plums" over "prunes." Focus groups confirmed that people thought of dried plums as fresh and appealing. The new name was more consistent with the image of plums, which many Americans knew from imports from Japan and elsewhere and associations with plum wine, plum brandy and the sugarplum fairy.

Marketers responded with a new array of the fruit: dried plums dipped in chocolate, individually wrapped, enhanced with lemon or orange essence, wrapped in snack packs for lunch boxes and back-packs. They can be pureed into an oil for baking brownies and cake.

Recently the board partnered with swimmer Natalie Coughlin (the most-decorated American female athlete in the 2008 and 2004 Olympics) promoting dried plums as part of a comprehensive nutrition, energy and fitness lifestyle.

PAPA JOHN'S PIZZA

When a franchise causes problems for a global corporation, the home office should be quick to respond. That's what happened when one of Papa John's franchise owners, a fan of Washington Wizards basketball, tried to distract an opposing team's star player during an NBA play-off game.

The franchise distributed "Cry Baby" T-shirts ridiculing LeBron James of the Cleveland Cavaliers, known for complaining about being fouled. One photo of the provocative T-shirt was posted on the SoGood.com food blog, and 12 hours later Cav fans had started a nationwide boycott of Papa John's.

Papa John's acted quickly with a Sunday afternoon emergency strategy session with its Fleishman-Hillard agency. The client first considered an advertising response, but public relations planners successfully argued the merits of a proactive media response.

First, the corporation distanced itself from the franchise with an apology to James, his fans and the city of Cleveland. Such distancing is standard with a diversionary response.

Then Papa John's maneuvered another diversionary response by offering fans two concessions. It donated $10,000 to the Cavalier's Youth Fund and an additional $10,000 to James' own foundation for kids. The corporation also prepared its 115 franchises in and around Northeast Ohio for a special promotion four days later, when it sold 66,000 pizzas for 23 cents each (reflecting James' jersey number).

The result was positive international news coverage of corporate philanthropy, thousands of happy customers, online chat rooms and blogs gushing with praise for the way Papa John's made up for one franchise's mistake, and in Cleveland a 15 percent increase in pizza sales that lasted several months.

REACTIVE STRATEGY 5: VOCAL COMMISERATION

Another family of strategies deals with ways in which an organization expresses empathy and understanding about a misfortune. The least apologetic of these is **concern** ("This is a serious and troubling situation") with the organization expressing distress but not admitting any culpability.

Condolence ("We are deeply sorry that this happened") is the next level, with the organization expressing grief over someone's loss or misfortune, again without admitting guilt.

Next comes **regret** ("Words cannot express how sorry we are for our role in this accident"), with the organization admitting its role but not necessarily accepting responsibility or admitting wrongdoing. This often is a crisis response endorsed by public relations practitioners who understand that publics generally need to see and hear that the organization is not minimizing its role in problem situations.

Occasionally organizations express regret for the actions of others. Congress incurred the wrath of the Turkish government when one of its committees passed a nonbinding resolution labeling as "genocide" the Turkish massacre of 1.5 million Armenians during World War I. Formal consideration of the resolution, which threatened US security interests in the Middle East, was stalled. The irony is that congress had yet to apologize to its own people for black slavery in the American South, the forced relocation of Japanese-Americans during World War II or the relocation and ethnic cleansing campaigns against American Indians.

The highest level of vocal commiseration is the **apology** ("We are sorry we did this; please forgive us"). With an apology, the organization publicly accepts responsibility and asks pardon. Particularly in crisis situations, public relations strategists point out that an apology often can shorten the lifespan of a crisis. A public apology also can minimize negative legal and financial consequences.

Strategists also are quick to point out the dangers of a **non-apology** ("I'm sorry if you took offense").

MATTEL TOYS

Like all strategies, an apology must be considered in light of both the public and the cultural context. That was the issue as concern grew about the safety of Mattel toys made in China, including lead paint in some of the toys.

A top Mattel official met with China's product-safety official to issue an apology to consumers. Mattel said it was sorry for the recall of millions of toys and that it would try to prevent future problems— at least, that's the version reported in Europe and North America.

The Chinese version went more like this: "Mattel is sorry for having to recall Chinese-made toys due to the company's design flaws and for harming the reputation of Chinese manufacturing companies."

Actually, the Chinese version got it right. It was a design flaw that had caused the recall of more than 17 million toys. Only 2 million of those were recalled because the Chinese firms used lead paint, which is prohibited in the United States.

China had previously been stung by a series of recalls undermining confidence in its manufactured goods (pet food, toothpaste, packaged seafood and baby cribs).

China needed the public apology, and it needed for the explanation to be clear that the fault was with Mattel which, critics agreed, deserved the bigger blame because of corporate policies to cut costs and speed up production.

REACTIVE STRATEGY 6: RECTIFYING BEHAVIOR

A positive response to opposition and criticism involves action on the part of the organization to repair the damage. One such strategy is **investigation** ("We are looking into the cause of this problem"). This may buy time for the organization, but it also sets up expectations that the investigation will be reported and acted upon.

Corrective action ("Here's how we will fix this problem") involves taking steps to contain a problem, repair the damage and/ or prevent its recurrence. This was part of Johnson & Johnson's response to the classic crisis of the cyanide murders associated with Tylenol. The company, clearly a victim along with its customers, took responsibility for repackaging the product to prevent future tampering, thus setting a new standard for the entire pharmaceutical industry.

Another rectifying behavior that serves the interests of both the organization and its publics is **restitution** ("Here's how we will make this right"). This involves making amends by compensating victims or restoring the situation to its earlier condition.

The strongest type of rectifying behavior is **repentance** ("We did something wrong, and here's what we are doing to make sure it never happens again"). This involves both a change of heart and a change of policy. It signals an organization's full atonement in the classic sense that it turns away from a former position and becomes an advocate for a new way of doing business.

DENNY'S

The story of Denny's restaurant chain is one of transformation from a symbol of corporate racism to a model of workplace diversity.

Denny's faced lawsuits for racial discrimination at several restaurants during the 1990s. One of the most notorious cases involved 21 members of the Secret Service. While 15 white agents were served quickly, a waitress and manager delayed serving six black agents for nearly an hour, allowing their food to get cold.

The ensuing publicity highlighted a series of lawsuits for similar acts of discrimination at other Denny's restaurants: Asian American students refused service and beaten by customers, Hispanic customers refused service, Muslim customers served pork after asking for a vegetarian menu, men of Middle Eastern descent kicked out of a restaurant and a blind woman refused service because she was accompanied by her service dog.

Denny's eventually paid $54 million (£34.5 million, €42.9 million) in legal settlements. The company's chief diversity officer later looked back on that "historic low point" in the company's history as presenting "huge opportunities. We had no place to go but up."

Dramatically, the company seems to have embraced the strategy of corporate repentance. It adopted an aggressive antidiscrimination policy that included hiring minority managers, training employees and firing those who discriminated. Denny's increased minority franchise ownership from 1 to 109 over 5 years (currently 40 percent of all Denny's franchises, and 44 percent of its board of directors are minorities and/or women.)

The company launched a $2 million (£1.2 million, €1.6 million) antidiscrimination advertising series. Each year it purchases goods worth more than $100 million (£63.8 million, €79.5 million) from minority vendors. It supports the King Center in Atlanta, civil rights groups and United Negro College Fund and has worked with the Hispanic Association on Corporate Responsibility and the NAACP.

A result of this turnaround is that Denny's ranked No. 1 in *Fortune* magazine's listing of best companies for minorities, two years running. It received similar awards from *Black Enterprise*, *Essence*, *Asian Enterprise* and *Hispanic Business* magazines.

This story is not without its irony. So successful is Denny's commitment to diversity, some white-nativist organizations called for boycotts because the company has become "too multicultural."

REACTIVE STRATEGY 7: DELIBERATE INACTION

Sometimes, the best response is no response. **Strategic silence** is the situation in which an organization does not respond to criticism, though it may take follow-up action. That was the case with Perrier, the upscale European company that produces bottled water. When cancer-causing benzene was discovered in some of the water, the company pulled millions of bottles from store shelves but refused to give any information to the news media.

A related approach is **strategic ambiguity**, the refusal to be pinned down to a particular response. This involves the artful dodging of a question, though often it's more a clear evasion of responding.

The final category is **strategic inaction**, neither making a statement nor taking any overt action. Instead, the organization simply waits it out and allows the situation to fade. While this may be a useful approach if the stakes are not too high, some problems do not fade away, especially those fanned by the opposition. By doing nothing, the organization risks allowing the problem to fester.

STATE DEPARTMENT

For years, the United States has walked a tightrope regarding the political status of Taiwan. China claims the island, but the US and a handful of other countries refuse to recognize this claim.

US diplomats have been deliberately vague, using strategic ambiguity to provide at least a semblance of options over the international dispute. The State Department uses terms such as "acknowledging" rather than "recognizing" a single Chinese political entity. US, UK and Canadian diplomats "take note of" rather than "support" Beijing's claim to be the legitimate government of China.

When President George W. Bush strayed from the standard party line and referred to Taiwan as a country, his aides quickly gave behind-the-scenes disclaimers that this was merely an informal designation and not a shift in US foreign policy.

WORKSHEET FOR STEP 5: FORMULATE ACTION AND RESPONSE STRATEGIES

Step 5 dealt with the "doing" part of a public relations campaign—what the organization does proactively or reactively. It grows from the notion that actions speak louder than words, reminding you to build your public relations message (in the next step) on a solid foundation of deeds.

Here are the basic questions to guide your planning for this step:

Action Strategies

1   If the organization is proactively initiating a public relations campaign, what kind of action or adaptation is appropriate?
2   What approach to news and information can be developed?

Response strategies

1   If the organization is responding to forces in its environment, to what extent is pre-emptive action appropriate?
2   ... offensive response?
3   ... defensive response?
4   ... diversionary response?
5   ... vocal commiseration?
6   ... rectifying behavior?
7   ... deliberate inaction?

PLANNING EXAMPLE FOR STEP 5

G^X is confident that its performance level is high. There have been no mishaps or embarrassments in recent years, and "graduates" of the engagement and exchange programs consistently give positive feedback. Additionally, the program involves careful training of staff and volunteers to provide high levels of service.

One strategy that G^X will undertake is to enhance *audience participation* by involving business leaders in planning for international activities. Another strategy is to forge strong *alliances* with like-minded organizations, particularly university exchange programs (which generally are long term) and shorter-term visits arranged through professional organizations.

G^X also will proactively seek to generate *newsworthy information* for local news media.

The one potentially negative incident involved a small but vocal group of single-issue dissidents in the community who rail against any international engagements because of an exaggerated sense of patriotism. Their message is that this country is No. 1 in its culture and thus does not need to engage with other countries. G^X will adopt a strategy of *strategic silence* toward these vocal opponents, who have shown from past incidents with other organizations that they are incapable of civil discussion and that, when they attract media attention, they discredit their own cause by their blatant and simple-minded diatribes against organizations that would participate in the international community.

STEP 6: DEVELOPING THE MESSAGE STRATEGY

Having identified publics (Step 3), established objectives (Step 4) and set into motion the way the organization is preparing to act to achieve those objectives (Step 5), it's time to turn your attention to the issue of how to communicate.

Effective public relations campaigns involve the sharing of information. Generally they also involve advocacy and attempts to persuade. Sometimes they aim for understanding, consensus building, conflict resolution and improved relationships. Communication is central to each of these models.

One way to approach communication planning is to look to the threefold analysis developed 23 centuries ago by Aristotle: Effective communication involves ethos, logos and pathos. That is, effective communication rests on a credible speaker, logical arguments and a sympathetic approach to storytelling.

ETHOS: SELECTING MESSAGE SOURCES

Years of research have produced a snapshot of an effective message source. This is someone who is credible, has charisma and exercises some kind of control over the audience.

Credibility is the power to inspire belief. Even audiences that don't understand an issue well often will accept a message from someone they think is believable. Credibility rests on how the audience perceives several qualities:

- The speaker is seen as an expert in the discipline being addressed.
- The speaker has a certain organizational or professional status.
- He or she is competent in speaking, remaining calm under pressure and able to articulate clearly.
- Finally, the credible speaker is perceived as being honest, both unbiased on the topic and not having a vested interest in it.

Charisma is the second characteristic of an effective message source. Charisma is a matter of perception, varying from one person to another. It has several components:

- A charismatic speaker is familiar to the audience.
- She or he is liked by the audience, at least to the extent that the audience thinks it knows the person.
- Generally, an effective charismatic speaker is similar to the audience, sharing (or appearing to share) its interests and values, and often reflecting demographic factors such as age, sex, race, ethnicity, religion, culture, sociopolitical perspectives and so on.
- Finally, and least importantly, a charismatic message source is seen as someone the audience considers to be physically attractive.

Control is the third quality of an effective message source. This is the extent to which a speaker has some command over the audience and the perceived willingness to exercise that control. It has three components:

- An effective speaker can exert a certain power over the audience, such as the ability to reward or punish.
- He or she may be in a position of authority, which implies that the audience more or less willingly has granted the right of control and thus will give obedience. The authority may be based on family, occupational, religious or some other important set of relationships in the life of audience members.
- The persuasive speaker has the ability to examine, giving scrutiny over members of the audience.

With this understanding of effective message sources, public relations strategists try to identify appropriate spokespersons to present their organizational message.

Some campaigns rely on celebrity spokespersons. Celebrities often are charismatic and familiar, but they aren't necessarily perceived as being credible. Nonprofit organizations such as charities for cancer and other diseases find that celebrities can attract attention to their cause. Social causes such as those focused on human rights, environmental issues and humanitarian concerns also find that star power can attract other supporters and donors.

But celebrities have baggage. Many organizations, both corporations and nonprofits, have been publicly embarrassed by their celebrity endorsers. Think of Tiger Woods, one of the highest-rated celebrities who annually earned $105 million (£63.8 million, €83.5 million) in endorsements before the scandal of his marriage and extramarital relationships.

Also, celebrities sometimes wish to avoid being linked with controversial products or partisan issues. Few celebrities would promote tobacco products, for example. While some feel strongly enough about politics to lend their name, others follow the example of Michael Jordan who, when asked to endorse a black Democrat in a senate election, refused "because Republicans buy sneakers too."

Some organizations rely on company spokespersons, on the notion that people close to the organization will be viewed as more expert. But expertise may not outweigh a perceived lack of credibility. Also, some company executives may not have the "stage presence" to be effective public spokespersons.

Your job at this point in the planning process is to identify the person (or perhaps several persons) to carry your message to the key publics.

CELEBRITY ENDORSERS

Businesses and nonprofit organizations have found that they need to exercise discretion in identifying celebrity spokespersons. Fame draws attention, but that attention is not always positive.

Soccer great David Beckham lost endorsements when British tabloid press reported that he had cheated on his wife. After the scandal died down, he emerged with a $10 million (£7.9 million, €6.3 million) contract with Gillette, followed by a $161 million (£103 million, €128 million) lifetime deal with Adidas.

Tiger Woods was earning $1 billion (£630 million, €800 million) in endorsements before his fall from grace (car accident, call girls, a bajillion extramarital affairs, public apology, messy divorce), which left him without his car, home, wife and endorsement contracts with Nike, AT&T, Gatorade and Gillette.

Other corporate sponsors have been embarrassed by their spokespersons: Michael Vicks (dropped by Nike, Coke, Hasbro, Reebok and Kraft for illegal dog fighting), Kate Moss (dropped by Chanel, Burberry and H&M Clothing after snorting cocaine on camera at a fashion show), Kirstie Alley (dropped by Jenny Craig after she gained more than a little weight) and Michael Phelps (dropped by Kellogg's after he was photographed taking a hit from a bong).

Cyclist Lance Armstrong began to distance himself from his own Livestrong foundation after being stripped of his Tour de France and Olympic titles and banned from the sport for life following numerous allegations of doping. He resigned as chairman of the foundation that originally bore his name and a few weeks later left its board of directors. Three months after that, the cyclist went on Oprah Winfrey's cable network to admit to the doping charges, despite his long-standing vociferous denials. Nike, Giro helmets, Trek bicycles, Oakley glasses, Radio Shack and Anheuser-Busch quickly canceled endorsement contracts worth an estimated $150 million (€113 million, £95 million), though several said they would continue to support Livestrong now that the cyclist had severed all ties with the cancer foundation.

Meanwhile, the social and political activism of some celebrities—Angelina Jolie, Sean Penn, Bono and Susan Sarandon, for example—has limited their commercial value as corporate spokespersons.

Some examples of wayward celebrity spokespersons fall into the "What were they thinking?" category. The Beef Industry Council dropped Cybill Shepherd after she revealed one of her beauty secrets: avoiding red meat. PETA publicly fired volunteer supermodel Naomi Campbell who had pledged not to wear natural fur after she wore it for fashion ads in Europe. And when Brylcreem sales dropped 25 percent after its celebrity hairdo guy David Beckham shaved his head, the soccer celeb lost his contract worth $7.9 million (£5 million, €6.3 million).

LOGOS: APPEALING TO REASON

Having selected the spokesperson, strategic planning next focuses on the content of the message. What will be said, and how will the message be framed?

Effective messages are built on solid reasoning, with clear claims and supportive evidence. The primary idea in a speech, editorial, advertisement, TV program or any type of communication—and there should be only one idea per message—is a **proposition**. There are four kinds of propositions:

- **Factual propositions** claim that something exists, such as urban air pollution or a link between education and income.
- **Conjecture propositions** state that something probably exists, such as likely outcomes of particular economic or political alternatives.
- **Value propositions** assert the merits or folly of something, such as health-care reform or school arts programs.
- **Policy propositions** identify courses of action and encourage adoption, such as advocating to change the legal drinking age or extending the school year.

Each proposition should be supported by evidence. When evidence is clear and indisputable, it's called **physical evidence**, and the proposition is easily provable. For example, if a city is spending more than it takes in, it clearly is dealing with an economic problem of major magnitude. As a factual proposition, that's an easy one.

But the parallel policy proposition—what to do about it?—may not be so easily resolved. Consider the various alternatives: raising taxes, selling off city-owned land, cutting services, reducing the workforce, reducing quality. Each of these impacts various principles and priorities, and there may be no clear solution on which everyone can agree.

Arguments for these alternatives rest on **verbal evidence**, which is less clear than physical evidence and open to varying interpretation. Verbal evidence takes various forms: analogy ("This problem is sort of like ..."), comparison ("This problem is similar to another"), example ("Here's an illustration of this problem"), statistics ("This data sheds light on the problem"), endorsement ("I'm famous, and I recommend this to you") and testimonial ("I've used this, and I recommend it to you").

PATHOS: APPEALING TO SENTIMENT

Human beings are not mere thinking machines. Much as we'd like to believe that we make decisions logically and based on evidence, we also rely heavily on feelings. Effective communication strategists take this into account and build an emotional appeal.

Some emotional appeals are positive. Here are a few types.

- A **love appeal** can feature various approaches: bittersweet poignancy, family togetherness, nostalgia, pity, compassion, romance, sensitivity, sympathy and more. Pleasant images lead consumers to remember the persuasive message because it makes them feel good.
- A **virtue appeal** can evoke any of the various values that society or individuals hold in esteem: justice, loyalty, bravery, piety, social tolerance and so on. Consider how natural disasters such as earthquakes and floods inspire volunteerism, blood donations and financial contributions to relief agencies.
- A **humor appeal** harnesses the power of comedy and amusement to gain attention and make the speaker more likeable. But humor gets old fast. In today's 24/7 news cycle, it's risky when politicians or organizational spokespeople repeat jokes or humorous incidents that were previously communicated to a wide audience. Additionally, for humor to be effective it should be relevant, tasteful, perhaps self-deprecating but not disparaging of others, and above all funny (not an easy thing to achieve when what is funny to one person may be droll, too cute, ludicrous or simply unfunny to others).
- A **sex appeal** can range from nudity to double entendres to shock. Messages with sex appeal can be effective in gaining attention, though whether the attention is positive or negative depends on the audience. But sex appeal is notoriously bad at linking the message with long-term retention and eventual action.

Persuasive messages sometimes are based on one of two negative emotions. Used in moderation, these can be powerful advocacy tools.

- A **fear appeal** is intended to arouse anxiety or worry among audiences. Political messages often are based on fear (such as pending economic doom, high taxation, erosion of rights and freedom). So, too, with advertisements for some health products (tooth decay) and grooming aids (body odor). For fear appeals to be effective, they should be moderate in the amount of anxiety they generate, and they should be capped with an easy-to-achieve resolution of the problem (buy this product, vote for my candidate, use that medicine).
- A **guilt appeal** is another common persuasive technique, particularly in the area of marketing communication and fund-raising. Like fear appeals, this approach is best done in moderation. For example, seeking support for refugees by making readers a bit uneasy in their relative comfort can become a turn-off if the guilt level becomes too intense. Also like fear appeals, guilt-based messages should feature solutions to the problem of conscience that they raise.
- A **hate appeal**, though sometimes effective in a short-term situation, is unethical at its base and is not used by true public relations professionals.

EFFECTIVE VERBAL COMMUNICATION

Both kinds of appeals—logical and emotional—can be communicated verbally or nonverbally. **Verbal communication** involves the right words, and the right use of those words. Here are some of the elements associated with effective verbal communication.

- **Message Structure.** Research suggests that one-sided arguments are useful in reinforcing opinions, especially among friendly audiences with low knowledge levels. Two-sided arguments that present both pros and cons are more effective with better-educated or undecided audiences. A common technique is to sandwich the message, first presenting your positive message, then refuting opposing points, and finally restating your theme.
- **Message Content.** Effective messages have several common elements. They use simple language that can be clearly understood by the audience. They offer what advertisers call the **unique selling proposition**, that clear statement of the benefit to the

audience. They involve **grabbers** or power words that get attention and are easily recalled ("eco friendly," "job creators," "human rights"). They also feature memorable quotes and strong product or program names. Finally, they use ethical language that does not stretch beyond the breaking point, as well as language that respects legal issues such as defamation and privacy.

Nonverbal communication occurs through actions and cues other than words. Some estimates are that 80 percent of what we learn comes to us nonverbally.

A whole range of body language issues can communicate information to us. These include eye behavior, facial expressions, touch and space between people. There also is a wide range of external aspects of visual communication. Here are some of these.

- **Symbols** can be powerful emotional elements of communication. Some are general, such as the national flag and wedding rings. Others are issue-specific symbols such as baby harp seals and pink breast-cancer ribbons. Certain photos take on a symbolic value, such as the attack on the World Trade Center or the iconic Vietnam-era photo of the running girl who was burned by napalm.
- **Corporate logos** identify businesses, nonprofit organizations and other groups. Some, such as the Nike swoosh or the Olympic rings have become so descriptive that often they no longer need the words.
- **Music** often has a symbolic value, such as the singing of a national anthem or songs associated with birthdays, holidays and religious events, even sport.
- **Language** itself takes on symbolic tones, often when it is used within religious traditions or in discussions of official national languages, such as some of the language issues in Quebec, many of the Southwestern states in the US, and among indigenous peoples throughout the world.
- **Physical artifacts and clothing** sometimes become symbolic—a judge's gavel, burning of a religious book, or wearing of a police uniform or religious garb. Clothing has symbolic significance in many countries and cultures.

- **People** such as the queen, the Dalai Lama and the pope sometimes are used symbolically.
- **Mascots** sometimes serve as symbols, such as Ronald McDonald, Smokey Bear or the Philly Phanatic, or more generically the koala or the panda.

BRANDING THE STRATEGIC MESSAGE

A concept drawn from marketing, **branding**, means the creation of a clear and consistent message for an organization. The purpose of branding, which is rooted in a strategic communications plan, is to foster understanding and goodwill and to encourage participation and support.

Corporations have been using branding for years. A car dealership has "the greatest deals in town." This toothpaste cleans "better than all the rest." That medical facility is "the hospital preferred by women."

Note that these branding statements have an implied comparison with the competition. Would it be appropriate for an educational institution to claim to be "the state's best university" or an environmental action group to proclaim itself "more effective than all the other tree-huggers put together"? Probably not, but the university may want to be known as "a top educator for science and technology" and the conservation group as having "proven results in saving the woodlands."

This step of the strategic planning process ends with attention to the message package. It may involve a **slogan**, a succinct catch-phrase that has been called a **verbal logo**. Nokia is about "Connecting People." At Allstate insurance, "You're in good hands." "Take action for the climate" is what Greenpeace wants.

Note that branding takes us back to the positioning statement in Step 4, where we began thinking strategically about the public relations situation and desired outcomes.

WORKSHEET FOR STEP 6: DEVELOP THE MESSAGE STRATEGY

In Step 6, you have considered the practical elements of the message: who will serve as spokesperson, how you might appeal to both logic and sentiment, how you can be effective in both verbal and nonverbal communication.

Here are the basic questions to get you started:

1   Who will be the spokesperson for this campaign? Why?
2   What is the logical part of the message (the proposition and evidence for it)?
3   What emotional appeal(s) can be used in this campaign?
4   How does this come together with a slogan or branded message?

Follow-up questions regarding the message source might deal with ways to enhance the perceived credibility of your spokesperson. When considering message appeals, consider the appropriate balance between the two.

Finally, flesh out verbal communication by giving your attention to creating a clear and understandable message and using powerful language in your message. Give attention to the various elements of nonverbal communication—symbols, logos, music and so on—that can enhance your message.

PLANNING EXAMPLE FOR STEP 6

There will be two *spokespersons* for this campaign.

- Sophie Mercier is G^X executive director. She is articulate in speech, professional in demeanor and quick with information and anecdotes about the exchange and engagement program and the benefits that past participants and companies have enjoyed.
- Kito Kawa-Jones is a young engineer with Serene Gardens Landscape Design in this community. He participated in a four-month exchange program in Japan, allowing his company to expand its professional services and increase its customer base.

The *logical element* of the message consists of facts and data about the low-cost, high personal benefits to participants and parallel benefits to employers in terms of productivity, professional networking and enhanced service to customers.

The *emotional element* consists of messaging about the value of personal development, the adventure of international work and significance of an added professional credential.

Branding will consist of several variations, from the humorous "Help your boss. Leave the country." to the more serious "Forging global alliances for local businesses."

7

PUBLIC RELATIONS PLANNING
PHASE 3: TACTICS

The tactical phase of the planning process focuses on the vehicles of communication. This chapter gives you an overview of the many and varied ways to present the organization's message and engage its publics.

If strategy is the skeleton and muscles for your communication program, tactics are the flesh. **Tactics** are the visible elements of a public relations or marketing communications program, the specific communication venues through which an organization interacts with its publics.

STEP 7: SELECTING COMMUNICATION TACTICS

Communication tactics range from websites to video news releases, tours to billboards, blogs to podcasts, tweets to brochures. They are the visible element of the strategic plan.

Various categories have been offered for communication tactics. Media are called controlled or uncontrolled, depending on the amount of influence the organization has over the message presentation. They sometimes are defined as internal or external media, reflecting their relationship with the organization. Another characterization is as mass media or targeted media, indicating the size of the audience.

Other designations include one-way versus interactive media, public versus nonpublic media, and popular or trade media. Sometimes they are designated by the means of production: print, electronic or digital media.

All of these descriptors can be useful in some ways. But for reviewing the full inventory of communication vehicles that can be used in a public relations campaign, consider a fourfold sorting as the media relate to the organization: interpersonal communication tools, organizational media, news media and advertising-promotional media. These are the categories we'll look at here. (Some of these should look familiar to you because they are included in the comprehensive listing of public relations writing formats at the beginning of Chapter 4.)

INTERPERSONAL COMMUNICATION TACTICS

The most persuasive and engaging of all communication tactics are those associated with **interpersonal communication**. Other tactics may be more prestigious or more cost-effective in communicating with large numbers of people, but in terms of persuasive effectiveness, interpersonal venues can't be beaten.

The premise underlying interpersonal tactics is that the organization takes its message directly to its publics. The tactics themselves usually are relatively inexpensive, though they often require personnel resources. These tactics are particularly useful with **information-seeking publics** (people who are actively looking for information about a topic).

Some types of interpersonal communication tactics focus on **personal involvement**. When the organization wishes to provide information and education or to engage in persuasion or dialogue, it often turns to tactics of personal involvement. These may be venues associated with the organization or audience sites.

Interpersonal tactics also include various kinds of **information exchange**. Various types of meetings provide an opportunity for both commercial and nonprofit organizations to meet face-to-face with their publics. These include educational gatherings, product exhibitions, rallies and speeches.

Another grouping of interpersonal communication tactics involves **special events**, which are activities created by an organization mainly to provide a venue within which to interact with its publics. The list of special events is bounded only by the imagination of the planner. Some of the common types include civic events, sporting activities, contests, holiday events, progress-oriented happenings, historic commemorations, social events, fundraising activities, artistic events and general publicity events. All seek to gain attention for an organization or its cause.

Here is a listing of various interpersonal communication tactics:

PERSONAL INVOLVEMENT

- Organizational site involvement (plant tour, open house, test drive, trial membership, free class, shadow program, ride along, sneak preview, premiere performance).
- Audience site involvement (door-to-door canvassing, in-home demonstration).

INFORMATION EXCHANGE

- Educational gathering (convention, council, convocation, synod, conclave, conference, seminar, symposium, colloquium, class, workshop, training session).
- Product exhibition (trade show).
- Meeting (annual stockholder meeting, lobbying exchange, public affairs meeting).
- Rally (demonstration, march, picket, boycott).
- Speech (oration, talk, guest lecture, address, keynote speech, sermon, homily, panel, debate, forum, town meeting, speakers bureau).

SPECIAL EVENT

- Civic event (fair, festival, carnival, circus, parade, flotilla).
- Sporting event (tournament, marathon, triathlon, outdoor spectator event, track meet, field days, rodeo, games, match, run).
- Contest (science fair, spelling bee, beauty pageant, talent contest, cook-off, dance-a-thon).
- Holiday event.

- Progress-oriented event (launching, procession, motorcade, ground-breaking ceremony, cornerstone ceremony, dedication, ribbon-cutting, tour, grand opening).
- Historic commemoration (founders' days, anniversary, centennial, play, pageant, caravan, re-enactment).
- Social event (luncheon, banquet, roast, awards dinner, recognition lunch, party, dance, reception, fashion show, tea).
- Artistic event (concert, concert tour, recital, play, film festival, art show, photo exhibit).
- Fundraising event (antiques show, auction, haunted house, pony ride, murder mystery dinner theater, fashion show, house or garden tour, tasting party).
- Publicity event (photo op).

ORGANIZATIONAL MEDIA TACTICS

A host of communication vehicles are managed by each organization and can be used at its discretion. These media generally are controlled, internal, nonpublic media, such as publications, direct mail, miscellaneous print media, and audiovisual or digital media.

Organizational media tactics can be the most useful tools for public relations, because they allow the organization to take its message directly to its publics, along the way controlling the timing, content, presentation and feedback. These tactics are most useful with information-seeking publics. These tactics can be expensive but, because they can be targeted to specific publics, often they are cost-effective in comparison with other types of tactics.

One type of organizational media tactic involves **publications**, which are materials published and printed by the organization. These can be serial publications such as newsletters or stand-alone brochures and fliers. Reprints also fit into this category, as well as progress and research reports.

Direct mail is another category of organizational media. These involve letters, memos and postcards, as well as catalogs.

Electronic media offer many opportunities for public relations. These include audio media such as phone messages and podcasts, video media involving non-broadcast video (also called corporate video) and electronic publishing.

Digital media allow for online publication of any of the print materials associated with organizational tactics. Digital media, which also involve mobile devices and websites, increasingly are becoming a mainstay of public relations message dissemination.

A final category of organizational tactics is **social media**, a still-emerging phenomenon that allows for much interaction with publics. These involve blogs and wikis, as well as social networking and file sharing sites.

Here is a listing of various organizational media tactics:

GENERAL PUBLICATIONS

- Serial publication (newsletter, bulletin).
- Stand-alone publication (brochure, flier, booklet, folder, pamphlet, tract, circular, fact sheet, FAQ).
- Progress report (annual report, quarterly report).
- User kit.
- Research report.
- Miscellaneous print media.

DIRECT MAIL

- Memo.
- Letter (appeal letter, marketing letter).
- Postcard.
- Invitation.
- Catalog (retail, full-line, specialty, business-to-business).

ELECTRONIC MEDIA

- Audio media (telephone, dial-a-message, recorded information, voice mail, toll-free line, demo tape, demo CD, podcast).
- Video media (non-broadcast video, videoconference, teleconference, videotape, slide show).
- Digital media (presentation software, e-mail, listserv, Internet, newsgroup, websites, web homepage, web-based television or radio, touch-sensitive computer, cell phone).
- Electronic publishing.

SOCIAL MEDIA

- Wiki.
- Blog.

- Social networking.
- File sharing sites.

NEWS MEDIA TACTICS

The **news media** are communication vehicles that exist primarily as businesses that present newsworthy information to various audiences. Print media includes newspapers and magazines of various types and categories. Broadcast media includes radio and television, which can be delivered over the air, on cable, digitally or via satellite. Increasingly, digital media provide for online dissemination of information and interaction between organizations and their audiences.

Whether print media, broadcast media or interactive news tactics, collectively they present many opportunities for public relations.

The advantage of working through news media is that they generally feature large and/or highly involved audiences. They offer a significant credibility to organizations they report on, offering what is called **third-party endorsement**. This means that media **gatekeepers** such as editors and news directors have considered all the information available to them and selected this information to share with their audiences. This vetting process gives credibility and prestige to organizational information disseminated through the news media.

A second major benefit of the news media is that publicity is free. There is no charge to the organization when an editor or news director decides to report news about the organization.

The downside is that the content of publicity is not controlled by the organization. With the benefit of third-party endorsement comes the loss of control over the content, timing and context. Even the decision of whether the information is published or broadcast at all is left to the media gatekeeper.

News reports generally are much briefer than the organization would write about itself.

The biggest limitation of working through the news media is that the information must be **newsworthy**. It must be something that media gatekeepers consider of relevance to their audiences, not merely information or data that the organization hopes to publicize.

Public relations practitioners provide media with **news subsidies**, a term for the information provided proactively by the organization or in response to media inquiries. Information subsidies are part of the reciprocal and symbiotic relationship between journalism and public relations. Journalists need public relations people to provide information and access so they can report the news. Public relations practitioners need journalists who provide the venue for their news releases, opinion pieces and other vehicles for information about the organization.

Here is a listing of various news media tactics:

DIRECT INFORMATION SUBSIDY

- News fact sheet (bulleted newsworthy information: who, what, when, where, why, how, quotes, background info).
- Event listing (brief about upcoming activity or event).
- Interview notes (transcript of interview with organizational expert).
- News release (news story written by a public relations practitioner and given to media gatekeepers to use edited or unedited; types include announcement, response, hometowner and news brief).
- Feature release (story on background aspect of the news, written by a public relations practitioner and given to media gatekeepers to use edited or unedited; types include biography, history, backgrounder, question-and-answer piece and service article/how-to piece).
- Actuality (sound bite for radio).
- Audio news release (radio release with actuality).
- B-roll (sound bite for television).
- Video news release (TV release with B-roll).
- E-mail release.
- Social media release (news report prepared for blogs, websites and other online forums).
- Media kit (collection of news releases and related material on a particular topic or news event).
- Online newsroom (organizational website with current and archived news releases and other direct information subsidies).

INDIRECT NEWS SUBSIDY

- Media advisory (note to media gatekeepers about upcoming news opportunity).

- Story idea memo (news-oriented tip sheet informing gate-keepers of interview subject or topic).
- Query letter (promotional letter urging media gatekeepers to do an interview or use something written by a public relations practitioner).

OPINION SUBSIDY

- Position statement (factual background with opinion-based conclusion; types include position paper, white paper, position paragraph and contingency statement).
- Letter to the editor.
- Guest editorial or op-ed piece.

INTERACTIVE MEDIA ENGAGEMENT

- News interview (question-answer session by reporter one-on-one with organizational news source).
- News conference (organizational announcement with group interview of organizational news source by various reporters).
- Studio interview (hybrid between interview and news conference; often reporter or commentator with individual or panel of news sources and opinion commentators).
- Satellite media tour (in-studio interview mediated by satellite, with reporter/commentator in one location and interviewees elsewhere).
- Editorial conference (meeting between organizational news sources with editors and editorial boards of newspaper or other news media).

ADVERTISING AND PROMOTIONAL MEDIA TACTICS

The final category of communication tactics involves media associated with advertising and promotion. The advantages are that these media can provide a large and/or highly specialized audience, and the organization can control the content, timing and presentation style.

The disadvantage is that these media are tremendously expensive. For example, a full-page in the *New York Times* can cost $158,000,

£30,000 for the *Daily Mail* in the UK, AUS$51,000 for the *Australian*, €417,000 for *Bild* newspaper in Germany. Television can cost £250,000 for a 30-second commercial in England, while in the US a half minute of network primetime advertising on a top-rated series can range up to $500,000. Cable network advertising targeted at key publics is considerably less.

When ad costs are considered on the basis of the number of viewers, media advertising can deliver a low cost-per-impression. But generally the advertising message spills over to many people who are not key publics for the organization and who have little or no interest in the message, thereby creating a significant waste of advertising money. Targeted media, thus, can be more cost-effective.

Here is a list of advertising and promotional media tactics:

PRINT ADVERTISING MEDIA

- Magazine advertising (full/partial page, center spread, advertorial, breakout ads that vary with geographic region or audience profile).
- Newspaper advertising (display ad, classified ad).
- Directory advertising.
- House advertising (such as program brochures).

ELECTRONIC MEDIA ADVERTISING

- Television commercial (network placement, spot local commercial, infomercial).
- Cable TV advertising (network placement, spot local commercial, cable crawl).
- Radio commercial (network radio, spot local commercial, online ad).
- Digital media advertising (pop-up ad, virtual ad).

OUT-OF-HOME ADVERTISING

- Outdoor poster (billboard, poster, digital billboard, wallscape).
- Arena poster (print or electronic ads in sport venue).
- Signage.
- Out-of-home video.

- Transit advertising (bus sign, train/subway car card, station poster, shelter poster, mobile billboard).
- Aerial advertising (blimp, airplane tow, skywriting).
- Miscellaneous media, such as outdoor public furniture, street fixtures and pavement notices or drawings.

PROMOTIONAL ITEMS

- Clothing.
- Costume.
- Office accessory.
- Home accessory.

WORKSHEET FOR STEP 7: SELECT COMMUNICATION TACTICS

In Step 7, you created a list of communication vehicles to carry your organization's message to your publics, selecting among various tactics associated with interpersonal communication, organizational media, news media, and advertising and promotional media.

Here are the basic questions for this worksheet:

1 What interpersonal communication tactics will be part of this strategic plan?
2 What organizational media tactics?
3 What news media tactics?
4 What advertising and promotional media tactics?

PLANNING EXAMPLE FOR STEP 7

G^X will use the following interpersonal communication tactics:

- Client-site seminars about the exchange program.
- Speeches before business–civic organizations.
- Sponsorship presence at golf tournament for junior and mid-level business professionals.
- Historic commemoration luncheon for 25th anniversary of the first G^X-sponsored exchange.

Organizational media tactics:

- Annual progress report for donors, sponsoring organizations, and prospective exchange candidates.
- Survey with follow-up research report on attitudes and opinions of area leaders in business, nonprofits, higher education and government on the value of international insight and experience.
- Online catalog of exchange possibilities.
- Enhanced website with exchange information, testimonials and placement opportunities.
- Online video presentation of 10-minute documentary of G^X programs.

News media tactics:

- News release to local newspapers, business publications, business radio programs and television stations announcing exchange opportunities (three per year).
- Story idea memo for interview opportunity with returning exchange participants.
- Feature release focused on returning exchange participants.
- Guest editorial on value of international experience for local businesses.

Advertising and promotional media:

- Advertisement in local business newspaper.
- Advertisement on local radio business program.

STEP 8: IMPLEMENTING THE STRATEGIC PLAN

Now that you have a full plate of ways to present your message and engage your publics, turn your attention to implementing these tactics. Try to turn the inventory of tactics into a logical and cohesive program.

The task here is to create a program or theme to bind the tactics together in a way that will appeal to the organization's publics. When you read a restaurant menu, you often make selections based on a particular culinary focus: Japanese, Tex-Mex, Southern, Italian, Middle Eastern and so on.

It's unlikely that you would start with tuna sashimi, add lamb-and-saffron harira soup with pita, feature jalapeño chili relleno as main course, add sides of grits and ravioli, and end with a flaming cherries jubilee for dessert, served with ouzo and Pepsi Max. Gastric nightmare!

Rather, you'd probably develop a culinary theme. You would creatively package your choices to concoct a special dining experience fitting the occasion, appropriate for your dining companions, and suitable to your resources, needs and interests.

The same is true with strategic planning for communication. Package your tactics to achieve your objectives. Make this more than a simple "to do" list. Consider how various tactics can be woven together, and group them around the themes associated with the strategic planning from Steps 5 and 6.

Think creatively as you approach this step. For example, if you have a new organizational logo to unveil, consider making it a real unveiling. How about a ceremonial removal of a sequined cloth covering the logo? One nonprofit organization introduced a new logo by involving five local political and media celebrities who each gave a short testimonial about the organization and then, one by one, placed together cut-out pieces of a giant jigsaw puzzle to create the new logo.

Some organizations have specially designed vehicles used for promotion and other public relations objectives. United Parcel Service has a miniature delivery truck to give its "Big Brown" branding visibility with potential customers. UPS uses these trucks in athletic arenas to deliver a coin for the ceremonial coin toss, such as at the start of football games.

Some award-winning campaigns have found their success through such creativity, such as the "man sled" race by Snausages (see Step 3, special events). Here are some other examples.

ORGAN DONOR PROGRAM

"Organ donor" is a negative reference to motorcycle riders, generally by four-wheeled folks who don't understand the passion for biking. But the nonprofit, Lifeline of Ohio, creatively embraced the term as a double entendre, changing it from an insult to a positive.

Its "Live on – Ride on" campaign involved face-to-face communication through booths set up at various biker events. The campaign also provided bold graphics, including a logo that could be added to motorcycles, as well as patches, T-shirts and other material for cyclists' clothing and gear.

The campaign received significant media coverage both in newspapers and on several blogs and other websites. It also had support through social media such as the group's Facebook page, creating new Facebook friends and Twitter followers. Search-engine traffic increased 91 percent during the campaign.

The result was that "Live on – Ride on" registered 3,000 new organ donors among motorcyclists in Central and Southeastern Ohio in its first year, with thousands more expected over the four-year cycle for renewing driver's licenses.

Since 2010, when Lifeline of Ohio won a Silver Anvil from the Public Relations Society of America for its campaign, similar donor-procurement programs in other states have looked at "Live on – Ride on" as a model.

SWINE FLU

AMResorts and its public relations agency got creative to combat health worries. The company's Mexican resort hotels were only half-full in 2009 because of fears of an H1N1 swine flu pandemic.

The company was convinced that the media-fueled fear was unfounded. It was so sure of this that it issued a "flu-free guarantee." The guarantee promised that any guest who contracted swine flu at one of its resorts would get free return visits over each of the next three years. Bookings shot up 140 percent.

Several other resort chains imitated the guarantee, and the Mexican government praised AMResorts for helping get Mexico's economy back to recovery.

CONFUSED.COM

A public relations agency in England helped raise brand awareness of Confused.com, an auto-insurance company. Goals included driving traffic to the company website, increasing visibility and generating requests for insurance quotes.

Company statistics identified the most accident-prone street in the United Kingdom: Somerville Road in Worcester. Eight people worked 12 hours to bubble wrap the entire street. Nearly 1,800 square yards (1,500 square meters) of bubble wrap covered cars and trucks, houses, bicycles, dog houses, swing sets, trees and shrubs, even garden gnomes.

The light-hearted publicity event carried a serious message about the dangers of winter driving, raising it well above the level of a mere publicity stunt. Rather, it was a means of attracting media attention to a serious issue of public safety.

The public relations planners contacted established news media, including major national newspapers. They engaged social media by posting photos on Twitter, Flickr and Facebook.

The combined buzz attracted more than 125 million viewers to blogs and articles, and the story was picked up by international news media in Australia and North America. The company website saw a 20 percent increase in visitors on the first day of the publicity event, which passed its objective of generating an additional 4,000 requests for insurance quotes.

In a final burst of publicity, the bubble wrap was donated to Oxfam, the international NGO, that used it to package aid being sent to earthquake victims in Haiti.

OXFAM

Oxfam is an international confederation of organizations that respond to humanitarian crises, work on the long-term development of sustainable livelihoods and campaign for changes in policies that reinforce injustice and poverty.

To call attention to an international conference on global climate change in Copenhagen, Oxfam wanted to highlight the danger of climate change in a creative way.

The organization set up the scene of a family living underwater, with a living room installed at the bottom of a shark tank at the London Aquarium. It was a typical family enjoying a meal together, except that parents and kids were wearing scuba masks and air tanks.

Oxfam invited news organizations and photographers to record the spectacle. The creative tactic was a top news story on BBC, Al Jazeera and Sky News beamed throughout the world. Blogs and Internet news sites featured it, as well as newspapers in the US, China and Australia.

PUTTING THE PROGRAM TOGETHER

Review the information gathered during the Research phase (Steps 1, 2 and 3), and the first part of the Strategy phase (Step 4). Then consider several different ways to package the tactics you have chosen. No particular format is best for every issue, so let common sense be your guide. Consider the most distinctive element of your program, and select the format that is likely to make the best impression on your colleagues, boss or client.

- **Packaging by Media Category**. This approach lists each tactic according to the outline of media categories from Step 7 (interpersonal, organizational, news and advertising/promotional tactics). With each tactic, list the relevant publics and objectives. This format may be a good starting point in organizing the tactics and in making sure that all publics and objectives are covered. But it usually is not the most creative approach.
- **Packaging by Public**. If the main focus of the campaign is appealing to several different publics, it may make sense to package the campaign that way. List the objectives and associated tactics for Public A, then for Public B, Public C and so on. This format clearly distinguishes among the various publics (for example, a hospital fundraising campaign that is reaching out both to former patients and to philanthropic donors).
- **Packaging by Goal**. If the plan has two or more significant goals, look at that as the distinguishing characteristic. For example, if a nonprofit organization has a campaign to increase visibility for a new program and to raise funds to support it, list

the publics, objectives and tactics associated with each of the two goals.

- **Packaging by Objective**. Similarly, if the plan is built around a single goal, perhaps the various objectives supporting it provide the best framework. List publics and tactics for each objective (awareness, acceptance and action).
- **Packaging by Department**. Sometimes the internal structure of the organization suggests a way to distinguish among the distinctive elements of the plan. Consider identifying goals, objectives, publics and tactics as they relate to various departments, divisions or organizational programs.

CAMPAIGN PLAN BOOK

The **campaign plan book** or more simply, the book—is the formal written presentation of your research findings and program recommendations for strategy, tactics and evaluation. This report should be concise in writing, professional in style, and confident in tone.

The plan book should include a title page, executive summary, an optional table of contents (if the plan book is detailed enough to warrant this), situation analysis (summarizing Steps 1, 2 and 3), strategic approach (summarizing Steps 4, 5 and 6), tactical program including schedule and budget (Steps 7 and 8) and evaluation plan (Step 9).

The book often ends with the consultant's credentials and resources, and sometimes includes a statement of principles indicating the philosophy and professional ethics that undergird the campaign.

Here's an example of a hypothetical outline for one tactic, an open house as part of a campaign proposal for a new graduate program in architecture at a university in a mid-sized city. This shows the internal linkage between the tactic, previously identified publics, already determined objectives and strategy, administrative details such as budgeting, and subsequent evaluation methods.

- *Public*: Professional architects (specifically, approximately 145 practicing architects within a three-county area).
- *Objective*: To increase the understanding of professional architects about the new program (50 percent of the professional

community prior to beginning the academic program; with 25 percent attending open house).

- *Strategy*: Attract attention of the professional community and create a core of opinion leaders; give specific attention to leading architects, particularly those who have received recognition from the Midstate Association of Professional Architects.
- *Tactical Elements*:

    1 Publicity elements including news release and fact sheets (no cost).
    2 Promotional materials including news release, e-mail invitations, Facebook note, and outreach to appropriate blogs ($100).
    3 Advertising: 1/8-page ad in local business/professional weekly newspaper ($500 value; actual cost $350 with non-profit/education discount).
    4 Information materials including an eight-minute video ($15,000 value; actual cost $1,000 with in-house production by broadcasting students).
    5 Information packet for visitors, with parallel information at website ($200).
    6 Open House logistical support including reserved space and parking arrangements ($100 for two student police aides).
    7 Open House hospitality: snacks and beverages ($1,000 value; actual cost $500 with catering by university students majoring in Culinary Arts as a promotion for their new catering service).

- *Budget*: $19,900 value; actual cost $2,250.
- *Evaluation Methods*: Attendance figures; follow-up mini-survey as part of a follow-up telephone call thanking people who attended.
- *Oversight*: Assistant Director of Community Relations.

In a complete proposal, each tactic would receive similar treatment. Even individual tactics might have multiple components. For example, the open house noted earlier might have additional publics, perhaps donors or potential students. Each of these would require its own statement of objectives and strategies, though the budget and evaluation methods may remain constant.

CAMPAIGN SCHEDULE

Implementing the strategic plan calls for establishing a timeline of when various activities need to be done. This involves two considerations: (1) the pattern and frequency of the communication tactics and (2) the actual timeline of tasks to be accomplished as the tactics are implemented.

Two concepts drawn from marketing and advertising are helpful in the implementation stage of a public relations plan. Message **frequency** deals with the number of times and the pattern (continuous, pulsing and so on) in which messages are presented to a particular public. Message **reach** refers to the number of different people who are exposed to a single message.

Research into message frequency shows that one presentation is never enough. That's why public relations practitioners look for multiple and overlapping ways to communicate with, and otherwise engage, their publics. The same message should be repeated and reinforced through various media and over time. Too-frequent repetitions seem unnecessarily redundant, but messages that are given only infrequently often fail to build awareness.

Your decision here is about how much and how often to communicate. If you are not sure, err on the side of too much (because it's almost impossible to communicate too much).

Planners also develop timelines of tasks, often working backwards from a key implementation date. For example, if a brochure is to be mailed by June 1, it may need to be received from the printer by May 21, with time remaining to add address labels and prepare it for mailing. To achieve this, copy would have to be delivered to the printer May 15, final copy approved May 10, first copy draft completed May 1, writing and design work begun April 15, and approval for objectives and budget by April 7. Thus planning would need to begin no later than April 1.

CAMPAIGN BUDGET

Identifying resources needed for each tactic is an important part of the implementation stage. At every turn of the planning process, you need to be practical. Consider budget constraints and limitations so the recommendations will be realistic, practical and doable.

Budgeting is about more than money. It deals with all needed resources, including personnel, material, media costs, equipment and facilities, and administrative costs. Here's how each category factors into the final budget.

Personnel items in a budget include the number of people and the amount of time needed to achieve the results expected of the tactic and the cost of this. Include both organizational and outside people (consultants, agency staff, subcontracted specialists and freelance workers). Make sure to account for salaried public relations staff within the organization. Though they may already be on salary, the value of their time associated with each particular tactic should be included in the full campaign budget.

Material items in a budget are the tangible "things" associated with each tactic. This may be paper for brochures, banners and food for an open house, media kits for a news conference, software for an online newsroom and so on. Each of these carries a price tag. A good budget itemizes each separately, allowing planners to make adjustments if the total cost estimate comes in over the expected budget.

Money needed to purchase time and space for advertising is part of the media cost. These costs are set by the publication, station or other advertising venue. The basic cost (such as the per-column-inch rate in newspapers or the per-second cost for air time) varies as placement frequency increases.

Budgets often include a 15 percent surcharge as a commission or agency fee or to cover in-house overhead expenses. Public relations agencies sometimes bill all out-of-pocket expenses at cost plus 15 percent.

There also may be costs for equipment and facilities. This budget category includes the cost of new computers or scanners needed for a newsletter, for example, or software to create a blog. Because these often are one-time expenditures, they might be calculated on a percentage basis to amortize the cost over potential uses after this campaign is completed. This category might also include expenses such as transportation fees for a portable outdoor stage or the cost of leasing a banquet hall.

Finally, administrative items also are included in the budget. These include the cost of telephone, delivery, photocopying and travel costs. Some organizations add a 15 percent surcharge to cover standard office expenses, often with a separate category for travel-related costs.

Make sure to include the full cost of all the tactics, even if some do not have a specific price tag. Note donated or contributed services, such as the value of volunteer time. Also figure financial support that nonprofit organizations sometimes receive, such as support from a corporation that offers to print its brochures, discounted consulting fees, or the actual cost of a video production that is produced pro bono by a media sponsor.

Also, try to provide a range of costs for tactics. This will help if the organization needs to trim costs. Rather than eliminate entire tactics, a cost range might allow the organization simply to choose some less-expensive options. For example, you might cost out a brochure for both one color and full color.

Finally, determine just how much success is necessary. Calculate this as the break-even point. Identify the total project cost; determine the dollar value for each desired outcome; and divide the total cost by that value. Let's say a private college will spend $160,000 of its recruiting budget for brochures, an informational video, paid radio commercials and billboards. Let's add $10,000 for salaries and freelance fees associated with the projects. Add another $10,000 for postage, travel, and other administrative costs. That's $180,000 for the total project cost.

Now let's presume that tuition at this college is $35,000. Apply the formula: cost $180,000 divided by outcome value $35,000 equals five-plus. That's the break-even point. Thus the brochure/video/commercial/billboard program has to recruit six new students just the pay for itself. After that, the income is profit.

Another useful tool is the per-capita cost, the total cost associated with the number of people needed to cover that cost. Using the college scenario, divide the project cost by the number of new recruits (let's say that's 1,600). Apply the formula: $180,000 divided by 1,600, which equals $113—the amount of money the college spends to recruit each new student through these tactics. That's about a third of a penny for every dollar received in tuition.

DEVELOPING A LONG-TERM BUDGET FOR PUBLIC RELATIONS

Budgeting is more than merely adding up the costs of various tactics for specific projects. It's part of the strategic management of an organization.

The question often comes up: How much should an organization spend on public relations? There is no simple answer, no one-size-fits-all formula. That's because so much depends on variables: the nature of the issue being addressed, the current relationship of the publics, the objectives sought, the tactics employed and so on.

Here are some various approaches to budgeting for public relations:

- **Competitive Parity**. This approach bases the budget on the level of similar activity by major competitors. Hospital A may set its budget for attracting new patients by matching the apparent budget of neighboring Hospital B. That involves guesswork, and it doesn't take into account the varying circumstances of each hospital.

- **Same-as-Before Budgeting**. This approach looks at how much the organization spent on a similar recent project and allows the same budget, perhaps adjusted for inflation. This presumes the first project was successful and worth imitating. It also assumes that the two projects are similar enough for the first to be a benchmark for the second.

- **Percentage-of-Sales Budgeting**. Drawn from marketing, this approach uses a percentage of income. For example, a university may earmark 2 percent of this year's tuition for next year's recruitment drive. The problem is that this can create a downward spiral. If recruitment was weak last year, probably more effort at more cost is needed, not less, as this approach would provide.

- **All-You-Can-Afford Budgeting**. This approach works best in good times, providing more resources when the organization's financial condition is stronger. Again, the real need may call for just the opposite, more funding when the organization is weak.

- **Cost-Benefit Analysis**. A budget based on this approach identifies the cost of implementing each of the tactics, and then compares this to the estimated value of the expected results. If an animal-protection group trying to raise $500,000, for example, calculates that spending money on social media could yield the same results as a more expensive TV advertising campaign, it would make sense to go with the social media approach.

- **What-If-Not-Funded Analysis**. This approach forces the planner to look at expected outcomes and to consider alternative ways to reach the same objective, or to re-think the relative priority of the objective in light of limited available funds.
- **Stage-of-Lifecycle Budgeting**. This approach looks closely at the phase of development of the issue. Starting new programs, for example, generally requires more financial resources than maintaining existing programs.
- **Zero-Based Budgeting**. This technique is rooted in current needs rather than past expenditures. Each tactic is ranked according to its importance. The cumulative cost of the tactics is calculated, and a cut-off line of a predetermined budget indicates the point at which the client or organization has run out of money. The disadvantage of this approach is that it allows pre-set budgets and calculators or computer formulas to determine what tactics can be undertaken, though an advantage is that zero-based budgeting can serve as a catalyst in re-evaluating priorities.

All of the above approaches to budgeting have problems. Some are arbitrary. Some fail to consider important variables. Some don't provide a way to rework a budget when the total is too high. But there is another way to budget that respects the decisions and priorities already made in part of this planning project.

This approach, more enlightened for public relations planning, is called **objective-based budgeting**. By focusing on objectives, this objective-based budgeting deals with already identified needs and goals. It aligns with decisions already made by the organization or client, building on the consensus check that concludes Step 4.

Because the tactics simply provide ways to achieve what already has been adopted as the objectives, the cost of these tactics is not seen as additional budget items for the organization. Rather the budget is an extension of these prior strategic decisions (and the implicit commitment to paying for them).

This suggests that the organization will assign the resources needed to carry out tactics that will achieve those objectives and the tactics that subsequently will impact them. Or the organization may need to scale back objectives. Either way, objective-based budgeting puts the responsibility on the organization or client to establish objectives that it will support with appropriate tactics.

WORKSHEET FOR STEP 8: IMPLEMENT THE STRATEGIC PLAN

In this step, you develop the creative theme that pulls together each of your proposed tactics and packages them in an effective way for both dissemination of information and eventual measurement of their impact.

Here are the basic questions for this worksheet:

1   What is the creative theme that links all the tactics?
2   How will be tactics be packaged?
3   What is the schedule for implementing the plan?
4   What is the budget for each tactic?
5   What is the total budget, both its full value and its actual cost to the organization?

PLANNING EXAMPLE FOR STEP 8

G^X will present a comprehensive program focused on each of the three key publics identified in Step 3: Young professionals; businesses, nonprofits and professional organizations; and media. It will unfold as a year-long program for the upcoming calendar year.

PUBLIC: YOUNG PROFESSIONALS

1   **Seminars**. G^X will solicit invitations from area businesses and nonprofit organizations for client-site seminars. These will take G^X speakers to the workplace of young professionals and graduating university seniors who have expressed an interest in the exchange program. Presentations with video or PowerPoint will include extensive question-answer periods.
    • Time: Six to be scheduled in consultation with businesses.
    • Cost: No cost
2   **Golf tournament**. G^X will sign on as a sponsor for a local golf tournament marketed primarily for junior and mid-level business professionals. This will allow G^X to be part of a leisure activity involving members of this key public.

- Time: May.
- Cost: $3,000 value ($1,500 sponsorship fee; $1,500 hors d'oeuvres). [May be no cost; board members will ask their corporations to underwrite the costs.]

3 **Invited informational presentation**. G^X will solicit invitations to provide speakers for business-civic organizations with significant proportion of young professionals. This will provide opportunities to discuss exchange opportunities and benefits in venues with young professionals who are actively seeking ways to enhance their professional lives.
- Time: Varies; Rotary International, March. Urban League Young Professionals, July. Jaycees, October.
- Cost: $300 for handouts and miscellaneous costs.

4 **Self-sponsored informational presentation**. Similar to the invited information presentations, G^X will sponsor a public presentation for young professionals who may not be part of an organization and graduating university seniors.
- Time: November.
- Cost: $800 value for venue (may be no cost; board members will solicit site from participating organization) $100 for handouts and miscellaneous costs.

PUBLIC: BUSINESSES, NONPROFITS AND PROFESSIONAL ORGANIZATIONS

1 **Progress report**. G^X will research, write and publish a progress report, with emphasis on the past year and current activities, with a summary of the organization's 25 years.
- Time: January.
- Cost: $1,000 for 500 copies (may be no cost; board members will seek corporate underwriter). $100 distribution cost.

2 **Anniversary luncheon**. G^X will invite approximately 250 current and past corporate representatives and exchange "alumni" to a luncheon, with an expected turnout of 150. The luncheon will commemorate the 25th anniversary of the business exchange program.
- Time: February.
- Cost: $4,000 for food; $500 entertainment; $1,200 value for venue rental (no cost if luncheon/meeting space can be successfully solicited from participating corporate sponsor).

3 **Survey**. G^X will conduct a survey on attitudes and opinions of area leaders in business, nonprofits, higher education and government on the value of international insight and experience among professional employees. Board members will be asked to identify a researcher from a local business or university to do the survey pro bono.
   - Time: July–September.
   - Cost: Pro bono $4,000 value; $100 in miscellaneous actual cost to G^X.

PUBLIC: MEDIA

1 **Editorial board meeting**. G^X will solicit invitations from the local metropolitan daily newspaper and from the weekly business newspaper to meet with reporters and editors to explain the organization's work and the benefits it offers to the local community.
   - Time: n/a.
   - Cost: $100 for leave-behind materials.
2 **News release**. Various topics including survey report, golf tournament, progress report, anniversary luncheon, upcoming public events and corporate/organizational presentations, application dates for exchange programs, and other relevant topics of newsworthy activities.
   - Time: Varies.
   - Cost: No cost.
3 **Story idea memo**. G^X will provide ideas for interviews and feature stories to reporters at the local metropolitan daily newspaper, weekly business newspaper, business radio programs and television newsrooms.
   - Time: April, September.
   - Cost: No cost.
4 **Feature release**. G^X will write and disseminate feature releases about local young professionals who are returning from an exchange visit. Following direct distribution to news media, feature releases will be posted at G^X website.
   - Time: Varies.
   - Cost: No cost.
5 **Guest editorial**. G^X will solicit an invitation from the local metropolitan daily newspaper to write a guest editorial on the

advantages that international exchange activities offer to local businesses. Following publication (or if publication is denied) G^X will post the editorial at its website.

- Time: Varies.
- Cost: No cost.

COMMUNICATION SUPPORT

1   **Progress report**. See p. 209.
2   **Website**. G^X will enhance its present website with a relaunch for its 25th anniversary. The new website will add a media/information page that will house contact information, news and feature releases, editorials and other opinion matter. The site also will catalog all past exchange programs with names of companies/organizations and individual participants (with some testimonials), as well as a current list of exchange opportunities.
- Time: April, with continual updates.
- Cost: $600 value. No cost to organization (board members will solicit pro bono web designer from participating organization to work with G^X staff on website project).
3   **Video**. G^X will invite a local university class in public relations production or broadcast documentary production to create a video of 7–10 minutes to showcase the organization's exchange programs. This video will be posted at the G^X website as a YouTube video and will be used in speeches and seminars sponsored by G^X.
- Time: January-March.
- Cost: Pro bono $5,000 value; $200 actual cost.
4   **Newspaper advertising**. G^X will purchase a 2×4 inch ad in the weekly business newspaper to invite participants to its self-sponsored public presentation on the exchange program.
- Time: November.
- Cost: $1,600 value; actual cost $1,080 with nonprofit/educational discount.
5   **Radio advertising**. G^X will purchase a six-day run of 30-second announcements on the top-rated business program on local radio to promote its self-sponsored public presentation on the exchange program.
- Time: November.

- Cost: Pro bono $200 value for production; radio station will donate this at actual cost; $600 value, with actual cost of $425 with nonprofit–educational discount.

BUDGET TOTAL

- Value: $23,310.
- Actual cost to organization: $11,815–$22,935 (representing a 2 percent to 49 percent saving) depending on board success in obtaining personnel and sponsorships from participating organizations.

8

PUBLIC RELATIONS PLANNING
PHASE 4: EVALUATION

> The strategic plan that began with research in Phase 1 comes full circle in this final phase of the process. In this chapter, you turn once again to research techniques, this time to evaluate the effectiveness of the tactics of Phase 3 in achieving the objectives you identified in Phase 2.

Books on strategic planning for public relations extol the virtue of evaluation. Awards competitions by the Canadian Public Relations Association and other national professional organizations expect to see evaluative research as part of winning campaigns. Surveys of public relations practitioners in all kinds of settings—agencies, corporations and nonprofit organizations—show that professionals see the need for evaluation.

Yet far too often, this phase of the planning process is given short shrift, or it's overlooked completely. Why? There are many reasons (excuses, really).

- It sometimes is hard to know what to evaluate and how to do so, in part because many practitioners have not studied research techniques.

- Public relations measures may not be as precise as those used in areas such as finance, operations and safety.
- Public relations campaigns and projects do not exist in a vacuum. Other forces are working on key publics while the organization is mounting its public relations activities, making it difficult to isolate the influence of public relations.
- Everything may be in motion, clouding the possibility of an accurate count of the evolving consequences of public relations activity.
- Some public relations measures are negatives—to what extent did criticism not happen, or how many negative opinions were minimized?
- Research takes time, resources and creative energy.

STEP 9: EVALUATING THE STRATEGIC PLAN

In this final step of the process of strategic communication planning, we look at various aspects of evaluative research: what, when and—most important—how, to evaluate.

WHAT TO EVALUATE

Public relations evaluation begins with a clear understanding of what it means to be effective. The research plan needs to consider several issues: the criteria to gauge success, timing of the evaluation, and specific ways to measure each level of objectives (awareness, acceptance and action). The plan also may prescribe particular evaluation tools.

The first decision point for an evaluation program focuses on **design questions**. What criteria should be used to judge the program? What information is needed to make an assessment? Who has this information, and how can it be obtained? Who will receive the final evaluation, and how will it be used?

Next come the **evaluation criteria**. These are called **metrics**, the standards of measurement to assess the outcome of a program or project. Each metric should be realistic and feasible, and it should be ethical and socially responsible. Here are some examples of realistic evaluation metrics.

- **To evaluate awareness objectives:**

  Metric: Media coverage and calculation of media impressions.
  Metric: Post-campaign awareness survey.

- **To evaluate acceptance objectives:**

  Metric: Tabulation of requests for information.
  Metric: Post-campaign attitude/opinion survey.
  Metric: Post-event audience feedback.

- **To evaluate action objectives:**

  Metric: Measures of ticket sales, attendance, donations and other
      results.
  Metric: Measure of improvement.
  Metric: Organizational or environmental change.

WHEN TO EVALUATE

There are three stages in the process of program evaluation related
to timing.

Implementation reports document how the tactics are being
carried out. Such a report may include a schedule of work to date
and an indication of the work remaining. Implementation reports
do not evaluate the quality of the work, only that it has or has not
taken place according to schedule.

Progress reports are preliminary evaluations in which planners
can make strategic modifications as they further implement
the program. Such mid-course corrections can keep the project
functioning at peak efficiency.

The **final report** provides a comprehensive review and overall
evaluation of the program.

RESEARCH DESIGN

How should you structure the evaluation in relation to the measurement standards? There are several possibilities.

The simplest research design is the **after-only study**. You simply
implement a tactic, measure impact and presume that the tactic caused
this impact. This approach is particularly appropriate for action
objectives with relatively simple metrics: measuring attendance,
votes, contributions, purchases and other easily measurable reactions.

But the simplicity of this approach is also its weakness, because this design presumes a cause-and-effect relationship that may not be accurate.

One way to overcome this flaw is to conduct a **before-and-after study** (also called a **pretest/post-test**). Before any public relations program is implemented, observe the key public. This initial observation serves as a benchmark or baseline. Then expose the public to the tactic, and measure the public again. Any change in the public's awareness, acceptance or action is likely due to exposure to your tactic.

But remember that public relations activities don't take place in a vacuum. Not every change in your key public can be linked, cause-and-effect fashion, to your programming, because the public most likely has been exposed to other messages from other organizations as well.

Therefore a more sophisticated evaluation tool is a **controlled before-and-after study**. This involves two sample groups drawn from the same key public. Do the baseline initial research with each sample. Then expose one group to a tactic, but do not expose the other group (which serves as the control group). Finally, measure each group again and compare the results of both groups.

The control group is likely to remain unchanged, while any change you find in the exposed group presumably can be linked to exposure to the public relations tactic.

How to accomplish the controlled study? Let's say you are working on a ridership campaign for an urban transit system. Identify a city similar to yours, and conduct the pretest both there and in your city. If both places are similar, ridership influences such as the price of gasoline, time of year, suburban sprawl and so on should make the results similar. The group in the other city serves as the control group for this study. After conducting your program in your city, retest both groups. Presumably there would be little or no change in the control group in the other city.

HOW TO EVALUATE

At the beginning of Step 9, you were asked to identify what information is needed in order to evaluate a program's effectiveness. Here are several levels of evaluation that can help you answer that question.

An evaluation made on hunches and anecdotes is **judgmental assessment**. It is informal feedback, based on personal observation. This sometimes can be pretty useless feedback: "The boss liked it." "The client asked us to continue." "Everybody said this was a success." "Hey, we won an award for this project." To make judgmental assessment more useful seek input from industry experts or perhaps public relations colleagues. The knowledge they have of the situation helps compensate for the informal way of gathering information.

While practitioners should draw on their personal insight, they should try to base program evaluation on more careful analysis. Thus another way of evaluating public relations activities is by measuring **communication outputs**. These are the things done by practitioners in implementing their tactics.

Output evaluation may focus on **message production**, such as the number of news releases written, brochures printed and blog entries posted. A bit more effectively, it may focus on **message distribution**, the number of news releases sent, brochures handed out, and blog entries posted.

Some outcomes focus on **message cost**, such as the amount of money spent on brochures or advertising—the presumption being that cost equates to value, not always a good indicator of success.

Related to this is **advertising value equivalency (AVE)**, a particularly knotty approach to evaluation that pretends to calculate the value of publicity by estimating how much it would have cost if the same amount of time or space in a news report had been purchased as advertising.

For example, you could focus on a story about your organization in a local newspaper. If the story totals 21 column inches (headline, story and photo), multiply 21 by the cost per column-inch of advertising (let's say $165 per inch). This calculation suggests that the publicity is worth $3,465.

But it's all smoke and mirrors. Publicity is not advertising. Actually, publicity has more credibility with audiences, though it offers less control for public relations.

Public relations experts from around the world met in Spain in 2010 to articulate standards and common approaches for evaluating public relations. One of the main principles of the Barcelona Declaration of Measurement Principles was a clear rejection of advertising equivalency. Some call it a game changer for public relations and a death knell for attempts to fix a dollar value on public relations by falsely comparing it to advertising.

So if judgmental assessment is too subjective and measurement of communication outputs of dubious value, what should be the basis for evaluating public relations? The answer is to look back to Step 4, where you established objectives. Now in Step 9, measure each of those objectives: awareness, acceptance and action.

Awareness evaluation focuses on the content of the message. One way to do this is to measure **message exposure**. Identify the number of people in key publics who were exposed to the message, such as by counting the number of people who log onto a website or who watch a TV news report. Focus also on **message content** by determining the extent to which a message was accurate and positive vis-à-vis the organization.

Another useful measurement tool is a **readability measure**. This means calculating the reading level of a message, usually translated into the level of education needed to easily understand the written content. There are a number of formulas for this, most notably the Gunning Readability Index, also called the Fog Index.

Message recall, a practice drawn from advertising, is another useful technique for evaluating awareness objectives. This involves interviewing people to learn the extent to which they recall a message, associate it with the organization and are able to describe the basic information provided in the message.

Acceptance evaluation looks at the second category of objectives. It goes one better than awareness evaluation by considering how publics internalize a public relations message.

Common techniques for this include **audience feedback**, which is based on the voluntary reaction of an audience. This often is linked with a measure of **audience interest**. Additionally, acceptance can be measured with a **benchmark study**, which is a more formal technique that provides a baseline that serves as a standard for comparing program outcomes.

Action evaluation ultimately is the way to consider the impact of a public relations program on bottom-line issues for an organization. One thing to measure is **audience participation**, such as by counting attendance figures. But be careful in interpreting this. Just because people attend a political speech doesn't necessarily mean that each person in the audience will vote for the candidate.

You might look also at **direct observation** as a way to measure program effectiveness. This simply means looking at the outcome. If your candidate wins the election, your objective was achieved. If you sought financial contributions of $12 million (£7.7 million, €9.5 million), count the total of donations and pledges.

Other examples of direct observation include passage (or defeat) of a piece of legislation, increased use of seatbelts and audience turnout. The outcomes for the legislation and audience size are easy to measure, but how would you measure the results of a seatbelt campaign? One way might be to place observers in highway toll-booths and at busy street corners. Over time, you also could monitor police and insurance data.

A final method of evaluating action objectives looks at **relative media effectiveness**. This evaluation compares one medium to others, attempting to help the organization determine venues for future editions of its campaign.

SEAWORLD

Public relations evaluation often uses several approaches. In 2007, SeaWorld San Antonio introduced a new roller-coaster ride, Journey to Atlantis. The theme park invited members of the media to try out the new ride. The park's public relations–marketing team decided to include social media in the mix.

Twenty-two blogs and online media forums were identified for their focus on roller coasters and invited to write about the new ride. Eventually 12 did so. The result was that SeaWorld San Antonio received 50 links from coaster-oriented websites. Media posted on YouTube, Flickr and other social media sites generated hundreds of thousands of downloads—providing a measure of message production, message distribution and audience interest. The team also received many positive comments, another measure of feedback and interest.

Additional audience feedback was solicited. Over two weekends two months later, a standard exit interview for SeaWorld visitors asked a typical question: Where did you hear about Journey to Atlantis? Forty-seven percent of respondents indicated social media as the source of their information.

> Finally, the research team turned its attention to relative media effectiveness. It looked at the various media used to promote the new ride (television commercial, newspaper ad, social media, radio spot, billboard and so on) and concluded that the cost per impression for social media was 22 cents, compared to $1 for each television impression.

DATA ANALYSIS AND REPORTING

Having gathered the data through a variety of measures, it is now time to analyze it carefully and match the results to your objectives from Step 4.

If the program failed to meet some objectives, try to analyze if this was the result of over-ambitious objectives, flawed strategy that undergirded the program or tactics that were inappropriate or poorly implemented. Consider also if there might be a flaw in the evaluation techniques used to gather the data.

Most program evaluations call for a written report, usually with an **executive summary** that outlines in one or two pages the more detailed findings in the full report. The evaluation often concludes with **recommendations**, such as the feasibility of continuing or expanding the program, applying a similar strategy to other situations, and so on.

WORKSHEET FOR STEP 9: EVALUATE THE STRATEGIC PLAN

In Step 9, you have considered the various ways to measure the success of the campaign. Most reliably, public relations evaluation centers on determining the extent to which previously agreed objectives were met.

Here are the questions for this worksheet:

1 How will you measure awareness objectives?
2 How will you measure acceptance objectives?
3 How will you measure action objectives?
4 What recommendations (if any) stem from this evaluation?

PLANNING EXAMPLE FOR STEP 9

Objectives for Public #1 (individual professionals):

1   To have an effect on the *awareness* of young professionals about G^X, specifically to increase their understanding of the advantages that G^X offers by 50 percent within one year.

This objective will be measured by tracking attendance at seminars and presentations about the exchange program throughout the year.

2   To have an effect on their *acceptance*, specifically to increase their interest in the engagement/exchange programs by 25 percent within one year.

This objective will be measured by tracking the number and content of questions and requests for follow-up information at seminars and presentations about the exchange program throughout the year.

3   To have an effect on their *action*, specifically to generate 10 applicants for long-term exchange programs and 40 for short-term engagement programs within one year.

This objective will be measured by counting the number of applicants throughout the year.

Objectives for Public #2 (organizations):

1   To have an effect on *acceptance*, specifically to increase the awareness of corporate executives and human resources staff about the G^X program opportunities (50 percent of identified organizations within one year).

This objective will be measured by tracking the number of organizations that act on information sent to them by G^X about the exchange program, such as by acknowledging receipt or requesting additional information. All e-mail transactions will be monitored to track when messages are read by the recipient.

2   To have an effect on their *acceptance*, specifically to generate feedback and inquiries from these organizations (15 percent within one year).

This objective will be measured by tracking the number of organizations that express some interest in scheduling seminars and presentations about the exchange program throughout the year.

3   To have an effect on their *action*, specifically to generate invitations for G^X to meet with organizational leaders (25 organizations within one year).

This objective will be measured by tracking the number of organizations that actually schedule a seminar or presentation during the year.

Objectives for Public #3 (news media):

1   To have an effect on their *awareness*, specifically to increase their knowledge about the G^X programs (journalists at 50 percent of identified news media and news blogs within one year).

    This objective will be measured by tracking the output of information in the form of media advisories and releases throughout the year.

2   To have an effect on their *acceptance*, specifically to generate inquiries from these journalists (25 percent of identified news venues within one year).

    This objective will be measured by tracking media requests for interviews and information throughout the year.

3   To have an effect on their *action*, specifically to see publication/broadcast of positive/neutral pieces by 10 percent of identified news venues within one year.

    This objective will be measured by tracking local media references to G^X throughout the year, then conducting content analysis at year's end.

WORKING THE PLAN

This concludes the strategic planning process for public relations. In the four main phases of Part II of this book, you have learned how to gather information (Phase 1), and you have made decisions about what you will accomplish and how you will approach your goals (Phase 2). You learned to create a plan effectively and creatively to use various communication vehicles toward your objectives (Phase 3) and finally you learned to fashion a way to evaluate the campaign once it is completed (Phase 4).

The nine steps thus have broken down this comprehensive process into manageable segments and points of action. This is a process used the world over by effective public relations strategists. It works for small cultural and charitable organization with few resources, as well as for multinational corporations with million-dollar budgets.

You've seen the warning: Don't try this at home. Toss away all such thinking. You *should* try this for yourself. It's good to have a guide, and that is what this process provides.

Certainly this is only a bare-bones approach to strategic planning for public relations, but it is complete. It covers all the bases. The questions posted in these nine steps allow you to answer them in many different ways. There are no preconceived right answers or wrong ones, only responses that reflect the realities of the organization you are working with—its needs, resources, and self-understanding of its personality and vision.

Let it serve as a template for you to create a public relations campaign for your company or nonprofit group. You should feel empowered to experiment with it. Adopt this planning process for your own needs, and adapt it to your own purposes. Let it guide you through the interrelated but not incomprehensive process of planning an efficient and effective public relations campaign.

[For more information on this process, see another book by this author, *Strategic Planning for Public Relations*, 4th edition, 2013, Routledge/Taylor and Francis.]

Appendix
CAREERS IN PUBLIC RELATIONS

In every part of the developed world, public relations is a growing field, ripe with opportunities for employment and advancement. Labor analysts predict that the demand for public relations practitioners will grow at least as fast as the general employment scene, and faster than many jobs.

That's good news for the public relations student and for people seeking entry-level jobs. The job search may take a while, but it should be successful.

CAREERS

Around the globe, public relations has a promising future. Most corporations and nonprofit organizations have public relations departments. In smaller organizations, public relations projects may be handled by employees who have additional jobs, often involving marketing, human resources, fundraising, recruitment and other areas of contact with the public.

On average, public relations agencies report that they are making a strong recovery from the global recession. As the economy in general improves, all kinds of businesses and nonprofit organizations turn to public relations to build markets, attract customers and serve their clientele.

In the US, the Labor Department's Bureau of Labor Statistics predicts that jobs in public relations are growing faster than average, with an expected increase of 25 percent through 2018. Growth areas for jobs in public relations are in health care, pharmaceutical, consumer, and high tech/social media fields. At the same time, the bureau expects competition to be keen for entry-level jobs.

Similar predictions come from the United Kingdom, Australia, Japan, South Africa and the European Union. The outlook for public relations is particularly optimistic in countries that are gearing up for significant economic growth: the BRICS countries (Brazil, Russia, India, China and South Africa) and in Middle Eastern nations such as Qatar and the United Arab Emirates.

The public relations industry has made a strong recovery from the worldwide recession of 2009. The Holmes Report, an industry analyst, estimates that public relations agencies generate nearly $9 billion (£5.1 billion, €5.7 billion) and employ 60,000 people worldwide.

That public relations is a lucrative international profession is clear from the statistics. Reports in 2011 indicated that the largest agency, Edelman, generated about $532 million (£420 billion, €339 billion) in fees and employed 3,753.

Close on its heels were other top-ranked agencies around the world: Weber-Shandwick, Fleishman-Hillard, Burson-Marsteller, Hill & Knowlton, Ketchum, Ogilvy, Golin-Harris, Ruder-Finn, Porter-Novelli (all US-based with an international footprint); MSL and EuroRSCG (France); FD, Brunswick, Grayling (UK); Dentsu, Kyodo (Japan), Media Consulta, CNC, Hering Schuppener (Germany); FSB (Brazil); Prime, Halvarsson, KREAB Gavin Anderson (Sweden); BlueFocus Communication (China); Barabino (Italy); Mostra, Interel (Belgium); Llorente & Cuenca, Infopress, Tinkle, Torres y Carrera, Marco (Spain); CROS, AGT, Pro Vision (Russia); Prain, KPR (South Korea); Professional Public Relations, Senate SHJ, Rowland, Wrights (Australia); AdFactors PR, Integral (India); Geelmuyden.Kiese (Norway); TRACCS (Saudi Arabia); ASMI, Bison & Rose, EPR (Czech Republic); Grupo Lift, C&C (Portugal); 124 (Thailand); EMG, Coebergh (The Netherlands); Pohjoisranta Oy (Finland); Partner of Promotion (Poland); and Meropa (South Africa).

SALARY

Salary comparisons are notoriously imprecise, especially with international comparisons. Salary information here is gleaned from various governmental, professional, academic and other sources. It is presented with the following cautions.

Salaries vary regionally. Even within the same country, they often differ geographically. Higher salaries are associated with larger metropolitan areas. For example, salaries in London and Southeast UK are higher than in Wales or Scotland. Similarly, North American salaries are higher in the large cities (New York, Toronto, Chicago, Los Angeles, Vancouver and so on) than in smaller areas.

Likewise, salaries vary within different organizational settings: public relations agencies, public relations divisions within marketing or advertising agencies, and in-house public relations departments. Within the latter, they diverge greatly depending on the type of organization—at the higher end for science, high-tech manufacturing, investor relations and high-performing industries such as pharmaceuticals and energy; at the lower end of the salary scale for nonprofit organizations, cultural groups, travel/tourism, education and religion.

Salaries also vary among groups of practitioners. Men still earn more than women, though the gender gap is not significantly different than in other professional areas. Practitioners (especially younger ones) with public relations degrees earn more than graduates with less-specialized career preparation.

In the United States, entry-level public relations jobs generally have salaries of about $28,000 (£18,000, €23,000) with more than 50,000 job openings each year. Experienced practitioners earn an average of $85,000 (£54,000, €68,000).

In the UK, entry-level salaries are about £25,000 ($39,000, £31,000). Salaries for experienced public relations managers are about £60,000 pounds ($95,000, €75,000).

The Public Relations Institute of Australia reports starting salaries of AUS$35,000 a year, (£22,000, €27,000), with seasoned professionals earning upwards of AUS$100,000 (£63,000, €79,000).

Perhaps a better way to compare salaries is to look at the pay in other professions. Public relations lies in the upper-middle income area.

- Public relations practitioners generally earn more than journalists, broadcasters, teachers, nurses, foresters, historians, police officers and game wardens.

- They earn about the same as funeral directors, insurance agents, college professors, copywriters, registered nurses, urban planners, audiologists, accountants, human resource specialists and archeologists.
- And they earn less than dental hygienists, accountants, market research analysts, biologists and other scientists, ship pilots, psychologists, fashion designers, sociologists and of course doctors, rock stars, Bill Gates and the Kardashians.

ENTRY-LEVEL JOB

Who's hiring in public relations? Here are some places to start looking for an entry-level job in the field:

- Public relations agency (general or specialists).
- Public relations section of advertising, marketing or fundraising agency.
- Public relations department in company: business, manufacturing, sports, health care, entertainment, travel/hospitality, industry association.
- Public relations/communication department in nonprofit or nongovernmental organization: education, charity, religious, arts, professional, advocacy.
- Public affairs unit in government or military: press secretary, public information, public affairs, communications specialist.
- Independent public relations consultant.

The PRSA Foundation, the research and education arm of the Public Relations Society of America, identifies five levels of job categories in public relations: technician, supervisor, manager, director and executive.

Students can expect entry-level positions that emphasize technical competence in writing and related areas at the technician level. Skills typically required for such positions include proficiency in preparing brochures, memos and letters, newsletter articles, news releases, proposals, reports, scripts and speeches. Related skills include conducting research, editing and interviewing. Virtually all entry-level job announcements call for applicants to be familiar with social media and new communication technology.

Look for openings with job titles such as public relations writer, public affairs or public relations specialist, media relations assistant, account assistant, and publications or web editor. Also look for generic job titles such as staff associate, coordinator and associate director.

A career-minded novice in public relations should be prepared to use an entry-level position as an opportunity to move toward the next level of positions. Cultivate interpersonal and problem-solving skills. Develop an expertise in a particular specialty such as public affairs, social media, research, investor relations or employee relations.

An excellent source of information for anyone seeking a job in public relations is The Public Relations Body of Knowledge, a compendium of articles, books and other published materials that deal with the profession. In its book, *Public Relations Professional Career Guide*, the PRSA Foundation identifies many sources of information related to the skills and knowledge expected of entry-level technicians in public relations writing and related areas. It also identifies articles associated with advanced career levels.

PRSA also published a Pack of Career Tactics, with 40 must-read articles for public relations graduates and job seekers. Information is available at prsa.org > "Career," "Job Seekers."

PERSONAL CHARACTERISTICS

Many personal traits are associated with successful public relations practitioners. Here is an alphabetical listing of some personal characteristics that are most often noted:

- accuracy and attention to detail;
- creativity;
- curiosity;
- honesty and integrity;
- personal responsibility and accountability;
- time-management and personal organization.

Additionally, here is an alphabetical listing of knowledge and skills that you should learn if you hope to be successful in public relations:

- listening skills;
- management ability;

- planning skills;
- problem-solving ability;
- research and analysis ability;
- understanding of communication technology;
- understanding of media;
- understanding of organizational behavior;
- writing ability.

This final characteristic deserves special consideration. Surveys point to declining writing skills among most young people, including those entering the public relations profession. Yet the profession still demands top writing talent. The Canadian Public Relations Society joined with PRSA and Michigan State University for a survey on entry-level public relations writing in North America.

Both Canadian and US public relations professionals—practitioners, educators, even students—ranked writing as the most important professional skill needed for public relations. Public relations supervisors in both countries were negative on the writing competency of junior-level practitioners.

Entry-level practitioners thought more highly of their writing abilities than their supervisors did. Supervisors rated the average writing skills of their entry-level employees 2.6 on a 1–5 scale, but the practitioners rated themselves at 3.1 on average. Translated into letter grades and numerical Grade Point Averages (GPAs), supervisors gave failing grades (Ds or Fs) for grammar (33 percent with failing grades, 1.94 average GPA on the standard 0–4 scale), spelling/punctuation (33 percent failing, 1.99), organized ideas (30 percent failing, 1.95) and stylebook use (45 percent failing, 1.72).

US supervisors said new public relations employees are least skilled in persuasive writing for fundraising appeals and proposals. Canadian supervisors rated that the second-weakest type of writing, with business letters and memos as the weakest.

Both groups gave the highest marks for writing for new media (blog/social media, e-mail and website content).

The Canada-US study showed that the two most common writing activities for entry-level practitioners are news releases/backgrounders (with 23 percent of a typical 40-hour work week) and conversational e-mail (20 percent). These are followed by newsletters/annual reports (14 percent of the work week), website content (13 percent), business letters/internal memos (11 percent), blogs/social media (8 percent), and fundraising appeals/proposals (4 percent).

North America isn't the only location for decreasing writing skills. Other studies have found similar perceptions of declining writing skills in the United Kingdom and Australia, such as various studies by Warwick University over the past decade about the perceived nationwide 'language crisis' in England, Scotland, Wales and Northern Ireland.

EDUCATION

The most useful advice for obtaining a job in public relations is to get the best education possible. The Public Relations Institute of Australia notes that some people begin in the profession through workshops and short courses. Some people transition from other areas such as journalism, teaching and law.

Increasingly, the most common and often the only dependable way of getting into the profession of public relations is to obtain a bachelor's degree in the field. The following categories of courses and knowledge/skill areas may help you plan your academic career.

PUBLIC RELATIONS

A report by the international Commission on Public Relations Education has recommended five specific and separate courses for undergraduates in a public relations major, minor or sequence:

- introduction to public relations, including theory, origin and principles;
- public relations research, measurement and evaluation;
- public relations writing and production;
- supervised work experience in public relations, such as an internship;
- an additional public relations course in law and ethics, planning and management, case studies, or campaigns.

The report cites an expectation that issues of diversity, communication technology and global implications be imbedded in public relations courses. It also recommends electives in advertising, broadcasting, photography, graphic design, persuasion and advanced media writing.

Here are several other areas of study that a would-be public relations practitioner should investigate:

WRITING

Employers consistently seek effective writers. Courses in public relations writing are especially useful, but don't stop there. Look to journalism and broadcast reporting courses. Look to courses in poetry, play writing, script writing and other types of creative writing. Investigate courses in professional and technical writing

ETHICS

The Commission on Public Relations Education cites professional ethics as an area central to academic preparation for entry into the profession. The recommendation is that ethics should pervade all content of public relations education. Consider also courses in philosophy.

ORGANIZATIONAL AND BUSINESS STUDIES

Increasingly, public relations is seen as a profession rooted not only in the communication arts but also in management science. Business courses enhance your value to an organization, particularly courses focused on marketing, research and management.

PROBLEM-SOLVING AND CRITICAL-THINKING SKILLS

Traditional areas such as logic and literature and newer areas such as creativity studies and organizational innovation offer opportunities to develop your competence in analytical skills sought by employers.

STATISTICS

Painful as it may be to some creative and literary types, skill in mathematics and statistics is a vital element of the education of a public relations professional. Practitioners often deal with budgets, surveys, evaluation reports and other topics that require proficiency in mathematics.

LIBERAL ARTS

The Commission on Public Relations Education recommends that 60 percent to 75 percent of undergraduate coursework be in liberal arts, social sciences, business and language study. The US-based Accrediting Council on Education in Journalism and Mass Communications echoes this expectation for professional programs including undergraduate public relations degrees. Employers prefer candidates who are well rounded. Expand your value to an employer by taking courses in the arts and humanities, natural and social sciences, and applied studies.

DIVERSITY

Likewise, an understanding of, and appreciation for, issues of diversity and inclusiveness are considered to be an essential part of public relations education. Look for courses in intercultural communication and diversity courses dealing with gender, religion, age and lifestyle, as well as race and ethnicity.

LANGUAGE AND CULTURE

Increasingly, organizations are finding themselves involved in an environment that is more global and more diverse. Public relations often is expected to lead this change. Job applicants familiar with another culture, conversant in an additional language, or knowledgeable about social or ethnic pluralism often catch the eye of employers. International study programs are a particularly good way to develop such cultural proficiency.

TECHNOLOGY

Employers often count on the fact that college graduates may have greater computer skills than practitioners already working in the field. Expose yourself as much as possible to computer applications for word processing, research, presentation, graphic design and Internet technology. Familiarity with social media and emerging communication technology is most important.

PRACTICAL EXPERIENCE

In addition to relevant courses, employers are looking for people with work experience. How do you get that before you have a job? Internships; part-time jobs; volunteer work; student organizations; student-run public relations firms.

Internships usually are available through colleges and universities, and many larger employers offer internships to college graduates. Part-time jobs and volunteer service are other ways to gain work experience; try to use these opportunities to show what you can do in public relations projects.

Student organizations, especially those related to public relations, provide opportunities for professional training. The Public Relations Student Society of America, which is affiliated with PRSA, has chapters on more than 300 campuses. IABC, the International Association of Business Communicators, also has established student chapters, and many colleges and universities have independent student public relations groups not formally aligned with either of the two professional organizations. Parallel organizations in other countries also have student members: IPRA internationally, CIPR in the UK, CPRS in Canada, PRIA in Australia, PRII in Ireland, PRSK in Kenya, and organizations in many other nations.

GRADUATE EDUCATION

The minimum academic qualification for a job in public relations is a bachelor's degree. Increasingly, competition for jobs includes people with master's degrees. Many universities throughout North America offer advanced studies in public relations, organizational communication and related areas.

Offering an international perspective, the Commission on Public Relations Education has recommended the following courses for a master's degree: communication theory, communication research, research methodology, communication in society, advanced public relations case studies, public relations management and a thesis project or comprehensive examination.

ACCREDITED DEGREE PROGRAMS

The public relations organizations in many countries have created a certification or accreditation program for universities offering programs of study in public relations.

PRIA in Australia offers an accreditation program that blends theoretical concepts, professional skills and industry engagement. Twenty-four universities there have accredited programs. In the UK, 59 degrees at 31 universities are recognized by CIPR, and the Public Relations Institute of Ireland accredits 9 colleges.

In the US, 28 universities hold a Certification in Education for Public Relations offered by PRSA, and public relations degree programs are included in the accreditation of most of the 109 institutions affiliated with the Accrediting Council on Education in Journalism and Mass Communications.

JOB SEARCH

There is no easy formula for landing your first job or getting a foothold in the profession of your choice. However, some techniques have been used by many job seekers and found to be effective. Following are several suggestions for breaking into jobs in public relations.

PERSONAL ASSESSMENT

You've heard it before: Life is too short to work at a job you hate, even a well-paying job. Before you plunge into the job search, give some time for a bit of soul searching.

- Do you like continual change or a routine and stable environment?
- Do you thrive on pressure, or does it grind you down?
- Are you willing to relocate for a job with potential?
- Do you have most of the skills needed for success in a job and can you learn the rest?

These are just some of the questions you should answer before preparing any job application.

Many types of personal inventories are available at career development offices in colleges and universities. These can help you assess your personal interests, aspirations and work styles, using the information to direct your career path.

EMPLOYMENT ASSESSMENT

Research the field. Learn who is hiring and where the jobs are. Investigate opportunities in other sections of the country or in other parts of the world. Look into job possibilities in related fields such as marketing, research, advertising and technical writing. Explore possibilities in both corporate and nonprofit organizations, as well as with agencies. Don't be afraid to ask for an information interview with a senior person in the public relations profession.

NETWORKING

Let everyone know that you are looking for a job. Ask friends to pass along your name to their friends and colleagues who may know someone looking for an eager public relations employee. Join the student chapter of a professional public relations organization, and transfer your membership to a professional chapter when you graduate. Try to participate in both local chapter meetings and national conferences.

Build an expanding network of professional contacts through your internships, class projects, shadowing and mentoring programs with practitioners, visitors to your campus and contacts with alumni of your school who work in your areas of interest.

COVER LETTER

A cover letter is your first introduction to a prospective employer. Make a strong first impression.

- *Ensure accuracy and professionalism.* Send an original letter, never a photocopy. Make sure there are no misspellings, smudges or other imperfections. If the application is online, attach an equally well-proofread cover letter. In either format, present a professional tone that reflects you without being humorous, overly confidant, cute or avant-garde.
- *Address the cover letter to a real person.* This is more effective than sending it to a nameless office holder such as Personnel Director or Public Affairs Manager. A search of the organization's website or a telephone call to the receptionist should yield the name you need.
- *Indicate your interest in the position.* State where you heard about the opening, indicate why you are interested in this job and express confidence that you can do it effectively. Keep the focus on what you can do for the organization rather than on your need for a job.
- *Briefly describe your philosophical approach.* Indicate what you think about this type of work, its importance and your commitment to it.
- *Summarize your qualifications.* Tell how they relate to the particular job for which you are applying. Restate from your résumé the two or three items that highlight your competence for this particular position.
- *Address each advertised qualification the employer is seeking.* The job posting will signal that the employer is looking for some very specific skills and experiences. Many applicants with otherwise excellent backgrounds will be overlooked because they appear not to have each qualification the employer is seeking. You are likely to be stronger in some areas and less experienced in others, but do not simply skip over one of those weaknesses. Address each in some way. For example, if the employer is

looking for someone with experience in running focus groups, you may realize that you not have done this on your own. But perhaps you can indicate that you helped lead focus groups as part of a team in one of your classes, that you have been a participant in other groups, or that beyond class you have studied on your own about how to conduct focus groups—don't exaggerate; get to a library and pick up a book on focus groups—and finally that you are eager to conduct focus group research for this company.

- *Ask for an interview.* End the cover letter with a specific request to obtain a response or to meet with the employer. If it is appropriate, offer to telephone for an appointment, or ask for a formal application.

PORTFOLIO

Every applicant for a public relations job should have a comprehensive portfolio of writing samples, graphic designs, research projects and other relevant materials. Preferably, the portfolio should be available both in hard copy and digitally.

At a minimum, the portfolio should include several news releases.

Ideally, it also will include a brochure, direct-mail package, fact sheet, newsletter article, opinion piece, pitch letter and public relations advertisement. Include a planning sheet for each piece of writing to give some context. If possible, also include clippings related to news releases and fact sheets.

Additionally, the portfolio should include a report on one of your research projects, particularly applied research using a focus group, survey or content analysis.

Display the portfolio in a professional-looking binder. Make sure that the digital or online version of your portfolio can be accessed from your online résumé.

In addition to the portfolio, copy several of the more impressive pieces and prepare a leave-behind packet.

RÉSUMÉ

Every job seeker needs a quality résumé, which is a listing of professional credentials and experience. This should be tightly written to highlight your strengths.

- *Keep the résumé to a single page.* This is sufficient for new graduates and other entry-level job seekers. One way of accomplishing this is to use résumé language that features action statements such as "edited newsletter" or "conducted focus group research" rather than complete sentences.
- *Use a summary rather than an objective.* Traditional résumé objectives focus on what you want, such as "position in public relations" or "challenging writing position with opportunity for advancement." Instead, consider using a personal summary highlighting what you have to offer. For example: "Recent graduate and agency intern familiar with research techniques. Diverse writing skills. Able to clearly present technical material. Experience with PRSSA accounts. Degree in public relations."
- *Design the résumé for eye appeal.* Especially in the field of public relations, where appearance is important and design ability is expected, would-be employers expect résumés that look professional. Use quality paper. Bold or underlined section heads with bullet items can be useful. People read from the left, so use the left side of the sheet for the most important information; save details such as inclusive dates for less-prominent positions.
- *Avoid gimmicks.* Neon-colored paper, personal brochures, techno typeface and bizarre graphics may be attention getters, but they often fail to generate a positive response. Stick with conventional and professional styles.
- *Avoid hype words.* Control the urge to call yourself "a dynamic, self-motivated go-getter" and avoid other such hyperbolic statements. Arrogance, self-praise and inflated ego have no place in a résumé. Instead, use objective words, numbers and strong verbs. Give examples of past success.
- *Use buzzwords.* Showing that you know the language can attract the attention of the person initially screening applications. Consider what is expected for the job you are applying for, and then use words to address those expectations. High on the list of most public relations employers are the following words: analyze, design, edit, evaluate, plan, research and write.
- *List professional experience.* Include paid employment, internships, volunteer work and military service. Indicate the company or organizational name, job title and dates (years, or months and years) of employment. If you have many part-time or summer

jobs unrelated to public relations, summarize these under one generic heading. List your professional experience concisely, using bullets and brief action statements. Don't exaggerate or use minute detail. Focus on tangible tasks rather than broad job categories, and use strong action verbs. Indicate not only your work projects but also their results. For example: "Increased student agency accounts by 35 percent." Many résumés present experience in reverse chronological order focused on jobs. An alternative is to focus on areas of skill or achievement, such as separate sections on writing, editing and research, followed by a brief work history.

- *List educational achievements.* Include the name of your school, major, degree, awards and special concentrations of study. Note if the major is accredited in public relations or communications. Indicate your grade average if it is noteworthy (3.0 or better on a 4.0 scale). List your most recent education first. Do not list high school unless it adds a particular credential, such as Academy for Visual Arts if you are citing experience in design. If you do not have much work experience, list relevant courses, using generic course titles, and don't overlook non-major courses in business, language and other disciplines.

- *List professional affiliations and memberships.* Even in an entry-level job search, you can show involvements with job-relevant organizations.

- *Provide an e-mail contact.* You may have to establish a new e-mail, if you have been relying on one provided by your college or university. It's probably a good idea to create an e-mail account just for job search and professional uses. Remember to check it often. Also, be careful about the name you choose. SuperKrak, Btchsbk, LilMama and StudMonkey17 may be okay for e-mails to friends, but they don't create the professional impression you need for business purposes.

- *Identify special skills.* Language fluency, computer skills and other personal capabilities relevant to employment should be listed. List organizational and volunteer activities if they are relevant to public relations or if they show leadership experience.

- *Monitor your social media pages.* Expect would-be employers to look at your Facebook pages, even if you try to limit access to your virtual friends. Be careful what you post online. Many job applicants have been scrubbed from the interview list because the company saw unflattering photos or negative information on their Facebook page. Google your own name (quotation marks around the name, plus city) and see what employees would find about you online.

- *Be selective with personal information.* Hobbies, political involvement and religious affiliation generally have no place on a résumé, unless your hobby relates to the potential job or if the position deals with political or religious matters. Marital status and other such personal information are out of bounds in a job search.

- *Do not list personal references.* Save these for a separate sheet including names, postal addresses, e-mail contacts and telephone numbers for people who have indicated their willingness to give you a good recommendation. Always ask permission to list a reference, and don't be shy about asking if that person feels comfortable about giving you a positive recommendation. Don't waste space on the résumé with the obvious note that references are available on request. Instead, be prepared to give this when you get an interview.

INTERVIEW PREPARATION

Employers receive hundreds of applications for a single job opening. Obviously, the cover letter and résumé are the initial screening devices. The competition is tough, but a few of the standouts make it through. If you are lucky enough to get an interview, make the most of it.

- *Research your interviewer.* Find out all you can about the organization: its mission, reputation, activities and successes. Investigate its standing within the community, perhaps with a call to the Chamber of Commerce or the Better Business Bureau. Do an online search to see if the organization has been in the news lately. Look into the organization's Facebook account if one exists. Check into biographical materials for information on its leaders. If the company CEO sits on the governor's taskforce on energy policy, let the interviewer know that you are aware of that fact.

- *Arrive early*. If anyone has to wait for the interview to begin, it should be you. Learn ahead of time how to get to the interview site and how long the trip will take. Plan to be in the building and on the correct floor at least 10 minutes before the scheduled time of the interview.
- *Dress professionally*. This should go without saying, but too many employers complain that job applicants dress in a way that suggests they aren't taking the interview seriously. Dress as if you already have the job, and then err on the side of being more formal than may be necessary. This doesn't mean to wear your best party dress, nor does it require purchasing an expensive business suit. But for most jobs, conservative professional attire means jacket and tie for men and parallel clothing for women.
- *Be an active listener*. During the interview maintain eye contact, look for nonverbal cues, concentrate on the discussion and evaluate the significance of questions before you respond.
- *Ask your own questions*. Prepare a list of questions relevant to the prospective position, questions that show you to be a person eager to make a contribution. Let these questions indicate that you will work hard, learn fast and quickly become a contributing member of the organization. Hold questions of salary, benefits, vacations and other personal concerns until you have a job offer. The Public Relations Institute of New Zealand suggests asking questions such as these: What skills are you looking for? What are your plans for the business? How do you differentiate your business from your competitors? What is the culture of your business? What are the key attributes of the people who succeed in your business? Which skills will I have the opportunity to develop? What formal and on-the-job training is available?
- *Show your portfolio*. Bring your portfolio to the job interview so you can show your work rather than merely talking about it. Offer it early in the meeting so the interviewer can glance at it during the discussion.
- *Have some leave-behinds*. Bring photocopies of the most appropriate portfolio items to leave with the organization. Prepare these as leave-behinds, and do not ask that they be returned. Also, provide a sheet with a link to your online résumé and portfolio.

- *Expect a writing test.* As part of the interview process, many employers hiring writers want to see how candidates perform under pressure. You may be given a set of facts and asked to prepare a news release. If so, do a brief planning sheet to make sure you are focusing on the appropriate publics and addressing their interests.
- *Expect a current affairs test.* Many graduates tell, often with regret, of feeling that they did poorly on a current affairs test that was administered as part of a job interview. Public relations professionals are expected to know what's happening in their community and beyond. You should develop a habit of following the news every day. When you go for a job interview, make sure you are aware of current happenings and that you know the names of key governmental and professional leaders.
- *Have an air of confidence and professionalism.* Maintain eye contact with your interviewer, and control any anxiety you may have. Remind yourself that this organization thinks you are good enough to consider hiring you. Dressing professionally can be an ego boost, and knowing that you are prepared can go a long way to calm your nervousness.
- *Follow up with a thank-you letter.* Immediately after the interview, mail a note or card that expresses appreciation for the opportunity to be considered for the position. Or go to a nearby coffee shop, write a note and deliver it to the receptionist where you just interviewed. Send a real card, not an e-mail note. Use this as another opportunity to restate your interest in the job and to reiterate your main qualifications.

GLOSSARY

Acceptance evaluation   approach to evaluation research that considers how an organization internalizes a public relations message

Acceptance objective   category of objectives dealing with what an organization wants people to think about it, thus focusing on interests and attitudes

Action evaluation   approach to evaluation research that considers the impact of a public relations program on bottom-line issues for an organization

Action objective   category of objective dealing with how an organization wants people to act toward it, thus focusing on opinion and behavior

Acute stage   stage in crisis communication when the crisis breaks forth on the public stage

Advertising value equivalency   discredited aspect of communication output research based on the false presumption that the value of publicity can be compared to the cost of advertising

Advocacy model   approach to public relations focusing on the use of two-way communication to modify attitudes and influence behavior; often used by competitive business organizations, causes and movements

After-only study   type of evaluation research design that reviews a situation after a communication project has been implemented (compare with **before-and-after study**)

Agenda-setting model   theory that observes relationships between the media agenda and the public agenda, observing that, by reporting an event or focusing on an issue, the media signal to audiences the importance of the event or issue

Apologia   formal defense that offers a compelling case for an organization's opinion, positions or actions

Audience engagement   proactive public relations strategy involving two-way communication between an organization and its publics

Audience feedback   aspect of acceptance evaluation based on the voluntary reaction of an audience; often considered a measure of audience interest

Audience participation   aspect of action evaluation based on measuring outcomes such as attendance figures

Awareness evaluation   approach to evaluation research focused on the content of messages

Awareness objective   category of objective dealing with what an organization wants people to know about it, thus focusing on knowledge, understanding and recall

Balance theory   theory that identifies the tension caused by inconsistent information

Before-and-after study   type of evaluation research design that reviews a situation before a communication project has been implemented, then investigates the situation again after the communication is completed, and compares the two (compare with **after-only study**)

Benchmark study   aspect of acceptance evaluation based on a baseline that serves as a standard for comparing program outcomes

Boundary-spanning capacity   attribute of contemporary public relations focusing on the role of practitioners as liaisons between an organization and its various publics

Branding   creation of a clear and consistent message for an organization; see **positioning**

Campaign plan book   comprehensive written public relations plan including research findings, strategic recommendations, tactics and evaluation techniques

Closed system   type of system in which organizations and publics cannot interact easily and frequently

Cluster sample   sophisticated approach to sampling that subdivides a complex population, drawing elements from each demographic subsection for the final sampling

Cognitive dissonance   theory that explores the role of psychological discomfort rooted in information that contradicts beliefs, values or attitudes

Communication output   approach to evaluation research based on things public relations practitioners produce to implement tactics

Communication theory   field of study focusing on various aspects of communication, such as source, sender, channel, receiver, message, encoding/decoding, and feedback

Community relations   specialty within public relations that manages the organization's relationship with people who live in the geographic or social community in which it operates

Concession   reactive public relations strategy in which an organization gives an aggrieved public something they both value

Condolence   reactive public relations strategy in which an organization expresses grief over someone's loss or misfortune without admitting guilt

Congruity theory   consistency theory with aspect of measuring attitudes

Conjecture proposition   type of proposition that argues that an outcome is probable

Consistency theory   attribute of contemporary public relations focusing on a category of theory that describes how people deal with information contrary to existing information, attitudes and biases

Content analysis   type of research based on unobtrusive and after-the-fact analysis of media artifacts such as newscasts, editorials or articles on a particular topic

Control   aspect of persuasion focusing on the message source's command over the audience

Controlled before-and-after study   type of evaluation research design that considers outside factors; involves two before-and-after studies with parallel sample groups drawn from the same population

Convenience sample   type of non-probability sample in which respondents are selected mainly on their availability

Corporate public relations   type of public relations that provides the vehicle for businesses to publicize products, gain customers, motivate productivity and maintain a communication link with investors, regulators and industry colleagues

Corporate social responsibility   commitment by many companies on contributing to the betterment of society while earning money for stockholders

Corrective action   reactive public relations strategy in which an organization takes steps to contain a problem, repair damage and/or prevent its recurrence

Crisis communication   process by which an organization plans for, deals with, and communicates in out-of-control issues

Crisis management   process by which an organization deals with out-of-control issues

Cultivation theory   theory that suggests the media shape or cultivate peoples' conception of social reality

Customer public   type of public that receives the product or services of an organization, such as consumers, clients, patients, fans, parishioners and members

Customer-driven response   attribute of contemporary public relations focusing on an organization's ability to take direction from its customers and other publics

Cyberactivism   see **online activism**

Democratic ideals   attribute of contemporary public relations focusing on standards of organizational behavior supporting equality and using persuasive communication

Design questions   aspect of program evaluation that considers what criteria should be evaluated

Diffusion of innovations   attribute of contemporary public relations focusing on the theory that identifies the role of opinion leaders as models in the process of mass adoption of new products or ideas

Direct information subsidy   category of news media tactics including information presented to the media in ready-to-use format, such as news releases or photos

Direct observation   aspect of action research based on measures of program effectiveness, such as money raised or members recruited

Disassociation   reactive public relations strategy in which an organization attempts to distance itself from wrongdoing associated with it

Donor relations   specialty within public relations, similar to **investor relations**, that manages the organization's relationship with donors and with regulators and watchdog organizations

Employee volunteer program   aspect of community relations involving an organization's support for employee involvement in the community

Enabler public   type of public that serves as a regulator by setting standards for an organization

Established media   attribute of contemporary public relations focusing on the role of traditional media (including newspapers, magazines, radio and television)

Executive summary   formal summary accompanying a public relations plan or evaluation report, designed for executives who may not have time to read a full report

External impediments   aspect of an organization's external environment involving identifying and dealing with extra-organizational obstacles that might impede a public relations program

Fear appeal   type of negative persuasive appeal intended to arouse anxiety or worry

Feature lead   type of lead used in feature stories

Final report   type of evaluation report that reviews a completed public relations program

Focus group   type of research based on small-group discussion/interview, in which a researcher guides a conversation about a particular issue

Formative research   first phase of the strategic communication process that gathers information about the public relations situation, the organization and the publics

Framing   manner in which the media provide a perspective or frame of reference that influences public discourse on a topic

Gatekeeper   media person who determines what information to present to audiences

Government public relations   type of public relations that includes agencies, military, legislative and judicial bodies to allow government entities to communicate with their publics; also a term involving lobbying of government entities by corporations and nonprofit organizations

Grabber   power words that get attention and are easily recalled

Guilt appeal   type of negative persuasive appeal attempting to arouse remorse or acceptance of responsibility

Hard news   information dealing with momentous events, such as accidents, crime, death, scandal and activities with immediate results such as elections, trials and sporting events

Hate appeal   type of negative persuasive appeal that is unethical and not used by public relations professionals

Herd mentality   observation that reporters from competing media tend to cover the same stories, usually from the same perspective

Humor appeal   type of positive persuasive appeal using comedy and amusement to gain attention

Hypodermic needle theory   see **powerful-effects model**

Identity system   tools used by an organization to project its identity, including name and logo, brochures, news releases, advertisements, social media sites and so on

Image restoration theory   theory that explains how organizations can understand and emerge from crisis situations

Implementation report   type of evaluation report that documents how tactics are being carried out

Indirect information subsidy   category of news media tactics including information presented for media guidance but not meant to be published or aired, such as media advisories and announcements of news conferences

Information exchange   category of communication tactics involving various types of face-to-face encounters between an organization and its publics

Information model   approach to public relations focusing on use of one-way communication to disseminate newsworthy information; often used by government, nonprofit organizations and business organizations

Information-seeking public   public that actively and consciously solicits information from an organization

Ingratiation   reactive public relations strategy in which an organization gives an aggrieved public something the public value but which is of little cost or significance to the organization

Inoculation theory   theory suggesting that persuasive information can sway unchallenged beliefs and attitudes, while attitudes that have been tested are more resistant to change

Integrated strategic communication   trend within organizations blending public relations and marketing so companies can coordinate promotional activities and use multiple tools to engage and communicate with customers and other significant publics

Interactive media engagement   category of news media tactics creating direct interaction between an organization and reporters, such as an interview or news conference

Intercessory public group that bridges the organization and its primary publics

Intergovernmental relations specialty within public relations through which government agencies engage their counterparts in other nations; see **public diplomacy**

Internal impediments aspect of an organization's internal environment involving identifying and dealing with intra-organizational obstacles that might impede a public relations program

Interpersonal communication aspects of person-to-person communication, as compared with communication via media

Investor relations specialty within public relations that manages the organization's relationship with shareholders, regulators, financial journalists and bloggers, investors, and both sell-side and buy-side analysts

Issues management process by which an organization tries to anticipate emerging issues and respond to them before they get out of hand

Judgmental assessment approach to evaluation research based on informal feedback drawn from personal observation

Key public publics identified as most important in dealing with a particular issue or situation

Lean resources attribute of contemporary public relations that recognizes the scarcity of money, personnel, supplies and other resources

Limited-effects model theoretical approach to communication that presumes that media have a loose and limited effect on audiences

Limiter public type of public that reduces or undermines the success of an organization, including competitors, opponents and hostile forces

Linkage aspect of systems theory dealing with the pattern in which an organization interacts with its publics

Litigation public relations specialty of public relations through which defense attorneys manage communication before and during legal disputes

Lobbying specialty within public relations through which organizations promote their causes and interests to lawmakers and government regulators

Magic bullet theory see **powerful-effects model**

Mean world aspect of cultivation theory observing that people who use the media heavily tend to be more fearful and more susceptible to social paranoia and conspiracy theories

Media change   attribute of contemporary public relations focusing on ongoing transformations in the technology of communication and the structure, finances, ethics and other aspects of various communication media

Media relations   specialty within public relations through which an organization communicates through various media (print, broadcast, electronic and digital)

Message content   aspect of awareness evaluation based on the extent to which a message is accurate and positive

Message cost   aspect of communication output research based on money spend on message artifacts

Message distribution   aspect of communication output research based on the number of message artifacts distributed, such as news releases sent or brochures mailed

Message exposure   aspect of awareness evaluation based on measurement of how many people were exposed to a message; see **reach**

Message production   aspect of communication output research based on the number of message artifacts produced, such as news releases written or brochures printed

Message recall   aspect of awareness evaluation based on the ability of a public to remember a message and associate it with the organization that produced it

Metric   specific standard of measurement to assess the outcome of a program or project

Models of public relations   theoretical approach to the evolution of public relations through four models: publicity, information, advocacy and dialogue

Moderate-effects model   theoretical approach to communication that presumes that media have a cumulative effect on audiences, moderated by other social influences

Multi-step flow of communication   theoretical model focusing on decision-making and how information affects people's choices, with a strong role for opinion leaders

News media   category of communication tactics involving print, broadcast and electronic media delivering audiences that may overlap with an organization's publics

News peg   linking an organization's message to something already in the news

News subsidy   term for information provided to media organizations by public relations practitioners

Nonprobability sample   series of techniques for selecting samples of a population not based on the principle of **probability**   (that each element within the population has an equal chance of being selected for the sample)

Nonprofit public relations   type of public relations conducive to education, health, cultural and religious groups, human service agencies, charitable organizations, and membership organizations

Nut graph   nutshell paragraph following the lead in a feature story that presents the key point of the story

Objective-based budgeting   preferred approach to budgeting based on implementation of tactics designed to achieve agreed upon goals and objectives of an organization

Online activism   use of digital and social media for social engagement

Online newsroom   media relations tool in an organization's website to present information, news, features, opinions, photos and videos

Open system   type of system in which organizations and publics can interact easily and frequently

Opinion leader   agent of information sharing who interprets information within his/her sphere of influence

Opinion subsidy   category of news media tactics including information presenting an organization's point of view, such as a guest editorial or a position statement

Organizational media   category of communication tactics in which organizations use media they can control for timing, content, presentation and feedback mission of an organization

Out-of-home advertising   category of promotional media tactics including billboards, bus signs and aerial advertising

Personal involvement   category of communication tactics involving direct interaction between an organization and its public

Policy proposition   type of proposition that identifies a course of action and encourages its adoption

Political public relations   type of public relations that focuses on the process of getting elected and staying in office

Position paper   media relations tool for presenting an organization's perspective on an issue

Positioning   process of managing how an organization wants to be seen and known by its publics

Post-crisis stage   final stage in crisis communication when an organization focuses on recovery (returning to normal activities, assessing the extent of physical and reputational damage, and planning to prevent a recurrence of the crisis)

Powerful-effects model   theoretical approach to communication that presumes that media have a powerful and immediate effect on audiences

Pre-crisis   early stage in crisis communication when an organization can anticipate and possibly prevent a crisis

Prebuttal   reactive public relations strategy that launches a pre-emptive strike rather than wait for others to report about an organization

Primary research   formal process of gathering new data

Principle of disclosure   one of seven principles of crisis communication, focusing on the need to communicate as much information as possible

Principle of existing relationships   one of seven principles of crisis communication, focusing on the need to communicate with employees, volunteers, stockholders, donors and other supportive publics

Principle of media-as-ally   one of seven principles of crisis communication, focusing on the need to communicate with publics through the media

Principle of message framing   one of seven principles of crisis communication, focusing on the desirability of managing the agenda to maintain some level of control over how the story unfolds

Principle of one voice   one of seven principles of crisis communication, focusing on the need to have either a single spokesperson or the coordinated message by designated multiple spokespersons

Principle of quick response   one of seven principles of crisis communication, focusing on the need to communicate quickly with key publics

Principle of reputational priority   one of seven principles of crisis communication, focusing on top priority of shoring up an organization's reputation

Probability sample   series of techniques for selecting samples of a population based on the principle of probability (that each element within the population has an equal chance of being selected for the sample)

Producer public type of public that provides input to an organization, including employees, volunteers, suppliers and financial backers

Proposition main idea within a speech or piece of persuasive writing

Public group of people sharing a relationship with an organization

Public diplomacy type of public relations involving government use of the media to impact public opinion in another country, non-governmental organization, corporation, political faction or nonprofit group

Public information term for **media relations** used by government agencies

Public interest attribute of contemporary public relations focusing on the well being of publics rather than of the organization

Publication category of communication tactics involving printed media such as newsletters and brochures

Publicity proactive public relations strategy of gaining attention through the news media

Publicity model approach to public relations focusing on use of one-way communication to disseminate information and gain attention; often used in entertainment, sports and marketing

Reach number of different people exposed to a single message

Reactive strategy public relations strategy through which an organization responds to influences and opportunities from its environment

Readability measure aspect of awareness evaluation based on the calculation of the reading level of a message

Relabeling reactive public relations strategy in which an organization changes a name or uses language to hide its association with wrongdoing

Relationship management goal category of goal focusing on how an organization connects with its publics

Relationship marketing attribute of contemporary public relations focusing on an emerging area of marketing that, public relations-like, deals with gaining long-term support

Relationship model approach to public relations focusing on use of two-way communication toward mutual understanding and conflict resolution; often used by regulated business, government, nonprofit organizations and social movements

Relative media effectiveness aspect of action evaluation that compares one medium to others

Restitution   reactive public relations strategy in which an organization makes amends by compensating victims or restoring the situation to an earlier condition

Reversal   reactive public relations strategy in which an organization under criticism tries to gain the upper hand

Risk management   process of identifying, controlling and minimizing the impact of uncertain events on an organization

Sample size   optimum minimum size for a sample to be considered representative of the population

Secondary research   formal process of collecting information by resorting data that already exists

Selective exposure   theory that people do not like dissonance and avoid information they think might oppose their bias, instead seeking information supporting existing attitudes

Selective perception   theory that people do not like dissonance and thus remember information that supports their attitudes and biases, ignoring contrary information

SiLoBaTi + UnFa   acronym to identify elements of news: significance, localness, balance, timeliness, unusualness and fame

Situational theory   approach to public relations that identifies publics as active or passive

Sleeper effect   aspect of communication research that notes that the persuasive impact of communication may increase as time elapses

Social judgment theory   theory that observes that individuals accept or reject messages to the extent that they perceive the messages are corresponding to their internal anchors (attitudes and beliefs) and as affecting their self-concept

Social psychology   attribute of contemporary public relations focusing on the scientific study of knowledge, attitudes, opinions and behaviors of groups

Soft news   type of news that is light information dealing with upcoming events and news programs, developments without major consequences, and activities and trends with more distant results

Specialized news   information of importance to particular publics and particular segments of the media, such as news about business, religion, sports, the arts, agriculture, science, health, home, fashion and so on

Spiral of silence   theory that observes that people learn through media reporting what appears to be the majority opinion, and that persons holding a differing opinion are likely to remain silent

Stage-of-lifestyle budgeting   approach to budgeting that considers the phase of develop, such as new versus continuing programs

Stakeholder   term indicating a group of people who relate to an organization; similar to **public**

Strategic ambiguity   reactive public relations strategy in which an organization attempts to dodge the issue by not responding

Strategic counseling   term used to indicate issues management plus a major role for public relations at the highest level of organizational decision-making

Strategic inaction   reactive public relations strategy in which an organization waits out criticism and allows a situation to fade

Strategic planning   attribute of contemporary public relations focusing on an organizational process of defining direction and making decisions on allocating resources to pursue that strategy

Strategic research   aspect of public relations planning that gathers data for insight into issues and publics and for guiding decisions on how an organization might address a situation

Strategic silence   reactive public relations strategy in which an organization does not respond to criticism, though it may take follow-up action

Stratified sample   sophisticated approach to sampling that ranks elements according to demographic factors, then draws elements from each factor to be part of the sample

Subordinate points   evidence supporting the proposition in a speech or piece of persuasive writing

Summary news lead   most common type of news lead, providing a one- or two-sentence overview of the information

Systematic sample   type of probability sample in which the researcher selects every nth name on a list

Systems theory   one of the theoretical underpinnings of public relations that explains an organization's relationship with its publics

Tactical research   aspect of public relations planning that gathers data to guide the production and dissemination of messages

Theory of accounts   theory about the use of communication to manage relations in the wake or rebuke or criticism

Third-party endorsement   benefit of using news media, which audiences understand to bestow added credibility because news reporting is vetted through reporters and editors

Two-step flow of communication   see **multi-step flow of communication**

Two-way communication   attribute of contemporary public relations focusing on the opportunity for organizations to engage in ongoing communication that can be initiated by either the organization or its publics

Unique selling proposition   marketing technique involving clear statement of the benefit

Value proposition   type of proposition that argues the worthiness or virtue of something

Virtue appeal   type of positive persuasive appeal evoking social or personal values

Volunteer sample   type of nonprobability sample in which the researcher invites people to participate if they feel strongly about an issue

Weighted sample   approach to sampling in which each demographic group is sized according to its proportion in the population to compensate for its being a small proportion

RECOMMENDED READING

Aronson, E.W. and Pinkleton, B.E. (2006). *Strategic Public Relations Management: Planning and managing effective communication programs* (2nd ed.). Lawrence Erlbaum.

Bardhan, N. and Weaver, C.K.I. (Eds) (2010). *Public Relations in Global Cultural Contexts: Multi-paradigmatic perspectives.* Routledge/Taylor & Francis.

Caywood, C. (2011). *Handbook for Strategic Public Relations and Integrated Marketing Communications* (2nd ed.). McGraw-Hill.

Curtin, P.A. and Gaither, T.K. (2007). *International Public Relations: Negotiating culture, identity and power.* Sage.

Cutlip, S.M., Center, A.H. and Broom, G.M. (2012). *Effective Public Relations* (11th ed.). Prentice Hall.

Freitag, A.R. and Stokes, A.Q. (2009). *Global Public Relations: Spanning borders, spanning cultures.* Routledge/Taylor & Francis.

Harris, T.L. (1999). *Value Added Public Relations: The secret weapon of integrated marketing.* McGraw-Hill.

Harris, T.L. and Whalen, P.T. (2006). *The Marketer's Guide to Public Relations in the 21st Century.* South-Western.

Hendrix, J.A. and Hayes, D.C. (2009). *Public Relations Cases* (8th ed.). Wadsworth.

Kendall, R. (1999). *Public Relations Campaign Strategies: Planning for implementation* (3rd ed.). HarperCollins.

Kotler, P., Roberto, N. and Lee, N. (2007). *Social Marketing: Influencing behaviors for good* (3rd ed.). Sage.

Levine, M. (2008). *Guerrilla PR 2.0: Wage an effective publicity campaign without going broke.* Harper.

Newsom, D., Turk, J.V. and Kruckenberg, D. (2009). *This is PR: The realities of public relations* (10th ed.). Wadsworth.

Parkinson, L. and Ekachi, D. (2005). *International and Intercultural Public Relations: A campaign case approach*. Pearson.

Phillips, D. and Young, P. (2009). *Online Public Relations: A practical guide to developing an online strategy in the world of social media* (2nd ed.). Kogan Page.

Reis, A. and Reis, L. (2004). *The Fall of Advertising and the Rise of PR*. Harper.

Seigel, L. (2011). *Public Relations Around the Globe: A window on international business culture*. Amazon Digital.

Seitel, F.P. (2010). *The Practice of Public Relations* (11th ed.). Prentice Hall.

Smith, R.D. (2012). *Becoming a Public Relations Writer: A writing workbook for emerging and established media* (4th ed.). Routledge/Taylor & Francis.

Smith, R.D. (2013). *Strategic Planning for Public Relations* (4th ed.). Routledge/Taylor & Francis.

Sriramesh, K. and Vercic, D. (Eds) (2009). *Global Public Relations Handbook: Theory, research, and practice*. Routledge/Taylor & Francis.

Stacks, D.W. (2010). *Primer of Public Relations Research* (2nd ed.). Guilford.

Stacks, D.W. and Michaelson, D. (2010). *A Practitioner's Guide to Public Relations Research, Measurement and Evaluation*. Business Expert Press.

Wilcox, D.L., Cameron, G.T., Ault, P.H. and Agee, W.K. (2011). *Public Relations: Strategies and tactics* (10th ed.). Allyn and Bacon.

Wilson, L.J. and Ogden, J. (2012). *Strategic Communications Planning for Effective Public Relations and Marketing* (5th ed.). Kendall-Hunt.

Wimmer, R.G. and Dominick, J.R. (2010). *Mass Media Research: An introduction* (9th ed.). Wadsworth.

JOURNALS AND PERIODICALS

American Journalism Review
Asia Pacific Public Relations Journal (Australia)
Case Studies in Strategic Communication
Consejo Profesional de Relaciones Publicas (Argentina)
Journal of Advertising Research
Journal of Business Communication
Journal of Public Relations Research
Public Relations Inquiry (UK)
Public Relations Journal
Public Relations Quarterly
Public Relations Review (UK)
Public Relations Strategist
Public Relations Tactics

Reputation Management
Revista Internacional de Relaciones Publicas (Spain)

REFERENCE AND STYLE BOOKS

Associated Press. *The Associated Press Stylebook and Briefing on Media Law.*
Reuters. *The Reuters Style Guide: Handbook of journalism.*
UPI. *UPI Stylebook and Guide to Newswriting.*

INDEX

Research Methods in *The Basics*

Research Methods: The Basics

Nicholas Walliman, Oxford Brookes University

Research Methods: The Basics is an accessible, user-friendly introduction to the different aspects of research theory, methods and practice. Structured in two parts, the first covering the nature of knowledge and the reasons for research, and the second the specific methods used to carry out effective research, this book covers:

- structuring and planning a research project
- the ethical issues involved in research
- different types of data and how they are measured
- collecting and analyzing data in order to draw sound conclusions
- devising a research proposal and writing up the research.

Complete with a glossary of key terms and guides to further reading, this book is an essential text for anyone coming to research for the first time, and is widely relevant across the social sciences and humanities.

November 2010 – 194 pages
Pb: 978-0-415-48994-2| Hb: 978-0-415-48991-1

For more information and to order a copy visit
http://www.routledge.com/books/details/9780415489942/

Available from all good bookshops

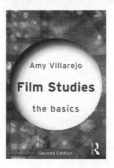